EDUCATIONAL PLANNING

Educational Planning

Strategic Tactical Operational

ROGER KAUFMAN, Ph.D.
Professor and Director, Center for Needs Assessment and Planning
Florida State University

JERRY HERMAN, Ph.D.
Professor, Administration and Planning
University of Alabama-Tuscaloosa

KATHI WATTERS
Associate in Research, Center for Needs Assessment and Planning
Florida State University

TECHNOMIC
PUBLISHING CO., INC.

LANCASTER · BASEL

Educational Planning: Strategic, Tactical, and Operational
a **TECHNOMIC** publication

Published in the Western Hemisphere by
Technomic Publishing Company, Inc.
851 New Holland Avenue, Box 3535
Lancaster, Pennsylvania 17604 U.S.A.

Distributed in the Rest of the World by
Technomic Publishing AG
Missionsstrasse 44
CH-4055 Basel, Switzerland

Printed in the United States of America
10   9   8   7   6   5   4   3   2

Main entry under title:
   Educational Planning: Strategic, Tactical, and Operational

A Technomic Publishing Company book
Bibliography: p.
Includes index p. 281

Library of Congress Catalog Card No. 95-60892
ISBN No. 1-56676-293-6

CONTENTS

Chapter 3: Strategic Planning Starts with the
Ideal Vision   39

Chapter 4: Identifying Mission Based on the
Ideal Vision   51

Chapter 5: Needs Assessment   75

PART TWO: TACTICAL PLANNING

PART THREE: IMPLEMENTATION

EDUCATIONAL planning seeks to create a learner-focused and societally relevant system which will measurably and continuously move
toward success, producing, hopefully, an educational system which is
deliberately designed to contribute to the kind of world we want for
tomorrow's children.

Most educational planning approaches target one or two aspects of a
total educational system: curriculum, quality management, strategic
planning, facilities, personnel, budget and finance, courses, educational
technology, and/or staff development. While each of these individual
pieces is important, they make their most powerful contribution when
they are integrated and related. The requirement for a process to generate
an "educational planning synergy" is what has motivated us to prepare
this book.

To relate the various elements of any educational system, including
all of the conventional ones, we have divided the book into three major
areas: *Strategic Planning, Tactical Planning,* and *Implementation.* The
two levels of planning should be linked and integrated in order that
implementation—what we use, do, produce, and deliver—will make a
useful societal and community contribution. In addition, we identify how
various usually independent educational efforts, including strategic
planning, (total) quality management, and needs assessment can and
should be integrated. This book is holistic in scope, combining the basic
elements of strategic planning with the usual areas of educational planning.

This book builds upon the previous works and ideas of the authors, in
addition to providing new material. Because the authors have published
extensively, some of the work will be recognizable, even in updated
form. This is, however, not a rehash, but rather a synthesis of what

works, with the addition of new concepts and tools. We particularly wish to thank the following publishers for allowing us to use, usually in modified and updated form, previously available material:

- Technomic Publishing Company, Inc.: Kaufman, ''Planning Educational Systems'' (1988); Kaufman and Herman, *Strategic Planning in Education* (1991)
- Corwin Press: Kaufman, *Mapping Educational Success* (1992 and 1995); Kaufman and Zahn, *Quality Management Plus* (1993)
- Sage Publishing: Kaufman, *Strategic Planning Plus* (1992)
- *Educational Technology, Performance & Instruction,* and *Training & Development* for various articles by Kaufman

We also wish to thank the many colleagues, students, clients, and educational systems who have used earlier materials and concepts and supplied useful (and sometimes uncomfortable) feedback on what to change, what to drop, and what to keep. Special thanks is given to Jean Van Dyke for spending many hours typing and checking this manuscript, and to Jason Strickland for his creative expertise with the graphics. Much thanks is especially due to Elizabeth Kirby for providing feedback on the initial draft, Phil Grisé for always being willing to discuss concepts and realities, and finally to David Wilkinson for the quality time he generously gave while enroute from Australia to Colorado. Your thoughts and comments also helped in shaping this book. But the ultimate test of educational planning concepts and tools is whether they are used and measurably improve the contribution the system makes to our collective and mutually interdependent future.

ROGER KAUFMAN
Tallahassee, Florida

JERRY HERMAN
Tuscaloosa, Alabama

KATHI WATTERS
Tallahassee, Florida

CHANGE

NEVER before, perhaps, have educators been required to do more. We have been asked to be surrogate parents, drug czars, and peace officers, as well as driving instructors, nutritionists, custodians, and health advisors. Legislation requires us to serve the increasingly diverse needs of people in disparate locations. And never before, possibly, has an educator's stock been lower. We work hard, but seem to be getting less respect and fewer results of which we can be proud. Change is a constant companion of education and the mega-environment in which education functions.

We have become a learning society; as such our educational systems must become a primary vehicle for assisting learners to become successful citizens in a world that demands knowledge, thought, problem solving, competence, and caring. Education must change much of what it does and how it does it in order to become a contributing partner to our new realities. Not that education is a complete and utter failure. It isn't (Cuban, 1994). In fact, education, given the myriad non-educational demands put on it, is performing as well, if not better, than can be expected (e.g., *Newsweek,* 1994). But we have reached the upper limit of our current abilities to respond (Branson, 1988) given the current demands and the conventional wisdom of what education is and how it should be done. Putting more money or muscle into the current system is to deny the changing demands put on us. The realities of our world dictate that we re-think and re-plan in order that the education of today will produce the useful citizens of tomorrow. Continuing our current mode of planning and operation will simply — as Peter Drucker warns us — make us better and better at doing what should not be done at all.

We must decide what changes to make, why we should make them, and for whom.

Most educational agencies are involved in change as are learners, teachers, parents, the media, and special interest groups becoming better organized in their demands. Usually, these groups are exerting pressure for or against specific educational programs and procedures. Changes are demanded of educators; frequently as if a single special topic or approach were the only critical element of an entire educational system.

Educational laws have grown bulkier and more intricate as legislators respond to special demands. They pass laws concerning educational practices, accountability, and procedures at a rate that requires most educators to be wizards. Many of these laws deplete the human and financial resources that should be focused on quality education. "Quality" is often mandated but not defined, and further demands for immediate returns just encourage quick-fix solutions. Whatever we are doing and delivering in education, there is an insistence for us to do it differently. There are new charges that education is missing the mark simply because it has wrong objectives based upon outmoded frames of reference, as well as not being responsive to international societal realities (Marshall and Tucker, 1992).

Because we are in the spotlight and because there are unyielding demands for change, we, as educators, have others making system-wide decisions for us. All too often we have behaved like bystanders, swayed by other's decisions and constantly *reacting* to situational crises. By merely *reacting* to demands for change, anarchy frequently results; we try to be all things to all people, probably satisfying not one of those whom were are attempting to serve. We must relinquish our role as bystanders and become proactive planners, active participants and contributors, to help create the kind of world we want for tomorrow's children.

Action requires purpose, confidence, and the defining of important expected results. When we *act* rather than *react*, we become accountable for both the educational processes and their payoffs. The responsibility is ours when we make a professional commitment to be proactive and successful.

An action-oriented, systemic approach to education requires that systematic, systemic, and formal planning, design, implementation, evaluation, and responsive revisioning take place. There is a constant effort to achieve relevancy and practicality for learners, so that they may survive, be self-sufficient, form satisfying relationships with others, and contribute to society when they leave our educational agencies (Kaufman, 1972, 1992, 1995). Open, observable, and accountable—a practical and realistic educational planning approach strives to derive a shared ideal vision, identify priority needs and requirements, and move continually to meet them efficiently and effectively. When we fall short of our objectives, the results signal a demand for revision.

Change—as inevitable as it is—seems to be threatening to most people. The question for educators is whether we will be the masters or the victims of change. Beals (1968) states it well: "'. . . the technological innovation which sooner or later arouses no resistance must be extremely trivial." When an educator decides to change (or innovate), preparations must be made to meet resistance from many sources—teachers, parents, administrators, the school board, business, politicians, and other members of the community until they can re-establish a new comfort zone for themselves. Old paradigms about school, society, and change are difficult to disrupt, but the price of not changing what must be changed is so severe that it defies rationality. In spite of the conventional pressures to fund and evaluate education on the basis of archaic standards, change we must in order to survive and contribute.

The threat from change is, unfortunately, a necessary price of relevance. The argument over our societal responsibilities is now beyond debate (Drucker, 1992, 1993). To remain static is to await decay and evolutionary extinction; to react is to risk dissipation of energy without achieving relevancy; to innovate and act to increase our responsiveness to other people is to invite criticism. Practical, functional, justifiable, planned change is a professional responsibility and societal imperative. It is suggested that the strategic planning approach[1] as provided here will help define and plan useful and functional change.

New educational methods and techniques are always being introduced and tried, although not always rationally. Educators often are accused of pursuing new methods with nothing but hope and faith to guide them. Useful planning must avoid change for its own sake, for there is nothing as frightening as ignorance in action. Therefore, action has the greatest chance for success when valid data are used to identify practical, useful,

---

[1]Later we will define the approach provided in this book as *Strategic Planning Plus* in order to first focus on societal—"mega-level"—results and consequences to define what an educational system must do and deliver.

and realistic purposes. Not to initiate innovative and responsible change is riskier than standing still (Drucker, 1985, 1992; Barker, 1993); otherwise the world and reality will overtake you.

A strategic planning approach which is rational and logical, rather than simply quick-fix-oriented or based on historical precedent, may be difficult to "sell" to people who operate only on an intuitive or "self-protective" basis. Change often comes with difficulty to "settlers" (Barker, 1993) who wait until everything is safe, wanting guarantees before adopting new ideas and methods. Yet meaningful progress has been made by the individual who, armed only with a valid requirement and a useful process, has set out and achieved an appropriate change. "Find a need and fill it" has been good advice that has been given to young people for some time. Change specialist Daryl Conner (1992) notes that until people realize that they have no other survival options than to change will they "take the leap." The approach to planning which follows provides a process for finding the needs and the best way of meeting them.

Happily, there is a trend in education away from the sole use of raw intuition, historical precedence, and conventional wisdom; and toward formal methods for information gathering and use. It is increasingly acceptable and expected for any agency to apply precision and reality in planning and subsequent activity. This shift is not in curriculum content alone, but in the design and management of the entire educational system.

This book provides guidance on moving from strategic planning through tactical planning to action. It moves from envisioning the kind of world we would prepare our learners to create to operating a successful school system. Thus, the book has been broken into three sections: *Strategic Planning, Tactical Planning,* and *Implementation.*

The essential concepts at the "heart" of strategic planning are elaborated on within the beginning chapters of the book. These provide the underlying foundation upon which strategic planning is based and tactical and operational planning are built upon.

As you progress through the concepts, you will begin to realize the importance of strategic planning and holistic thinking—where each part is a piece of a greater whole. Without defining our intended destination and mapping our journey, how do we measure or evaluate our en route accomplishments? It is not good enough to manage a school, administer a policy, or a plan of instruction without an awareness of a shared ideal vision to guide us.

Politics, Comfort Zones, Pragmatism, and Mega-Planning

Some people get the closest to being creative when they are trying not to leave their comfort zones. Their reasons for not changing are myriad, ranging from ''We've tried this already'' to ''The politicians will never let this happen'' to ''This kind of idealism (or Utopianism, or any pejorative term will do) won't work in the real world.'' To refuse to create a better world and an associated responsive and responsible educational system is at best unrealistic and perhaps cowardly or unethical as well. Usually, however, concerns about the practicality and political viability of mega-level planning is based in the discomfort caused by the possibility that everything one knows and does might be subject to revision or obsolescence. When we are tempted to retreat to the comfortable, Drucker reminds us that (1) we are getting better and better at doing that which should not be done at all, (2) it is more important to do what is right than to do things right, and (3) every organization should prepare for the abandonment of everything it does. In his works, quoted in this book at length, Drucker would have us create the future instead of simply mourning the past. We agree enthusiastically.

The basic pragmatism of using mega-level planning—with an ''ideal vision'' as the starting place—and deriving everything else from there is provided in Table 3.2. For those who are concerned that we cannot get to the ideal vision right away, they are right . . . we only have to move ever-closer to it, even if it takes several generations (see Chart 5.1).

But why shift out of today's comfort zones? Why buck the politicians and those colleagues who see excuses behind every turn, in the way of any suggestion?

The first *Critical Success Factor* (Chapter 1, page 12) upon which all of the others depend, encourages people to venture beyond the known, acceptable, and conventional. If we stick to only what is comfortable, we will likely only increase our speed in reaching outmoded, incomplete, or even wrong destinations. The world is constantly changing. Old and outmoded ground rules, frames of reference, boundaries, assumptions, and frameworks must be discarded. Fundamental deep change in the way we think about education and its public service partners' contributions and activities are long overdue. We have to be open to doing what's right, not what's conventional or comfortable.

Pushing beyond our comfort zones and identifying new and useful objectives will bring success beyond just fitting into the conventional wisdom. Having the right destination and heading there, in the final analysis, is less risky than continuing on a conventional path because it is comfortable. Define what is right and useful to deliver, not what is simply safe.

Joel Barker in his *The Business of Paradigms* (1989) and *Paradigm Pioneers* (1993) shows how formerly great enterprises, such as the Swiss watch giants, suffered because they did not recognize a paradigm shift. They failed to note that the old boundaries and ground rules didn't work anymore. In education, we have gone beyond the old paradigms (all learning happens in schools, teachers are the primary delivery agents, textbooks drive the curriculum content, longer school days and years bring more learning, time-on-task is the only basic variable, and money, much more money, is required to get the necessary results). There are many items of conventional wisdom that are under serious (and long overdue) attack (Kaufman, 1993, March).

The importance of changing our frames of reference, even though we have been successful up until now, is gaining increased attention. Several contemporary authors (e.g., Argyris, 1991; Barker, 1992; Drucker, 1993; Garratt, 1987, 1994, 1995; Martin, 1993; Popcorn, 1991; Marshall and Tucker, 1992) suggest that the very frames of reference and approaches that have brought individuals past success might be the same that will lead to today and tomorrow's failures. The past is prologue. The future requires different paradigms and different planning approaches.

Successful and useful strategic planning requires that we be open to new missions, new needs, and new realities. Futurists (such as Toffler, 1990; Naisbitt and Aburdene, 1990) tell us that the world has changed. Policy experts, such as Osborne and Gaebler (1992), and educational planners (such as Kaufman, 1992a, 1995) reinforce the fact that education is being planned back-to-front, with an emphasis on dollars, resources, and processes instead of defining the societal contribution to be made: it is thus not driven by outcomes . . . or societal reality.

Without critical consideration, one might be tempted to dismiss mega-level planning on the basis that the politics of reality would preclude ever developing and delivering curriculum that does not fit current conventional wisdom. That would be a convenient but basically irrational response.

For example, an ideal vision might provide the basis for developing learners who would be more than ''lifting and moving,'' minimal competency, minimal-intellectually skilled graduates while there is a resounding popular demand for them. There is a contemporary passion for creating jobs (regardless of how menial) under the assumption that people have to work. They ignore the fact that the future has arrived and that menial and low-thinking-skill jobs are being exported to third-world nations. Yet the conventional wisdom is often that we have to create more jobs regardless of their nature and complexity. While we should constantly help learners to ''think for a living'' (Marshall and Tucker, 1992) we must not turn our backs on those who choose to provide the most basic services. We must help others make any productive contributions to themselves and our society they can.

There are, of course, transient quick fixes such as this that are popular but are contrary to what is known about the ''future that has arrived.'' Such process-oriented initiatives come our way and are usually driven by politics and power rather than interventions that will move us ever-closer to the achievement of an ideal vision. Well-meaning solutions in search of problems include school prayer, outcome-based education, moral education, busing, and ethnic/racial/gender-based courses to name a few. These passionate yet unproductive methods-means will soon fade if we keep our basic focus only on the proactive contribution to a better society . . . a focus on the ideal vision.

Instead of being reactive and responding to politics, polemics, and pressure, we would be better off if we heed Drucker's advice that if we cannot predict the future, create it. This is different from the political option—although once you start that game it never ends for you—to pander to power rather than taking the ethical road of doing what is right. When being attacked or pressured by one power broker or another, it is safer, saner, and more realistic to define needs in terms of gaps in results rather than gaps in processes that please small groups with narrow agendas.

Mega-planning provides the reality and data that make one resistant to the reactive approaches that have landed us in the trouble we now often find ourselves. To reiterate and add to Marshall and Tucker (1992), you cannot solve today's problems with the same tools, techniques, and paradigms that caused them . . . including the politics of here-and-now quick fixes regardless of how comfortable they seem.

Where are we going? Why do we want to get there? What results are intended? Each piece is important as it impacts upon the ''world view.'' Are we ready to jump out of our comfortable familiar patterns and engage in a new more effective adventure? Let's accept the challenge and discover its rewards.

PART ONE

STRATEGIC PLANNING

CHAPTER 1

Why Plan Strategically?

CHAPTER FRAMEWORK: What It Costs to Plan or Not Plan Strategically • An Educational Strategic Planning Framework—*Strategic Planning Plus* • What Strategic Planning Is and Contributes • Educational Results . . . Today and Tomorrow • Working Harder, Not Smarter • Shifting Our Educational Paradigm—How We View and Interact with Our World • The Rediscovery of System Thinking

KEY HIGHLIGHTS: Differences between reactive and proactive planning as they relate to useful strategic planning • Holistic strategic planning framework (*Strategic Planning Plus*) • Significance of the identification of a strategic plan's basic client and beneficiary • Importance of strategic planning and its relationship to societal change • Critical significance of changing our way of thinking regarding organizational planning and its relationships to society and our children's future • Value of system thinking for strategic planning • Critical success factors involved in strategic planning

IN his book *Future Shock,* Toffler makes the following point:

> Arguing that planning imposes values on the future, the anti-planners overlook the fact that nonplanning does so, too—often with far worse consequences.

Education is one generation's contribution to those that follow. It is a costly enterprise and should be treated as an investment, not simply a payout. In many states education has the highest share of the state's budget, and most cities allocate funds with a sigh and stubborn hope that productive citizens will come out the other end of the schooling pipeline. However, our world has changed from what we remember as learners to a new and demanding one requiring people to "think for a living" (Marshall and Tucker, 1992) and not simply depend upon a job market that requires only lifting and moving. We cannot sensibly continue to expect education only to do better what it has been doing in the past. A new reality of our shared world has emerged and our education must

3

focus on creating, with other partners, a new tomorrow, not reacting to yesterday. Educators want to do better, but how to define "better" and how to re-engineer education still, unnecessarily, escapes most of us and our educational partners. Various groups offer solutions, but none stem the tide of alleged (but not always documented) learner ignorance and disappointing results.[2] We have implemented excellence, quality, and accountability programs, lengthened school days and years; added "tough" subjects and deleted "electives," increased credentialing requirements, and made teachers pass tests. Still, these solutions (however well intended) don't seem to prepare learners properly for the kind of life and work required by our new realities. We can continue to implement more quick-fix solutions and throw more dollars at the problem, or we can plan and think strategically—moving from reactive to proactive planning. Education works now, but doesn't contribute what it must to help create a better tomorrow. We must improve, not blame.

Strategic planning is a forward-looking, proactive option. It seeks to create a better future by encouraging educational partners to join together in defining and achieving important results and contributions. The results, along with our conventional educational planning and doing efforts, are seriously wanting; simply attempting to increase the efficiency of our current efforts is choosing to work harder without working smarter. Drifting into the future without setting a proper course is reactive and hopeful—relying on luck to turn things around. Just as Naisbitt (1982) reminded us in the early 80s that things were rapidly changing, he now assures us that they will continue to transform dramatically in the future (Naisbitt and Aburdene, 1990). Simply wandering into tomorrow *without* (1) knowing the prevailing forces and trends, and (2) actively attempting to create the reality we want, is to miss the opportunities of creating a better life. Toffler (1990), Naisbitt and Aburdene (1990), Marshall and Tucker (1992), Osborne and Gaebler (1992), and Drucker (1992, 1993, 1994) signal that a business-as-usual approach will certainly fail us.

Strategic planning, as described here, can help you move systemati-

---

[2]Education does much good. But it could be more successful if it were to rethink its roles, responsibilities, and objectives and to align its efforts to a new set of social realities. Some argue that education only requires more money, better paid teachers, and more resources in order to be successful. We suggest that we are missing the definition of what we should achieve in terms of the kind of world we want to create, together with our educational partners, for tomorrow's children. It is not a matter of working harder or investing more, it is a matter of defining what we are to deliver.

cally toward defining and creating a better world. Education is nested within societal good (Figure 1.1) and all we use, do, and deliver must have payoffs to society. It is necessary that we define and deliver education as part of society, not as an isolated splinter which is not integrated with the larger whole. Or put another way, "If education is the solution, what's the problem?"

We will define a basic framework, and show how it integrates other approaches that stop short of being as powerful and potent as possible. We suggest a fundamental referent—a mega-planning focus—which will better assure that learners and society are well served. This strategic planning process identifies how to provide the rationale database for

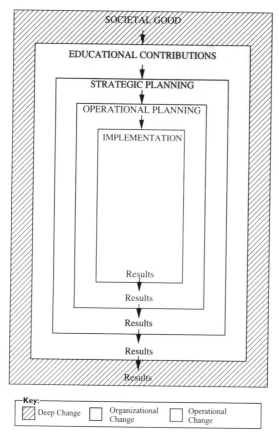

Figure 1.1. *Educational Purposes and Delivery Are "Nested" within Societal Good* (© *R. Kaufman, 1995*).

defining educational interventions, including curriculum and learning experiences, which will be responsive and responsible.

The framework presented here has been the basis for operational applications which range from public to private sector organizations. It has been and is being applied from the U.S. to Australia, Canada to Mexico, and from England to Chile. It is pragmatic and practical, yet will offer a paradigm shift to challenge the comfort zones of many who would rather continue doing what they are doing in the manner in which they are currently doing it.

AN EDUCATIONAL STRATEGIC PLANNING FRAMEWORK

Figure 1.2 provides the framework of our strategic planning model that is described in detail in further chapters and used to organize the discussion throughout this book.

It has a number of functions, answering the question concerning the primary focus, or frame of reference: Who is to be the primary client and beneficiary of what gets planned and delivered? The framework has three major clusters:

- scoping
- planning
- implementation and continuous improvement

What Strategic Planning Is and Contributes

Strategic planning has attracted serious attention. In some form or another, most organizations indulge in it. Unfortunately, much of it has had better intentions than results. Our approach adds some additional dimensions to other approaches, especially the focus on societal good, and planning on the basis of an ideal vision. An ideal vision defines the kind of world we want for tomorrow's child and then selects the part which the educational system commits to deliver. We term this societally focused approach *Strategic Planning Plus* in order to recognize the potential usefulness of conventional approaches. While existing approaches to strategic planning are not wrong, they are incomplete. After all, it seems sensible to have each and every organization focused on making societal contributions in addition to meeting its own requirements for contribution and survival.

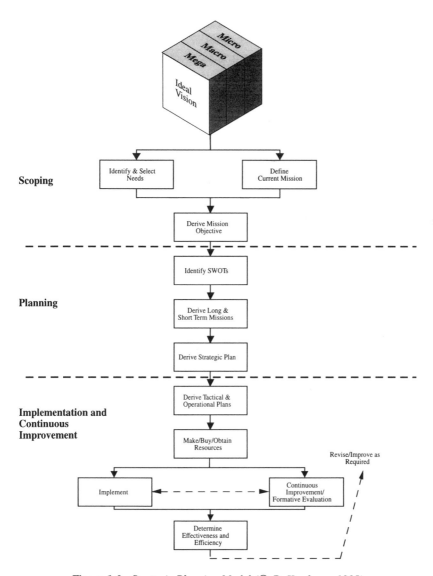

Scoping

Planning

**Implementation and
Continuous
Improvement**

Figure 1.2. Strategic Planning Model (© R. Kaufman, 1995).

Strategic Planning Plus is a dynamic, active process. It identifies the future we want for tomorrow's child, before scanning current and future opportunities and realities. From an ideal vision of the future, we may identify useful strategies and tactics for arriving at that better tomorrow. It is not a prescriptive, rigid, linear, lock-step, authoritarian process; nor is it built on hunches and raw feelings. It encourages the educational partners to define and support the educational purposes and missions. It provides blueprints for results-oriented progress and renewal.

While it is vital for our children's future, as well as our own, that sensible, valid, and useful strategic planning for education be accomplished, there is a lot of confusion among educators and planners as to what that planning should be. People often call just about anything "strategic planning." As a consequence, many conventional models and approaches are muddled, or at best, myopic. Some approaches are intuitive, while others focus on individual programs and projects. While most approaches have something to offer, almost all of them are incomplete.

Strategic Planning Plus, if done correctly, isn't very different for varying contexts; people are people, and organizations are organizations. They all serve the same society. The key difference in Strategic Planning Plus lies in a basic purpose: Who are its basic clients and beneficiaries, where is the organization headed, and why is it going there? Our approach starts from the understanding that the primary client and beneficiary of any educational enterprise is society. This humanistic approach intends to improve learner accomplishments and contributions both in school and in later life. It cares enough about people to be results-oriented. It empowers the educational partners — learners, educators, and citizens — to define an ideal vision and develop a strategic plan and related tactical plan to achieve educational success with long-range payoffs.

EDUCATIONAL RESULTS . . . TODAY AND TOMORROW

Educational realities and purposes have changed dramatically. Challenges are part of our lives . . . we have seen them in the past as we reacted to Sputnik; currently as we encounter increasing overseas competition for our markets; and in the future with unknown but anticipated surprises. No longer do we exclusively get middle-class learners with homogeneous cultural background values and language, but learners with a rich array of personal characteristics, problems, and expectations. But conventional education still attempts to do better by working harder and spending more instead of by defining what its business is. Everyone seems to know *how* education should be done, and they let others know. We miss defining and justifying *where* we are headed before selecting how we get there; we select means before defining useful ends.

Albert Einstein observed that our world is characterized by a proliferation of means and a confusion of goals (cited in Kaufman, 1972). We argue about *how*—in terms of resources and process—education should do its job, but we do not have clear purposes toward which to chart our course. We are working as hard now as we know how. But that won't improve education's contribution to learners and our shared world until we set useful destinations.

WORKING HARDER, NOT SMARTER

It is widely recognized that American education has been troubled for many years. We argue about the sources of the trouble (see, for example, Banathy, 1991, 1992; Branson, 1988; Cuban, 1990, 1994; Kirst and Miester, 1985; Marshall and Tucker, 1992; Newmann, 1991; Perelman, 1990; Pipho, 1991; Rasell and Mishel, 1990), but without a clear—and shared destination there will be no resolution.

Simply changing the labels for what we do ("restructuring," "back to basics," "local control," "downsizing," "outcome-based education," "total quality management," "re-engineering," and the like) will not work. We must change the way we think about education—our education paradigm—and shift from budget-driven strategies to strategy-driven budgets. We must become visionary *Strategic Thinkers* if we are to succeed in this ever-increasing change and technologically impacted mega-environment. The rhetoric in education has for too long been inferring results, while the practice regresses into placing new labels on old process- and resource-related activities. We find ourselves in what George Odiorne called the "Activity Trap." Performance—useful performance—has to take center stage. The demand for clear purpose—education mission objectives—is clear and beyond doubt. Yet many reform/restructuring/change initiatives assume that the objectives for education are known, clear, and shared. Not so! We keep turning to changes in how we do education without first defining where we are headed, and we must be specific about why we want to get there. We must also obtain a shared commitment for both the destination and the journey.

SHIFTING OUR EDUCATION PARADIGM—HOW WE VIEW AND INTERACT WITH OUR WORLD

We still teach subjects and not learners. We accept without question that the sum total of conventional courses (math, science, music, and so on) and experiences (drama, athletics) will provide learners with the skills and abilities for current and future survival, self-sufficiency, and well-being. Figure 1.3 shows the conventional subject-based planning tactic. But what about the "blank spaces" (total requirements for future functioning) not covered by conventional subject areas? How will learners master what is not available in the curriculum?

We splinter our curriculum and content and thus miss both the coverage of vital areas as well as the synergies among topics and areas. If we start educational (and curriculum) planning with a big picture — what learners have to know and be able to do in tomorrow's world — the educational experiences will be more complete, responsive, and useful.

We now must enlarge our educational paradigm from teaching to learning and then from content mastery to success in today and tomorrow's world. We have to be holistic and responsible for our learner's success both in school and in life, as part of our shared responsibility for a better tomorrow.

THE REDISCOVERY OF SYSTEM THINKING

We are rediscovering system approach concepts (see Senge, 1990; Marshall and Tucker, 1992). Instead of splitting, dissecting, and dissociating parts of a system, the holistic view of organizations as subsystems of a larger world is becoming reaffirmed (see, for example, Banathy, 1987, 1991, 1992; Banghart, 1969; Bertalanffy, 1968; Churchman, 1969, 1975; Cleland and King, 1968; Corrigan and Corrigan, 1985; Corrigan and Kaufman, 1966; Gagne, 1962; Kaufman,

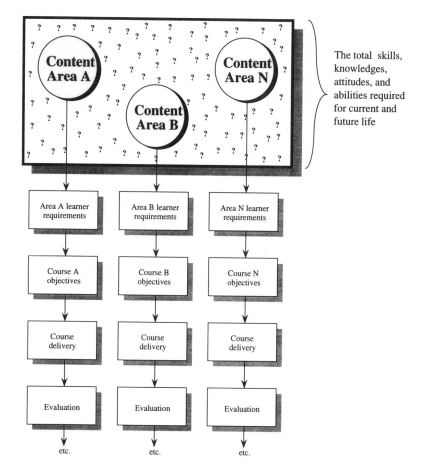

The total skills, knowledges, attitudes, and abilities required for current and future life

Figure 1.3. By Dividing and Delivering Curriculum and Learning Sequences into Discipline, or Content Areas, We Don't Include the "Blank Spaces" of What Education Should Deliver and Accomplish (© R. Kaufman, 1994; based on Kaufman, 1992b).

1968, 1972, 1988b, 1991b, 1992a, 1992b, 1995; Marshall and Tucker, 1992; and Morgan and Chadwick, 1971). A system approach views education as the sum of the independent parts working together and individually to achieve a common – ideally societal – purpose. A change in any part changes all others.

The basic secret for defining and achieving success is to find the correct destination for the system before tinkering with the internal parts and resources. To set a useful direction, we have to be open both to considering changes in what we now do and also to rethinking where we should be headed. As previously stated, Peter Drucker suggests, if we cannot predict the future, we had best create it.

Strategic planning, in its most powerful use, identifies results based upon an *ideal vision.* This measurable description of the world for tomorrow's child becomes the basis for linked achievements at three levels: societal, organizational, and individual/small group.

Conventional strategic planners usually have the greatest apprehension (or difficulty) in addressing societal outcomes, and often ignore or assume them. In such instances, so-called strategic planning actually stops at short-term, stop-gap objectives, and a useful strategic plan is never developed or accomplished. Instead of first defining—in measurable performance terms—the ideal vision of the world in which we want our grandchildren to live, attention is immediately diverted to courses, content, and subjects with the blind assumption that societally useful results will follow; some would prefer to stay well within their comfort zones rather than defining useful results and payoffs for society.

Useful strategic planning depends on people being able to appropriately get out of their comfort zones and enlarge their paradigms. This is so important that it forms our first strategic planning critical success factor:

Critical Success Factor #1: Shift your paradigm to be larger and more inclusive—focus at the mega-level, and think globally as you act locally.

There are six critical success factors for successful strategic planning (Table 1.1). They will be discussed within the next few chapters. An initial overview of these factors follows.

SUMMARY

At each and every level, education has purpose. It is not an experience for its own sake. Educators and educational agencies are chartered by the public to provide learners with the skills, knowledge, abilities, and values to be contributing citizens—not a casual commitment.

Educational planning intends to create a better future for individuals, groups, organizations, and a shared society. Planning identifies where to go, it justifies why, and shows how we get there. It provides the basic criteria for assessing if and when you have arrived at your destination and calibrates your progress. Poor planning will take us to unwanted,

Table 1.1. Six Critical Success Factors for Planning and Thinking Strategically
(© R. Kaufman, 1994).

Critical success factor #1	Move out of today's comfort zones and use newer and wider paradigms for thinking, planning, doing, and evaluating.
Critical success factor #2	Differentiate between ends and means (focus on "what" not "how")
Critical success factor #3	Use and link all three levels of results (mega/outcomes, macro/outputs, and micro/products)
Critical success factor #4	Use an ideal vision (future-oriented) as the underlying basis for planning (don't be limited by current restraints or only develop a vision for your organization).
Critical success factor #5	Prepare objectives—including mission objectives—which include indicators of how you will know when you have arrived (mission statement plus success criteria).
Critical success factor #6	Define "need" as a gap in results (not as insufficient levels of resources, means, or methods).

unintended, and often dangerous destinations; ones even worse than those currently being reached. Planning should ask and answer important questions about purpose and payoffs. Responsive, responsible, and useful education is results-based and results-oriented. What education delivers is preferably more important than focusing solely on how it does its job. First define the results to be delivered and then select the best ways to get them accomplished.

A Paradigm Shift for Education

Paradigms—the boundaries and ground rules we use to filter and respond to our external world—are with us for education, economics, society, and life (e.g., Barker, 1989, 1992, 1993; Kuhn, 1970). Our current educational paradigm is about courses, instruction, teachers, and learners. It has taken us to today but it will likely fail us for the future.

We cannot solve today's problems with the same paradigms which created them. It is now time to accept a new frame of reference for education: the mega-view.

The mega referent identifies the society of tomorrow we wish to create as the basis for educational planning, doing, delivery, and improvement. Instead of the primary client and beneficiary of the educational system being itself, the mega-level starting place is with an ideal vision of the world we wish to create.

For most, this new frame of reference will require a paradigm shift and will likely intrude on current comfort zones. When we leave our comfort zones there are a number of predictable responses: (1) we dismiss it all as jargon or academic, (2) we call it new words for what we do already, (3) we deride the proposal of what is new, and, if none of these work, (4) we just don't listen. Regardless, the shift is vital if we are to survive.

This is a book for educators who care enough to change what should be changed . . . who care about useful results, and about learner individuality and performance, about helping learners create a better future for themselves and society. The "strategic planning plus"[3] process provided in this book is about how to define, build, and manage a successful, responsive, and responsible educational system. The approach details a way of thinking and acting that can help serious professionals create the results that they have long desired. It is designed to help achieve human success and dignity where they do not exist, and to increase them where they only partially exist. It is creative and concrete. Above all, it is practical.

This holistic planning approach has a number of distinguishing characteristics:

(*1*) It is results- and accomplishments-oriented vs. means- or process-oriented.

(*2*) It places individual learner performance and success in school and beyond at the center of planning and management.

(*3*) It is a precise and rigorous way of assuring that the social and personal uniqueness of each person is formally brought to the forefront of planning, and used as an enhancer, not as an obstacle.

(*4*) It emphasizes that both a learner's current and future success are vitally and centrally important.

(*5*) It focuses on society — now and in the future — as the primary client of education.

---

[3]For those impatient for a definition, one may be found in the glossary at the end of the book.

Not everything in today's education is wrong or useless. In fact, much of what is currently done should be continued by design, not by default. By energizing valid, thoughtful, and responsible rethinking, redesign, and restructuring (transformation) of education, we will bring new vitality and responsiveness to our schools, curriculum, learners, and citizens. Unlike a dose of vitamins here, or a workout there, this approach integrates the useful old with the robust new to provide educational methods and payoffs which will guide us successfully into future generations. Successful planning has to be positive, built with the contributions of all educational partners, and must result in solid, understandable, and valid changes. These are not one-shot quick fixes, but systemic improvements and additions to our educational system.

Applying the material in this book to your educational professional planning and doing should help you and your educational partners to continuously improve and deliver educational success. It will challenge your paradigms, nudge your comfort zones; and if you will apply it consistently, positively change your payoffs.

CHAPTER 2

Mega-Planning: A New and Practical Paradigm

CHAPTER FRAMEWORK: Time to Work Smarter • Ends and Means: Another Critical Success Factor • Asking and Answering the "Right" Questions • The Organization as Client • The Individual or Small Group as Client • The Society as Client • Mega-Planning: There Is No More Real Argument • Educational Efforts, Results, Consequences, and Payoffs • The Common Good • Inside-Out Planning • Outside-In Planning • Planning Perspective: How We View Our World • Rolling Up: The Inside-Out Approach • Rolling Down: The Outside-In Approach • Rolling Down/Rolling Up: A Consolidated Approach

KEY HIGHLIGHTS: Differences between ends and means and their significance in strategic planning • Relationship in educational planning approaches and the identification of the primary client and beneficiary of deliverables • Difference between conventional planning and mega-planning upon educational consequences • Illustration and discussion of the Organizational Elements Model and its relationship to strategic planning • Importance and relationship of various world views upon strategic planning

TIME TO WORK SMARTER

BLAME hasn't helped. Restructuring, downsizing, and reengineering hasn't either! Caring is not enough. Changing is not enough. Spending more money won't turn the trick. Raising standards is not enough. In fact, each of the single-issue, quick fixes imposed upon education might be failing because they don't address the underlying problems and opportunities. Educational success is more than writing measurable objectives for courses. Success requires more than preparing new and tougher graduation or vocational standards.

It is imperative to view and treat education from a different perspective, i.e., a different paradigm. Using a different frame of reference usually requires that we temporarily suspend judgment on the understandings, beliefs, values, and ways that we relied on up to now — *shifting, instead, outside of our comfort zones.*

We educators have been selecting and pursuing means (hows) before agreeing upon the ends. It is now time to get ends and means sensibly related. Being strategic is defining what to achieve, being able to justify the destination, and then — and only then — finding the best ways to get there.

ENDS AND MEANS: ANOTHER CRITICAL SUCCESS FACTOR

Another important element to successful strategic thinking and planning is to know — and act on — the difference between ends and means. Perhaps no other area is more confusing and more simple to resolve.

Ends are results, consequences, accomplishments, and pay-offs. There are several different levels of ends, but they all deal with results. Educational ends include students who become self-sufficient and self-reliant citizens, graduates, completers, people who have earned a license, learners who have acquired a specific skill, passed a test or course, or completed a recital.

Means are the ways to deliver ends. For strategic thinking and planning, means include resources (time, money, people, and facilities) and methods (teaching, learning, supervising, planning, thinking, and developing).

$$Means \rightarrow Ends$$

$$Means \neq Ends$$

Differentiating between ends and means is an absolutely vital action, yet one that people find most difficult. It's like knowing that a healthy diet will allow you to live longer if you can give up the greasy hamburgers and fatty french fries.

Critical Success Factor #2: Differentiate between ends and means (distinguish between what and how).

If you start looking at the world, including education, as relying on the differences — including relationships — between ends and means, you will focus on "what" is to be accomplished before deciding "how" to proceed. By distinguishing between ends and means, the differences between mastery and competence (results, or ends) versus teaching and learning (how-to's, or means) become clear.

Some education-related ends and means appear in Table 2.1. Cover the two right-hand columns with a sheet of paper and sort each of the items into their appropriate classification, they will either be ends or means. Then compare your answers with those in the right-hand columns of the table.

We spend most of our time and money on means, but starting with means before defining useful ends is backward. It is vital to identify first what results (ends) we should accomplish. Looking back upon the myriad of educational reforms, note that almost all of them (distance learning, authentic assessment, decentralization, child care programs,

Table 2.1. Some Typical Educational Ends and Means.

	End	Means
Restructuring		X
School-based managing		X
Accountability		X
Quality management		X
Teaching		X
Learning		X
Course grade	X	
Graduation	X	
Employment	X	
Budget		X
In-service education		X
Computer-assisted learning		X
Reengineering		X
Downsizing		X
Unionization		X
Law		X
Policy		X
Curriculum		X
Classrooms		X
Child care program		X
School lunch program		X
Total quality management		X
Strategic planning		X
Tactical planning		X
Needs assessment		X
Distance learning		X
"Outcome-based" education		X

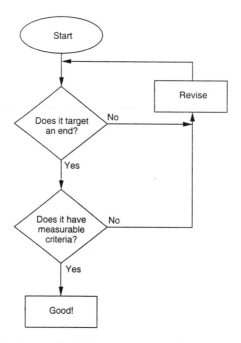

Figure 2.1. *Setting Used Objectives Job Aid (© R. Kaufman, 1994).*

computer-assisted learning, total quality management) are means to loosely defined ends. In fact, most of our professed educational ends are really means. To prove this, retrieve your district's education mission. As you did in Table 2.1, sort the various elements into means and ends and note how much attention is given to means.

Figure 2.1 provides an algorithm—in this case a job aid that contains yes/no questions and related functions—for determining if your objectives are ends related (later we will add considerations of whether they relate to what learners must accomplish in school and beyond).

Use these questions to determine whether your objectives are ends related and whether they relate to what learners must accomplish in school and beyond.

ASKING AND ANSWERING THE "RIGHT" QUESTIONS

Strategic thinking, and consequent planning and accomplishments, depend upon useful direction finding:

(*1*) Where should our educational system be headed?

(*2*) Why do we want to get there?

Seven questions that any education organization may consider as well as the primary level of concern for each, is shown in Table 2.2. When asking the questions in Table 2.2, you will notice that the differences in educational planning approaches are dependent upon who is identified as the primary client and beneficiary of the ''deliverables.'' Who are we

Table 2.2. Asking the Right Questions: Seven Basic Questions All Educators Should Ask (and Answer).

	Strategic Planning Question	Type of Planning	Primary Client/Focus
Ends/results	1. Do you care about and commit to deliver the success of learners after they leave your educational system	Mega	Society
	2. Do you care about and commit to deliver the quality— competence—of the completers and leavers when they leave your educational system?	Macro	Organization/ school system
	3. Do you care about and commit to deliver the specific skills, knowledges, attitudes, and abilities of the learners as they move from course to course, and level to level?	Micro	Small groups/ students, educators, staff
Means	4. Do you care about and commit to deliver the efficiency of your educational programs, activities, and methods?	Quasi	Processes
	5. Do you care about and commit to deliver the quality and availability of your educational resources, including human, capital, financial, and learning?	Quasi	Resources
Consequences	6. Do you care about the worth and value of your methods, means, and resources?	Evaluation	
	7. Do you care about the extent to which you have reached your educational objective?		

planning for? If education is the solution, what's the problem? One way to clearly determine different varieties of planning is to identify who really benefits from the results—who the primary clients are. Three major client choices are available:

(*1*) Citizens, taxpayers, residents, and members of the society and community
(*2*) The school or school system itself
(*3*) Individuals or small groups—internal clients (such as teachers, learners, subject matter areas, lobbyists, unions)—within the school or system

When the primary client and beneficiary is the society and community, then planning is at the *mega*-level. When the clients are the school or educational system itself, planning is at the *macro*-level. When the beneficiaries are individuals and small groups, then planning is at the *micro*-level. Who is the primary client? Who really benefits? Everyone should.

Of course, one really should choose to plan and include all three client groups. Let's take a closer look at each, in the sequence of the most usual (but not the most useful).

THE ORGANIZATION AS CLIENT: MACRO-PLANNING

Most approaches to planning (especially those labeled "strategic") assume the organization's survival is paramount and any planning must deliver organizational continuation, well-being, and growth. While concern for the student, taxpayer, economy, or environment is often expressed (and even meant), it is the organization which typically benefits from any plan. While this mode of planning might identify learner performance both in and out of school, the underlying primary focus and concern tends to be on making the system more successful, not necessarily on the benefits to the learner, community, and/or taxpayers. Such self-interests as organizational funding levels, personal liability, salary levels, facilities acquisition or improvement, prestige, and additional territory often drive this type of planning focus.

This is not to say that the well-being of the organization or its associates is not extremely important. It usually is. Any educational organization must be chartered to deliver and have competent, well-equipped, properly supported, caring and concerned professionals. The critical, and often uncomfortable, primary issue is not just the organization's survival and continuation but whether the organization should be the *primary* client and beneficiary. Some—but unfortunately not all—"restructuring" in schools today results from realizing the stark reality that simply "doing what we are now doing but better" will not suffice . . . it will hurt us.

THE INDIVIDUAL OR SMALL GROUP AS CLIENT: MICRO-PLANNING

Organizations are composed of people (and, of course, the resources that support them). Often, an individual or small group becomes the primary focus and beneficiary of planning. Educational organizations might target learners and their course-level (or test) performance, and/or teachers, and/or programs. Individual-as-client planning foci could be the improvement or mastery of the capitals of the world, sentence structure, home electrical wiring techniques, the ability to communicate with visual symbols, development of social and job skills, or passing a competency test. Such an individual competency focus can be very useful and productive; it is the basic rationale for programs such as those in instructional improvement, instructional systems design, competency-based education, computer-assisted instruction, communication improvement programs, and criterion-referenced assessment.

Another variety of individual (or small group) as client foci is gaining resources for the math department, getting a salary increase, or capturing a bigger budget. When the payoff is for individual position or power, we often call this approach "school politics."

But what good are microlevel results—products—if they do not contribute to success in school and in later life? Just passing courses will not assure future contibutions.

THE SOCIETY AS CLIENT: MEGA-PLANNING

A much rarer approach to educational planning is one where the current and future good of society is the primary focus and commitment. From this perspective, any educational system part (such as a district, school, course, activity, or program) is a means to societal ends.

When using the society-as-primary-client planning mode, you bring to center-stage current and future societal opportunities, requirements, and problems. This starting point includes: (a) defining current results and future requirements, and (b) identifying educational requirements for helping to bring about genuine societal good.

This approach operates on the basis of that which is good for society is also good for the organization and its people. Even though legislators, government executives, educational managers, and educational planners should be taking this approach, being human they tend to quickly slip into the organization-as-client mode or the me-as-the-client mode.

MEGA-PLANNING: THERE IS NO MORE REAL ARGUMENT

The conventional education organizational paradigm—the way we view the world and the ground rules we use to make decisions—has shifted. Societal good as the primary objective of every educational organization is now part of the new organizational planning and doing paradigm (Drucker, 1992, 1993; Kaufman, 1972, 1988a, 1991a, 1992, 1995; Kaufman and Herman, 1991; Kaufman and Zahn, 1993; Popcorn, 1991).

Even the revered management expert Peter Drucker (1992, 1993) agrees with the mega-level of planning as basic and vital. He notes that:

- . . . a sharp transformation has occurred
- . . . a society of organizations: the purpose and function of every organization, business and non-business alike, is the integration of specialized knowledge into a common task.
- . . . the rising demand for socially responsible organizations.
- . . . every organization must prepare for the abandonment of everything it does.
- For the organization to perform to a high standard, its members must believe that what it is doing is, in the last analysis, the one contribution to community and society on which all others depend.

Mega-level planning (Kaufman, 1992, 1995) views the society *and* the educational clients, now and in the future, as the basis for everything the educational system uses, does, and delivers. Other planning approaches have lower levels of primary clients and beneficiaries. One way to view those who choose different labels is on the basis of who are leaders, executives, or managers/administrators.

Table 2.3. Relating the Three Levels of Planning to Type of Sponsors and Levels of Results.

Level of Planning	Type of Sponsor	Level of Results	Level of Payoff
Mega	Leader/steward	Outcomes	Societal/community
Macro	Executive/ superintendent	Outputs	Organization
Micro	Manager/ administrator	Products	Small group

If you select the mega-level, then you are taking a leadership role.[4] Leaders link what your school or system uses, does, produces, and delivers to achieving positive payoffs for all, including society. If you select the macro-level, you are primarily looking after the organization but without any substantial commitment to both the client and our shared world (Kaufman, 1992b). If you choose to pursue micro-level results, you are only concerned with individual jobs and tasks (and usually taking the risk of assuming that lower-level results will integrate with what the organization delivers and the outputs' usefulness).

Societal good—mega-planning (linking educational efforts, organizational results, and societal payoffs)— is a paradigm which has been a long time in the forming. It is here! Mega-planning incorporates and integrates macro- and micro-planning as well.

People, outside of their comfort zones and alienated from the conventional wisdom, will continue to strain to make the old paradigm work. It won't, and it hasn't for some time.

The mega-level of planning is quite rational if you step back from previous paradigms: if an educational system (or school) doesn't make a contribution by helping fashion a responsive and responsible society for today and tomorrow, then what good is it? No amount of internal shifts and changes, no level of restructuring, and no increases in total quality management processes will help an organization which isn't headed in a useful direction.

Barker (1992) notes that a paradigm shifts when there are just too many cases which the old one cannot explain or handle. We have had a

---

[4]Peter Block (1993) attributes many of these characteristics to what he calls "stewardship," but seems to limit the term to macro-level concerns. Also see Hogan, Curphy, and Hogan (1994) for the attributes of leadership.

paradigm shift in organizational orientation because the old ones just ran out of steam:

- from viewing educators and staff as interchangeable parts to team building and organizational development
- from supervising to empowerment
- from increasing efficiency to delivering results
- from results to client satisfaction and total quality
- from results and total quality to positive societal contributions and payoffs

The new paradigm speaks to client satisfaction *and* societal contribution. And while we are thinking about this new paradigm, what could make more sense than aligning what an educational organization uses, does, produces, and delivers to what is good for both the client and for society? Illiterate learners and leavers don't often pay taxes and contribute to the common good, nor does it make much sense if we are turning out graduates who are happy with the system but cannot be self-sufficient and self-reliant good neighbors. Delivering a positive return on our educational investment[5] to citizens, parents, educators, and learners is not only sensible, but the only way in which education will survive. We should examine the relationships between our educational costs and the societal consequences. If we only respond to wishes for more education simply because it is "good" to do so, we will often lose funding to another competing "good" such as health, environment, housing, and the like. Sooner or later we must justify what we spend and do in terms of the societal contribution we make. By using the mega-level for deciding what we do and deliver, we are relieved from making inappropriate selections of programs or activities based on immediate costs rather than societal contributions.[6]

---

[5]Economists would have a more rigorous definition of "return on investment" which would consider many of the contributing variables to both costs and results (such as opportunities lost, who pays, what monies eventuate to the individual and society, etc.). For the purposes of this work, we are referring to "Costs/Consequences" which simply examines what monies and resources were put into the system and what payoffs result from its operation. The basic and minimal relationship for an individual after completing or leaving the educational system is that their consumption (C) will be equal to or less than their production (P). (Kaufman, 1992a,b; Kaufman and Sobel, 1989).

[6]Some in Europe, Australia, and New Zealand warn against "economic rationalists" who simply look at what costs for doing or not providing an intervention, service, or course. To the extent to which one makes decisions, economic or otherwise, only at the micro- or macro-level, their concerns are real. However, by using the mega-level, societal good may be estimated, and, more likely, achieved.

With societal return-on-investment in center focus, we can both do good and be successful, rational and practical. Value-added human capital and societal capital are achievable and imperative results.

Education and educators can be one of the very few groups which can have a singular interest in the stewardship of our planet. The public-trust mission is to help people be contributing members of society – now and in the future. Education, and schools, are clearly means – potentially potent and useful – to societal ends.

EDUCATIONAL EFFORTS, RESULTS, CONSEQUENCES, AND PAYOFFS: THE ORGANIZATIONAL ELEMENTS MODEL

A useful aid, or template, to use in relating what your educational organization uses, does, and delivers is a five-unit framework called the *Organizational Elements Model* or *OEM* (Kaufman, 1988b, 1992a,b, 1995). The OEM identifies three types of results (one for each level of planning: mega, macro and micro) and two types of means and resources. Any educational organization may be described as employing and relating these five elements. Table 2.4 shows the five elements of inputs, processes, products (results at the micro-level), outputs (results at the macro-level), and outcomes (results at the mega-level) along with some examples of each.

When being strategic, all of the organizational elements must be integrated and linked. For example, the existing facilities, teachers, and learning resources (inputs) may be used in delivering learning opportunities/teaching (processes.) These, together, should deliver mastery in courses and proficiency in the application of principles, values, and decisioning (products) that, when gathered together, lead to graduation or certification (outputs). All of the internal organizational elements – inputs, processes, products, and outputs – can and should deliver people who are self-sufficient, self-reliant, mutually contributing citizens of today and tomorrow (outcomes). The relationships among the organizational elements, levels of planning, emphases, and typical examples are shown in Table 2.4. Notice that there are three levels of planning (mega, macro, micro) for which there are three levels of results (outcomes, outputs, products). This is the basis for the *Third Critical Success Factor:*

Critical Success Factor #3: *Plan using (and linking) all three levels of results.*

Table 2.4. The Organizational Elements Model (OEM) and an Educational Example of Each—A System Model (© R. Kaufman, 1995; based in part on Kaufman and Herman, 1991; and Kaufman, 1995).

Organizational level	Inputs (resources, ingredients, starting conditions)	Processes (how-to's; means; methods; procedures)	Products (en route—building-block—results)	Outputs (the aggregated products of the system that are delivered or deliverable to society)	Outcomes (the contributions and consequences of outputs in and for society and the community)
Examples	Existing personnel; identified needs, goals, objectives, policies, regulations, laws, money, values, and societal and community characteristics; current quality of life, learner entry characteristics, teacher competencies, buildings, equipment, etc.	Total quality management—continuous improvement; teaching; learning; in-service training, managing, accelerate learning; site-based managing; accountability; etc.	Course completed; competency test passed; skill acquired; learner accomplishments; instructor accomplishments; etc.	Graduates; completers; dropouts; job placements; certified licensees; etc.	Self-sufficient, self-reliant, productive individual who is socially competent and effective, contributing to self and others; no addiction to others or to substances; financially independent; continued funding of agency, etc.
Cluster	Organizational efforts		Organizational results		Societal results/ consequences

Table 2.4. (continued).

Scope	Internal (organizational)		External (societal)
Planning level	Micro	Macro	Mega
Primary client or beneficiary	Individual or small group	School system or school	Society/community
Strategic planning question	Do you care about the specific skills, knowledges, attitudes, and abilities of the learners as they move from course to course, and level to level?	Do you care about the quality—competence—of the completers and leavers when they leave the educational system?	Do you care about the success of learners after they leave the educational system and are citizens?

29

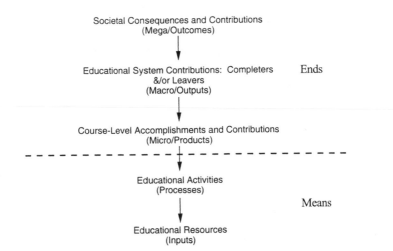

Figure 2.2. *An Educational Results Chain, Which Shows the Relationships among the Organizational Elements (© R. Kaufman, 1995).*

When thinking and planning strategically, we start with the outcomes (mega-level results) we desire and then identify the internal elements (outputs, products, processes, and inputs) that will efficiently deliver those. The educational system's success is based on how well educational resources contribute to useful processes, and those must deliver successful en route mastery for graduation and citizenship. This chain of results that links educational resources, interventions, and the three levels of results may be shown in "shorthand" using the terms from the OEM and noting the three levels of educational planning (see Figure 2.2).

Notice the arrows which connect the five organizational elements: mega/outcomes; macro/outputs; and micro/products, processes, and inputs. If there is any misalignment or lack of "fit" between any of the elements, the system—and all of its clients—is at risk. Linking and integrating all the levels provides effective and efficient educational consequences—if we have first chosen the correct outcomes.

Figure 2.3 provides a job aid for assuring your objectives are useful and link one with the others.

THE COMMON GOOD

The degree to which organizational purposes are identical and contribute to societal purposes is the extent to which an educational agency will be successful. Shared visions, purposes, and missions will provide a common set of results, destinations, and consequences—a "North Star"—toward which all educational stakeholders and partners may steer and contribute. When there are shared purposes and payoffs, a common good is created leading to a win-win situation and a cooperative environment.

INSIDE-OUT PLANNING

If one plans *for* the organization as the primary client, it is as if one were looking from within the organization outside into the operational world where learners complete, graduate, or get certified; and where citizens live, play, and work. This focus is on what is good for the

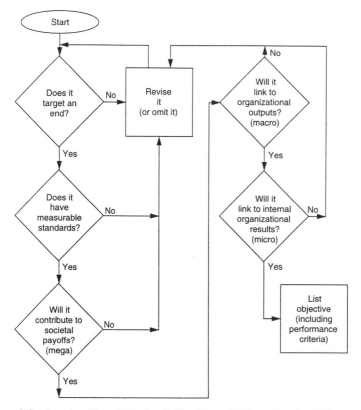

Figure 2.3. *Assuring Your Objective Is Useful at All Three Levels of Planning and Results (© R. Kaufman, 1995).*

organization and its continuation—a macro-level-limited perspective. It usually carries assumptions that make major change difficult, such as altering a major mission of the system or identifying opportunities and problems which currently do not exist. Inside-out planning is reactive and usually projects the current educational mission(s), goals, purposes, and activities forward in time.

Inside-out planning represents the bias and world view of those who feel more comfortable fixing things which are broken while assuming that they are worth fixing. Such people start work analyzing the problems and then seek methods for repairing the damage. The success of any reactive approach hinges on current objectives and purposes being valid and useful—both today and tomorrow.

OUTSIDE-IN PLANNING

If one plans *for* society as the primary client, then an alternative perspective—an enlarged paradigm—is gained. Planning in this way is as if one were looking into the organization from outside—from the vantage point of society back into the organization and its results and efforts. Social good, now and in the future, becomes paramount and primary. The role of the educational organization as only one of many means-to-ends (providers) becomes obvious. In this type of planning, the client is all of society, as well as all of the educational partners.

Outside-in planning is proactive. It is a paradigm—or frame of reference—that constructively challenges the status quo (not just criticizes or derides it) while identifying possible new opportunities, purposes, and payoffs. This perspective is the rationale for most professionals who seek positive change and growth, not just damage control methods or ways to increase the efficiency of current operations.

PLANNING PERSPECTIVE: HOW WE VIEW OUR WORLD

The differences between these two planning perspectives is how one views the world—who one selects as the primary client and beneficiary. In the inside-out mode, the client (and beneficiary) is the organization; its survival and well-being will likely be paramount. The outside-in mode sees the basic client (and beneficiary) as society, and anything which the organization can or should contribute is identified and considered in that light.

Figure 2.4 shows the two different "views." We argue that the outside-in view is more realistic and practical. It clearly recognizes that education and educational agencies are means to societal ends. Its use reduces the likelihood that the primary client and beneficiary of education will be the organization itself or its associates while ignoring those who pay the bills.

When an educational organization's mission contributes to the well-being of today's and tomorrow's society it is likely to be successful. In practice, there are different "fits" among society, school, curriculum, educator, and learner. Based on the degree of alignment, there are different possibilities regarding optimism for the contributions and future of the educational agency, as shown in Figure 2.5. The upper segment of the figure shows how different aspects of an educational operation, when splintered and unrelated, will likely lead to an ineffective system. The middle section of Figure 2.5 shows overlap among the various aspects which (if they are moving together) offer some hope for positive payoffs. The lower part of the figure shows an integration of the various facets which bodes well for educational success.

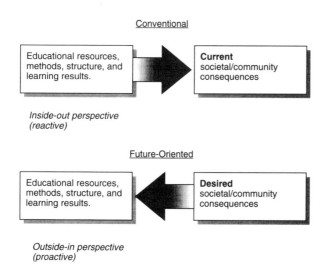

Figure 2.4. Inside-Out and Outside-In Perspectives for Educational Strategic Planning (© R. Kaufman, 1995).

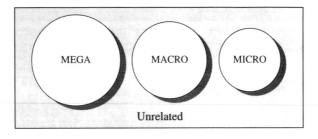

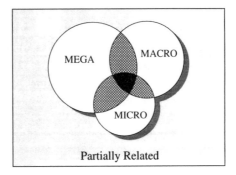

Figure 2.5. Different Aspects of an Educational Organization (© R. Kaufman, 1995).

Related to outside-in/inside-out approaches to planning is the direction in which we actually do our planning and improving.

ROLLING UP: THE INSIDE-OUT APPROACH

Most approaches to strategic planning move from inside-out. They build from lower levels of organizational efforts and results, and progress upward to the organizational mission . . . building a house of blocks from the lowest levels hoping the roof and even hoping (or assuming) that the whole structure will be safe and usable – that the ground upon which it is built is firm and stable. They will build an entire educational system from the subject matter learning objectives in each course to deliver satisfied clients. Using this typical tactic, each class, then course, then department, then school is asked, in turn, to set in place a ''strategic plan.'' These, in turn, are used to build the levels above. In this sequential fashion, the whole array of individual strategic plans are ''rolled up'' together to construct the would-be total educational strategic plan. The consequence of this tactic is an internally consistent plan where each part is linked to all parts from lower to higher levels of the organization: from tests and courses, to curriculum and courses, to buildings and teachers, to the school years, to the graduates, to the levels of self-sufficiency and self-reliance. Typical of this approach would be an organization with several operating schools and levels (elementary, middle, secondary, vo-tech) where each part's strategic plans would be ''rolled up'' together. With this inside-out approach, you better be sure you have the right destination the structure is responsive to the environment before building an increasingly efficient educational system – you could get completers who pass all the courses and still have no marketable competencies or social skills!

ROLLING DOWN: THE OUTSIDE-IN APPROACH

Uncommon is the approach which defines the external environment and human condition to be achieved, and then derives – moving (or rolling) downward – defining what each part of the educational establishment must contribute to the whole, as well as the ways each part of the system must cooperate and mutually contribute to the collective educational mission. Planning, using this tactic, might move from a self-sufficient society, to drug elimination and an educated citizenry, to curriculum, to incentive programs; from citizens who are healthy, down to the practices and procedures of hospital location and patient intake. By starting from the outside of the system with the specification of what should be created (or maintained), the strategic plan is free from ''how we always do business.'' It is thus released from the restraints of existing philosophy, politics, materials, approaches, content, and methods. Instead of only seeking efficiency, the rolling-down approach provides the opportunity to create a modified (or even a new) organization, courses, methods of instruction, location, and content. This will contribute to a continuously successful school system, including graduates and completers' survival and well-being, and an improved and continuously improving current and future world.

ROLLING DOWN/ROLLING UP: A CONSOLIDATED APPROACH

Most school organizations are currently successful in some of the things they do and deliver. They should continue that which is successful while seeking what to change, modify, add or delete. It is not unlikely that entirely independent new school systems will be built. It is possible that new delivery avenues and techniques might be created and existing ones disbanded or modified extensively. As shown in Figure 2.6, it is reasonable to both roll-up and roll-down planning results as a continuing and seamless process. Compare the inside-out and outside-in perspectives, and revise wherever required: develop the up-from-the-bottom strategic plan, and, at the same time (ideally independently), develop the down-from-the-top plan and see if they meet and match.

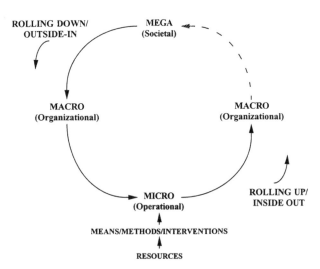

Figure 2.6. Rolling Up or Rolling Down — Which Better Assures Success (© R. Kaufman, 1995)?

If there are mismatches between elements of the plan, then changes should be made. For example, suppose the rolling-up plan calls for improving *efficiency* by increasing school hours and the number of school offerings of an inner-city school. This, in turn, calls for more teachers, more books, more media, and more computers. Now, if the top-down plan shows that there should be, more than increased efficiency, useful results — no completer without a job-readiness skill and the ability to identify and resolve problems, an increase of at least 60% of those who go on to college, and an increase of 100% who get and keep jobs — then the rolled-up plan with its early selection of means and resources which might not deliver the required results is likely incompatible with the rolled-down plan. Based on the probabilities of future happenings and consequences (tougher educational standards, demonstration of return-on-investment, etc.), and the priorities the strategic planning partners have selected, alternative tactics and resources may be identified, verified, and chosen. This selection of the roll down results because it is unlikely that the roll-up recommendations for throwing more money, time, and people at the existing situation will meet future realities or even deliver useful results. It is not likely that any roll-up process will deliver a positive return on the fiscal contribution made to the system.

A disadvantage of employing the roll-up approach alone is that new opportunities, targets, and visions may be overlooked by moving from the bottom reaches of organizational efforts, resources, and results upward in increasing building-block fashion. By using both approaches — analogous to getting dressed by rolling down a sweater from the top and pulling up slacks from the bottom — you and your educational organization might get the best of all possible worlds . . . by using both proactive and reactive modes to identify a useful future for all concerned.

SUMMARY

One important theme that runs through this book is that there are different levels of results. The choice of a planning frame of reference — level of focus — has major implications for the success of any effort. A useful guide to assist planners is a five-unit framework called the Organizational Elements Model (OEM). If one chooses too narrow a frame of reference, the result will likely be a very well-developed component that does not contribute to the whole. If one selects a frame of reference that only extends the current educational goals and purposes into the future, possible new objectives and payoffs might be overlooked. If one just gazes at the future without taking care of today, the whole adventure might be disastrous. Picking the most useful and practical frame of reference is a serious responsibility of planners and partners entrusted with the future of their systems and citizens.

Planning and planning literature often focus on the here and now, with a view to meeting urgent crises and political considerations, and they should not be minimized or ignored. But there is another, equally important, frame of reference: creating the future to benefit society — mega-level strategic planning.

It is important to note that although we should plan to achieve outcomes such as self-sufficiency and self-reliance, we will probably never realize them completely; we can only attempt to get as continuously close as possible.

Armed with such strategic thinking, we can now begin our strategic planning.

CHAPTER 3

Strategic Planning Starts with the Ideal Vision

CHAPTER FRAMEWORK: Identifying the Ideal Vision • Continuous Improvement toward the Ideal Vision • Ideal Visions Are More Similar than Different • Getting Agreement on the Mega-Level: Starting with an Ideal Vision

KEY HIGHLIGHTS: Relationship between the ideal vision and mega-level strategic planning • Critical significance of an ideal vision to strategic planning • Relationship of en route results and the ideal vision within the strategic planning process • Similarities among ideal visions • Importance of a shared ideal vision and agreement among the planning partners

IDENTIFYING THE IDEAL VISION

STRATEGIC planning is long-range planning to define and achieve an ideal vision—to create the future we want tomorrow's child to help produce and live. At this first scoping phase, the planning partners identify, define, and plan to create a preferred future. At this juncture, it is vital that all partners agree on the mega-level scope of strategic thinking and planning.

Planning Partners

The selection of a planning partners' group must assure that key experiences, perspectives, understandings, values, and constituencies contribute to identifying the ideal vision/preferred future as well as developing the system's related mission objective. Without a broad-based group of planning partners, the ideal vision will be a limited, superficial one. When identifying and selecting the educational planning partners, assure that they are really representative of their constituencies. If ethnic and age composition are important—and they usually are—obtain a representative sample. Scan the demographics of your system and service area and make certain that no group, including

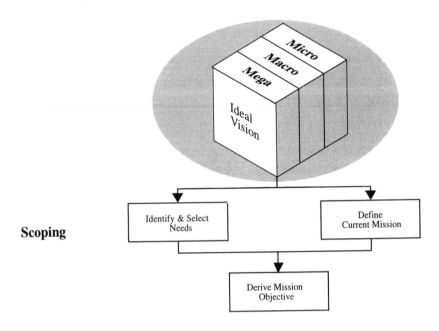

© R. Kaufman, 8/94

learners, is left out. We also urge that you compose the planning partner group of a "vertical slice" of the constituency. A "vertical slice" has within it representatives at all levels of the stakeholders and organization, including those from the very top[7] (the learners, parents, and society/community) right down the organization to include teachers, administrators, sweepers, and drivers. It is crucial that you locate influential opinion-formers and key communicators, and include them in your planning group.

Including Beliefs and Values, but Not Starting Strategic Planning with Them

It is important to define an ideal vision before restricting oneself with uncovering and considering unchallenged beliefs and values. Although it is customary, under many strategic planning approaches, to begin with

---

[7]While it is convenient to talk about levels, we urge that all people, at all levels, are seen as and included as equal partners.

identifying values and beliefs, our approach avoids some possible conflict introduced by beginning with unchallenged perceptions.[8] By first defining the ideal vision the planning partners are unencumbered by premature adherence to unexamined values.

Although it is conventional strategic planning practice to define beliefs and values first, it is not a productive approach. Doing so allows the strongly held "philosophies" and ways of viewing the world to drive and bias the future view rather than allowing the ideal vision to drive what we do and accomplish today and tomorrow. Starting with the identification of beliefs and values assumes that the educational partner's attitudes and perceptions are immutable and unchangeable. Worse, starting with existing beliefs and values assumes that they are all correct and useful. Recall the many positive changes we have had wrought recently where we first had to overcome previously strongly held beliefs and values concerning ageism, sexism, racism, ethnocentrism, and anti-intellectualism.

Strategic thinking and planning focuses on results before selecting the means or beliefs and values.

The initial strategic planning task is to define the kind of world we want for tomorrow's child. As this cooperative process unfolds, and as partners define the ideal vision in results terms (devoid of means, resources, processes, and funds), some people will have an initial tendency to include means and resources in their vision. These premature leaps to solutions usually come from individuals imposing their beliefs and values. As the partners get comfortable with the ends orientation, they will start asking themselves (and each other) "If we did get this means, methods, or resource, what result could I expect to achieve?" Each time there is a disagreement over the content of the ideal vision, it will usually signal that someone is insisting on a means (computers, values education, vouchers, outcome-based education, back-to-basics) before defining what kind of world to create.

If there are disagreements about the elements of the ideal vision, they usually come from arguments over means, not ends. Reconciling differences is usually straightforward when (1) there is a firm emphasis on ends and not means; (2) the ideal vision is targeted to the mega-level;

[8]In the chapters which follow, and especially when discussing needs assessment, we will be suggesting methods and approaches for collecting perception data. The difference will be that those perceptions will focus on results, not on unchallenged notions of means and resources.

and (3) all involved understand how their own comfort zones might limit them from seeing new vistas, approaches, and payoffs. People's beliefs and values will come into productive play as they cooperatively identify the ideal vision, and they should not allow these perceptions to blind them to new vistas and new possibilities.

After Agreeing to the Mega-Planning Level, Derive an Ideal Vision: Define the World in Which We Want Tomorrow's Child to Live

Strategic planning, in its most powerful form, identifies results based upon an ideal vision: a mega-level "dream" (Kaufman, 1992a, 1992b, 1995; Kaufman and Herman, 1991; Kaufman and Grise, 1995). Martin Luther King, Jr. had a dream, and Walt Disney said that if you can dream it, you can do it—so we should develop our own ideal vision.

The ideal vision is just that—the ideal. In what kind of world do we want our children and grandchildren to live? From this ideal, we set steppingstone strategic objectives—including our mission objective—that will move us from current results ever closer to the ideal. We construct a results ladder that will link our three levels of results (Figure 3.1).

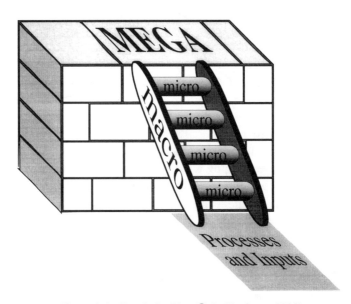

Figure 3.1. *Results Ladder (© R. Kaufman, 1995).*

Starting at the mega-level to develop the ideal vision is very pragmatic and practical. Setting your sights on what it is you and your colleagues want to become is called "practical dreaming" (Kaufman, 1992b; Roberts, 1993). If you don't intend to move ever closer to the ideal, where are you headed? If you don't intend to make everyone a winner,[9] who chooses the losers and the disenfranchised?

Although it is rational to start at the mega/ideal vision level, planners sometimes have the greatest initial discomfort with addressing societal outcomes — the mega-level — and often ignore or assume them. In such instances, so-called strategic planning actually stops at short-term, stop-gap objectives, and a true strategic plan is never developed or accomplished. Instead of first defining the ideal vision of the world in which we want tomorrow's child to live and help create, attention is immediately diverted to courses, content, and subject matter with the assumption that societally-useful results will follow.

Critical Success Factor #4: Use an ideal vision as the underlying basis for planning (don't be limited by current restraints nor limit the vision to your organization alone).

Collecting the Data for an Ideal Vision

Partners should derive the ideal vision with a results-only orientation. Table 3.1 provides a format for obtaining planning partner perceptions of an "ideal vision" (or preferred future), and a commitment to link organizational results and efforts to that ideal. This format breaks the agreement into two stages: first, a statement (free of means and resources) of the ideal; and, then, an identification of criteria that could be used to measure success and progress.

It is not unusual for first-time vision creators to keep including means and resources in their initial responses. Keep asking "If I successfully applied these means/resources, what result and payoffs would result?" By repeatedly revisiting this question, there will be a shift to ends. Keep repeating this question until the ends are at the mega-level. If there are partners who feel very strongly about a means or resource, write it down and post it in front of the entire group and note that it will definitely be considered when selecting the methods and means for the organization to achieve its vision and mission.

[9]Similar to Leon Lessinger's 1970s concept of "every kid a winner" (Lessinger, 1970).

Table 3.1. Obtaining Planning Partner Perceptions (© R. Kaufman, 1994).

Ideal Vision
Describe the world in which you want tomorrow's child—your children and grandchildren—to live:

ENDS/Results Criteria
(e.g., no suicides, no deaths from toxic substances, no murders, no rapes, no species becomes extinct from unintended human causes.)

Double Checking the Ideal Vision

After the groups have derived an initial statement of their ideal vision, identify which elements of it are at the mega-, macro-, and micro-levels. Also identify if any means (processes) or resources (inputs) have been included. For each vision element which is not at the mega-level, ask "If I got this result, what contribution to the mega-level would it make?" After answering that question, it is likely that the original statement (at the macro- or micro-levels) will be replaced with the mega-referenced statement. If any input or process statements are included, convert them to ends-related criteria.

Although some (using old paradigms) will dismiss the developing of an ideal vision as a "pie in the sky," without an ideal vision we limit the thinking and planning to reactive, here-and-now, quick-fix tactics. Devising a shared ideal vision is so important that several authors have identified it as critical to contemporary thinking and planning (e.g., Kaufman, 1992a, 1992b, 1995; Nanus, 1992; Senge, 1990). With a shared ideal vision, each person can know how to contribute, in his or her unique way, to that journey. We use it as a North Star for steering and orchestrating our educational processes.

A shared destination may be intrinsic (create tomorrow's ideal world) or it may be extrinsic (having the highest number of Merit Scholars; winning a Baldridge Award). The intrinsic works better (Senge, 1990). Simply meeting the challenge of competition (having more success than private schools; having the lowest dropout rates, or lowest levels of truancy) is transitory and does not obtain commitment to continuous improvement and a holistic, societal-contribution destination. It also overlooks possible opportunities others have not discovered.

Ideal visions that speak to defining and achieving a shared "perfect" destination allow alignment between the society, your organization, and the personal aspirations of all members. The concept of an ideal, even perfect, vision of the world is increasingly encouraged. Senge's book *The Fifth Discipline* (1990) devotes a chapter to the topic and quotes a number of "practical" executives on the importance of generating and using an ideal and perfect vision to drive all organizational contributions. For example, Senge quotes Kazou Inamori, of the Japanese Kyocera Corporation, as urging people to aim for a perfect world (a societal view), not simply being the best; or a societal vision, as opposed to merely an organizational one.

If we want an ideal world for tomorrow's child—a world at peace, with no deaths or disabilities from drug addiction, no requirement for welfare, no crime, and so on, those factors should form the ideal vision. Issues of practicality should not be considered here (otherwise we would limit ourselves to that which we are currently achieving or know we can deliver). If we don't reach for a better future through strategic planning, how will we ever know the direction for the first step to begin the journey?

Nay-sayers will disparagingly carp about these being "utopian." Forgive them. They are using old and outmoded paradigms which keep them in their comfort zones. We must set an ideal standard, even if we never get there in our lifetime or that of our children, so that we know what direction in which to continuously move and for us to plot our progress to identify what is working . . . and what is not. From this ideal, we set building-block strategic objectives that will get us from our current results ever closer to the ideal vision.

CONTINUOUS IMPROVEMENT TOWARD THE IDEAL VISION

The achievement of the en route results on the way to the ideal vision will take time and consistent effort. Micro results might start to appear this year; macro results, within the next several years; mega results in four to ten years; and the ideal vision, twenty years or more in the future.

For example, if part of our ideal vision includes everyone obtaining and keeping a job above the poverty level, our schools could commit to achieve that by the year 2010. The building-block results would have at least ninety-five percent of graduates and completers mastering the requisite skills, knowledge, attitudes, and abilities by the year 2000; and the building-block competencies will start to be demonstrated by learners starting next year. The ideal vision from which this all flowed might have been this: "Every learner, graduate, or completer will be self-sufficient and self-reliant. They will not be under the care, custody, or control of another person, agency, or substance."

IDEAL VISIONS ARE MORE SIMILAR THAN DIFFERENT

Any ideal vision speaks to a perfect future. Regardless of the type of organization (a technical high school, a school district, health agency, or the Coast Guard), ideal visions will be very similar. Because all organizations, educational ones included, are means to societal ends, their ideal visions will be similar. When getting your planning partners to think about the world they want for their children and grandchildren, a very appealing place gets defined.

For example, here is an ideal vision developed by one public sector health and human services organization:

Our citizens have a bright future. People take charge of their lives, become healthy and stay self-sufficient. Families are strong, self-reliant, and productive. Neighborhoods are safe, supportive, and prosperous, and residents contribute to the achievement of peace and harmony for their community. This vision will become real as we trust people, as we earn the public's trust through our own excellence, and as we are full partners with people, families, and neighborhoods as they achieve success.

Compare that ideal vision with one for a mining company:

The world will be safe for every living thing. There will be no species which becomes endangered or extinct from human causes. There will be no murder, rape, war, psychological or physical abuse. People will acquire the skills and abilities and will be self-sufficient and self-reliant and will assist others to acquire those same skills and values so that less than one percent of the population will ever be temporarily (less than six months) requiring social welfare. Water will be available and clean, so that no one will get ill or die from contamination. No one will die from starvation, thirst, contamination in their homes, lands, food, water, or air.

Here is an educational organization's ideal vision:

There will be no murders, rapes, or crimes, nor debilitating substance abuse. The world will be at peace. It will be free of infectious disease, and every child brought into the world will be a wanted child. Poverty will not exist, and every woman and man will earn at least as much as it costs him/her to live unless he/she is going to school and moving toward preparing him/herself so that he/she is increasingly close to being self-sufficient and self-reliant. People will take charge of their lives and be responsible for what they use, do, and contribute. Personal, intimate, and loving partnerships will form and sustain themselves. Government's contribution will be assisting people to be happy and self-sustaining, will reinforce independence and mutual contribution, and will be organized and funded to the extent to which it meets its objectives. Business will earn a profit without bringing harm to its clients and our mutual world.

Useful, practical, proactive strategic thinking and planning depends upon an ideal vision as its primary referent. Remember *Critical Success Factor #4: use an ideal vision as the underlying basis for planning (don't be limited by current restraints nor limit it to your organization alone)*. Going directly to macro- or micro-level planning should not be given into easily — it just is not safe to do so.

GETTING AGREEMENT ON THE MEGA-LEVEL: STARTING WITH AN IDEAL VISION

An Agreement Table

Often skeptics, outside of their comfort zones, have not really considered what their customary ways of viewing the world and their organization really mean. They have been successful in the past, and the discomfort of change might "blind" them to the full array of organizational questions to be asked and answered (see Figure 2.2).

Table 3.2 provides an educational strategic planning agreement table which asks educational partners and stakeholders to actively respond to a series of questions. These questions, each requiring a "yes" or "no"

Table 3.2. Educational Strategic Planning Agreement Table (© R. Kaufman, 1995).

	Response			
	Stakeholders		Planners	
	Y	N	Y	N
1. Each school, as well as the total educational system, will contribute to the learner's, as well as society's, current and future success, survival, health, and well-being.				
2. Each school, as well as the total educational system, will contribute to the learner's, as well as society's, current and future quality of life.				
3. Learner's current and future survival, health, and well-being will be part of the system's and each of its school's mission objective.				
4. Each educational function will have objectives which contribute to #1, #2, and #3.				
5. Each job/task/activity will have objectives which contribute to #1, #2, #3, and #4.				
6. A Needs Assessment will identify and document any gaps in results at the operational levels of #1, #2, #3, #4, and #5.				
7. Educational learning requirements will be generated from the Needs identified in #6.				
8. The results of #6 may recommend non-educational interventions.				
9. Evaluation will use data from comparing results with objectives for #1, #2, #3, #4, and #5.				
10. Data from evaluation will be used to continuously improve the contributions of #1, #2, #3, #4, and #5.				

signature forces the partners to consider the total array of important variables and considerations for planning and doing.

If a partner decides that they do not want to operate at the mega-level, then they (1) initial under the "no" column, and (2) realize that if there are no results at that level they "own" the responsibility for not even attempting to get there! By working through the Strategic Planning Agreement Table, most people realize the full array of questions and variables which are to be formally considered.

While, for some, competition motivates action and improvement, any vision should not be centered on rivalry (e.g., better test results than Canada, or fewer drop-outs than Michael County), rather it motivates and encourages everyone to enroll in the adventure of creating the future. Walt Disney was right, if we can dream it, we can do it. Martin Luther King, Jr. had a dream and we are moving toward it. Peter Drucker advises us if we cannot predict the future, create it!

The ideal visions identified in this chapter are ''consensual'' — based on what diverse groups agreed upon to begin initial strategic planning and thinking—and thus include elements that are ''comfortable'' to them. They include some means and non-mega level results. Appendix C provides a basic and minimal ideal vision that eliminates process-oriented elements.

SUMMARY: STRATEGIC PLANNING IS PRACTICAL DREAMING

In its most powerful form, strategic planning first identifies results based upon an ideal vision: a mega-level practical dream. To be useful, an ideal vision has to:

(*1*) Be future oriented—unfettered by any constrained or negative thinking; it is an ideal and, as such, defines the kind of world we want for tomorrow's children

(*2*) Identify a clear set of conditions, written in a format using all the elements for measurable objectives

(*3*) Be completely devoid of means, methods, and ''how-to's'' and, instead, focus on tangible results

(*4*) Project hope, energy, and destination; not despair, distrust, or negatives such as competition

CHAPTER 4

Identifying Mission Based on the Ideal Vision[10]

CHAPTER FRAMEWORK: A Mission Objective Is Derived from the Ideal Vision • Defining the Mission • Mission Statements vs. Mission Objectives • Preparing Useful Objectives—Including Mission Objectives • Everything Is Measurable. Everything. • Preparing Mission Objectives from Mission Statements • Templates for Developing Useful Objectives • Beyond Just Efficiency: Optional Template 4 • Hypothetical Mission Statement: An Example • Deriving the Mission Objective from the Ideal Vision • Identifying Existing Policies, Rules, Laws, and Regulations as Part of the Determination of Mission • Some Curriculum Considerations

KEY HIGHLIGHTS: Critical significance of the ideal vision to the organizational mission and the mission objective • Differences between a mission statement and a mission objective • Importance of the mission objective in the strategic planning process • Four key components of a mission objective • Differences among the types of results and their relationship to scales of measure • Importance of transforming a mission statement to a mission objective • Templates for converting mission statements to mission objectives • Importance of proactive planning and its relationship to the future and "what should be" • Examples of mission objectives • Significance of current policies, rules, laws, and regulations when determining performance requirements as they relate to the mission objective • Critical value of the relationship of the ideal vision to measurable objectives and their relationship to new transformations that could emerge

AN organization's basic mission identifies where the organization is headed. It supplies the declaration of purpose and destination. A mission

---

[10]A system approach, such as the one used in this book, has a number of advantages and some initial disadvantages. The advantages include the recognition that all parts of the system have to operate according to specific criteria *and* contribute to a common purpose in the interaction of one with all of the others. An initial disadvantage is that the holistic concept of all parts interacting is very difficult to portray in a linear medium such as a book. This chapter provides such a potential stumbling block: it will not be until the next chapter that we get to the real details of how you move from the ideal vision to the basic mission objective, but for accuracy we have to note this roll-down relationship here. Please, as you read this and other chapters, remember the interactive/transactional nature of our approach . . . it is what keeps it from being arbitrary, linear, authoritarian, and prescriptive.

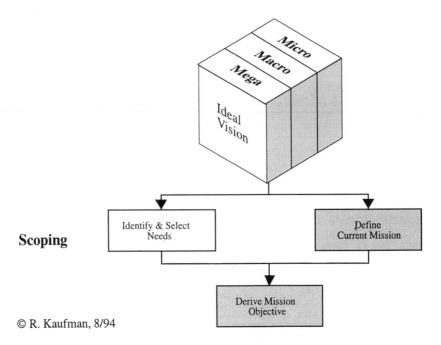

Scoping

© R. Kaufman, 8/94

objective identifies, in *measurable performance terms,* where the organization is headed. In this chapter we identify:

- the characteristics of a mission objective (which is like any other objective in being specific)
- how to write a useful mission objective (and objectives in general)
- how to roll down from an ideal vision to determine a related mission objective

A MISSION OBJECTIVE IS DERIVED FROM THE IDEAL VISION

The identification of the ideal vision is important to our defining an organizational mission. Figure 4.1 depicts the general relationship of the mission to the ideal vision.

As noted in Chapter 2, strategic planning rolls down from the ideal vision, which provides the continuing and developing basis for results at the macro- and micro-levels, and provides substantiation to processes and inputs. This relationship is shown in Figure 4.2.

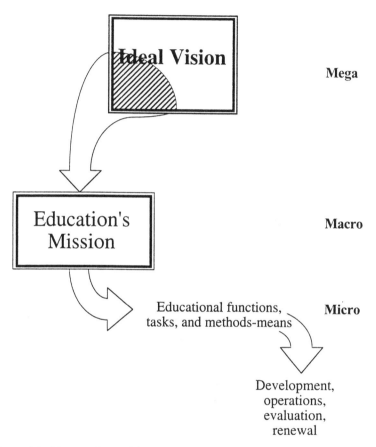

Figure 4.1. *Missions Derived from the Ideal Vision. An Organization Will Select What Portion of the Ideal Vision It Commits to Address and Plans and Does from There (© R. Kaufman, 1995).*

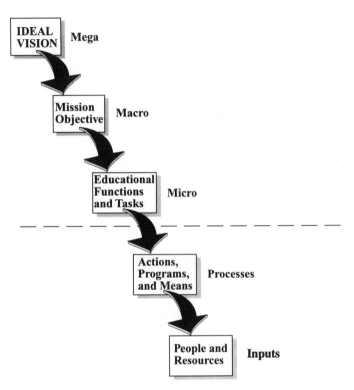

Figure 4.2. *The Three Levels of Planning (Mega, Macro, Micro) and Their Relation to Inputs and Processes (© R. Kaufman, 1995).*

54

DEFINING THE MISSION

A mission identifies the elements of the ideal vision that the organization commits to deliver, and states the over-arching educational purpose which measurably contributes to that vision. The mission will state precisely the destination which allows all educational partners to:

(*1*) Agree to that journey
(*2*) Set their contribution ''compasses'' to enable them, individually and together, to steer toward that common mission (and also toward the ideal vision)
(*3*) Decide what they want to spend — in time, resources, and effort — to get there
(*4*) Evaluate the extent to which they are progressing toward, and arriving at, the shared result

Unfortunately, the missions of educational systems are often stated in well-intentioned, yet global and rambling terms, such as ''The mission of this district is to help learners grow and develop in a multi-cultural environment in a cost-effective and continuous improvement manner so they will be competitive in a global economy.''

Such statements are much too vague. When doing a strategic plan, the common ''North Star,'' toward which all can steer, has to be both precise and measurable.

Strategic planning depends on precise, measurable, valid mission objectives that state the purpose and the destination of the organization along with the precise criteria for assessing success.

MISSION STATEMENTS VS. MISSION OBJECTIVES

A *mission statement* is a general description of purpose. (As we will see later, mission statements are measurable on nominal or ordinal scales, while mission objectives are measurable on interval or ratio scales.) A mission statement can be motivational, inspirational, and directional. It states a destination, but it does not include tight, rigorous, measurable specifications for determining when the mission has been accomplished. A *mission objective* states both where the organization is headed and provides precise criteria for determining accomplishment.

— A *mission statement* is a general, overall destination; an intended organizational result.

— A *mission objective* is a precise and rigorous statement of where the organization is headed and provides the criteria—stated as an output—for assessing when one has arrived.

If we are going someplace, we should know exactly where that "someplace" is located. A mission statement provides intention. We must know the exact criteria for the location of where we are headed. The measurement of location, for both planning and evaluation purposes, is central to planning. (Examples of mission statements vs. mission objectives are provided later in this chapter.)

PREPARING USEFUL OBJECTIVES—INCLUDING MISSION OBJECTIVES

A Focus on Ends, Not Means

Where are we going? How do we know when we have arrived? Mager (1975) set the standard by identifying that an objective should state, without confusion,

(*1*) Who or what will demonstrate the performance

(*2*) What performance is to be demonstrated

(*3*) Under what conditions the performance will be observed

(*4*) What criteria will be used to determine success

A vital characteristic of an objective is that it relates only to results. Objectives never should state *how* we will achieve the result, only the performance to be exhibited, by whom or what will it be demonstrated, where it will be shown, and what criteria will be used to measure it. Thus, in preparing any objective, including a mission objective, we address ends, not means, as in " *Critical Success Factor #2: Differentiate between ends and means (distinguish between what and how).*"

Table 4.1 shows a format for preparing "Mager-type" objectives, built on an ABCD framework.

Table 4.2 provides a hypothetical example of an objective using the ABCD elements.

Table 4.1. Mager-Type Objectives (© R. Kaufman, 1994).

A Format for Preparing Measurable Objectives: As Easy as ABCD
A: Who or what is the *Audience,* target, or recipient?   B: What *Behavior,* performance, accomplishment, end, consequence, or result is to be demonstrated?   C: Under what *Conditions* will the behavior or accomplishment be observed?   D: What *Data*—criteria, ideally measured on an interval or ratio scale—will be used to calibrate success?

Table 4.2. A Sample Completed ABCD Form.

A Format for Preparing Measurable Objectives: As Easy as ABCD	
ABCD Element	Hypothetical Objective
A: What or Who is the *Audience,* target, or recipient?	100% of all learners, completers, and leavers who enrolled at the Grise Unified School District after August 17, 1996.
B: What *Behavior,* performance, accomplishment, end, or result is to be demonstrated?	Will be accepted to accredited post-secondary education, and/or get and keep a job which pays at least as much as it costs them to live. None will drop out without meeting state requirements, and all will be self-sufficient.
C: Under what *Conditions* will the behavior or accomplishment be observed?	Both in school and beyond, as certified by an independent audit of in-school registrations and district records, as well as placement and follow-up of completers and leavers.
D: What *Data*—criteria, ideally measured on an interval or ratio scale—will be used to calibrate?	There will be zero drop-outs, and zero previously enrolled learners who did not get accepted to an accredited post-secondary program and/or who did not get and keep a job for at least six months (barring seasonal or economic lay-offs) as reported and certified by the superintendent and/or the State Department of Employment.

Based on Kaufman, 1995 (with permission)..

Table 4.3. A Taxonomy of Educational Results.

Type of Result	Description/Label	Scale of Measurement
Naming—no implied direction	Goal, aim, purpose	Nominal
Rank order—relative position		Ordinal
Equal scale distances with arbitrary zero-point	Objective, performance indicator, performance	Interval
Equal scale distances with known zero-point	criteria	Ratio

Based, in part, on Kaufman (1972, 1988b, 1992b) and Kaufman and Herman (1991a).

Table 4.4. Some Hypothetical Educational Mission Statements, Objectives, and Their Associated Scales of Measurement.

Educational Intention	Scale of Measurement			
	Nominal	Ordinal	Interval	Ratio
Develop each child to his/her own capacity	X			
Creating excellence in higher education	X			
Create a Total Quality System	X			
Better jobs		X		
Learning for the 90s and beyond	X			
90% of all learners graduate			X	
Happy children make successful students	X			
A learning place	X			
All learners get and keep a job				X
Higher standards for exceptional learners	X			
Higher performance for at-risk youngsters		X		
Students come first	X			
Building better students for tomorrow's world		X		
Score at or above 90			X	

EVERYTHING IS MEASURABLE. EVERYTHING.

Everything is measurable. Table 4.3 provides a taxonomy of educational results.

The only differences among types of results lie in the reliability of the measurement. Interval and ratio scale measures involve much more precision than nominal or ordinal scales. Sometimes we don't know enough about variables (such as self-esteem or learning style) to develop true interval or ratio scale measures, so we simply write goals, or purposes. When we do know enough about a phenomenon to write true objectives (using an interval or ratio scale), then ethically we should do so. But pretending that some things are not measurable, or "intangible," avoids reality and places important – and often very humanistic – results and achievements in question.

Using some examples of mission statements, we can begin to identify nominal and ordinal measures as shown in Table 4.4.

PREPARING MISSION OBJECTIVES FROM MISSION STATEMENTS

An important step in strategic planning is to translate, as is usually required, the current statement of educational purpose (often inaccurately called the "mission" or "objective") into measurable performance terms. This translation is important because it will allow the strategic planner to identify objectives already in place in the agency and also to identify those that have to be modified or deleted.

Most educational agencies have an existing mission statement, but it must be turned into a measurable commitment for results. An important strategic planning task is likely to take existing statements of purpose, and, from them, derive mission objectives which will (1) state our direction and destination, (2) add rigorous criteria, and (3) provide the basis for strategic and tactical, as well as sensible, planned accountability for results.

Objectives at all levels – mega, macro, and micro – can and should include all of the elements highlighted in the ABCD format. Frequently, objectives for the entire educational organization only deal with intentions and thus are best called "mission statements." We should prepare mission objectives and not be content with motivational statements of intent, such as "education for all" or even "educational excellence for all learners."

Although a mission statement (i.e., "a learning place," "excellence in teaching," "develop each child to his or her greatest potential") sets a direction, it is hardly the stuff for strategic thinking, let alone strategic planning. We must, if we are serious about getting useful results, state both where we are headed and how we can measure (on an interval or ratio scale) when we have arrived:

mission statement + measurable criteria = mission objective

Measurability, best on an interval or ratio scale of measurement, is vital to setting educational purposes and destinations. Even when deriving our ideal vision (see Chapter 3), we define each element of it in measurable performance terms . . . as objectives. From the measurable elements in the ideal vision, we identify which parts of it we commit to deliver and move continuously closer toward.

The differences among objectives are only in terms of level, not in substance or content. This is so important that it is *Critical Success Factor #5:*

Critical Success Factor #5: Prepare all objectives—including mission objectives—to include rigorous, precise, clear statements of both where you are headed and how you will know when you have arrived.

"TEMPLATES" FOR DEVELOPING USEFUL OBJECTIVES

It is crucial to understand that objectives have two fundamental uses, one proactive and the other reactive, to (1) identify what results (or mission) to accomplish, and (2) provide criteria for assessing success or failure. Objectives can target each or all of the three types of ends (products, outputs, outcomes) and, thus, mega-, macro-, and micro-levels of planning.

There are three characteristics of a useful objective:

(*1*) They differentiate ends from means (and eliminates means and/or resources).

(*2*) They measure results, ideally in interval or ratio scale terms.

(*3*) They encompass the range of three results—products, outputs, and outcomes—of the five organizational elements.

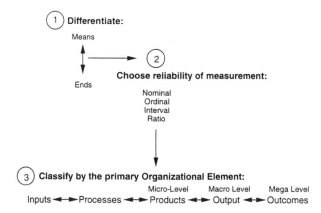

Figure 4.3. *The Relationship among the Three Performance Templates (based on, with permission, Kaufman, 1988).*

Figure 4.3 provides a series of templates for preparing, reviewing, or converting intentions to measurable objectives. Any of these templates may be used . . . ideally all of them. The relationships among the templates are provided. The steps are numbered, and include:

(*1*) Differentiate means from ends.

(*2*) Select the reliability of measurement.

(*3*) Classify the primary organizational element upon which to focus.

BEYOND JUST EFFICIENCY: OPTIONAL TEMPLATE 4

Strategic planning is best when it is proactive, that is, oriented towards creating a better future, not just making the current operations more efficient. Some conventional mission intentions (and other educational purposes) are framed only to improve current consequences without examining their validity and usefulness—just improving ''what is.'' If you are confident of the validity and utility of current objectives and the educational mission, then Templates 1 − 3 will suffice. However, if you choose to ask if the objective/mission to be accomplished is worth doing in the first place, then Template 3 may be extended to include the two planning dimensions of ''what is'' and ''what should be,'' as shown in Figure 4.4.

An added bonus for using this additional template surfaces when doing an evaluation mandates continuous improvement. By examining both "what is" and "what should be" for results, an evaluation may be planned to compare three types of results (or levels) and then two types of means (resources and processes). This will allow a contrasting of "what was intended" with "what was accomplished" for each of the organizational elements, instead of lumping all means and ends together or confusing different levels of evaluation and improvement.

Table 4.5 shows the scope of each of the three levels of strategic educational planning where each will be concerned with both "what is" and "what should be."

Table 4.6 provides the characteristics of a mission objective. It also provides a format and process for assuring the levels of your objectives and for determining if your mission objectives are really objectives, and

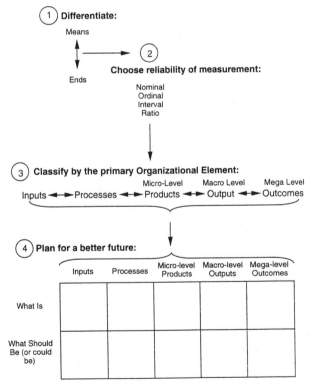

Figure 4.4. *Four Possible "Templates" for Developing Useful Objectives. Any or All May Be Used. The Numbers* ① *to* ④ *Show a Recommended Sequence (© R. Kaufman, 1994).*

Table 4.5. The Areas of Concern of Mega-, Macro-, and Micro-Planning for the Organizational Elements (including both "what is" and "what should be") (© R. Kaufman, 1990).

	Inputs	Processes	Products	Outputs	Outcomes
Mega	X	X	X	X	X
Macro	X	X	X	X	
Micro	X	X	X		

Table 4.6. Conditions of a Mission Objective (© R. Kaufman, 1994).

Conditions	Characteristics
1. What accomplishment is to be displayed in order to demonstrate completion? 2. Whom or what is to demonstrate completion? 3. Under what conditions is it to be demonstrated? 4. What criteria will be used to determine if it is accomplished? (How much or how well is it to be done?)	Objectives must communicate successfully to all users and evaluators. All of the conditions for measuring results must be specified and must contain the basis for evaluation; they must be in measurable performance terms which are valid and will leave no room for confusion.

Table 4.7. A Format and Procedure for Assuring That Your Mission Is Useful, Deals with Ends and Not Means, and Has Mega-Level Expectations (© R. Kaufman, 1994).

Mission Elements:	Target		Results/Ends Level		
	Means	Ends	Micro	Macro	Mega
a) b) c) etc. . . .					
Step: 1) List each element of the mission. 2) For each element, determine if it relates to a means or an end. 3) If an element relates to an end, determine if it is focused at the micro, macro, or mega-level. 4) If an element relates to a means, ask "What result—and payoff—would I get if I got or accomplished this?" Keep asking the same question until an end is identified.					

not statements. Table 4.7 will assist you in translating mission statements into mission objectives at the mega-level and for assuring that you have all three levels of results covered and related.

This process is useful for any derivation of objectives, whether at the mega-, macro-, or micro-levels. It is essential, in keeping with *Critical Success Factors #2* and *#3,* to assure that objectives deal with ends and that all three levels of ends are considered and linked.

HYPOTHETICAL MISSION STATEMENT: AN EXAMPLE

Now, consider the following hypothetical mission statements in terms of whether they provide enough specificity to guide strategic planning:

Unacceptable: Develop better citizens for the 21st Century. (This is a statement of general intent, or mission statement, not a mission objective.)

Better: Before January 2, 2010, at least ninety-seven percent of the learners who have completed the graduation requirements from our district will be self-sufficient and self-reliant as indicated by follow-up data (such as job tenure, credit levels, etc.) certified as valid by a state university. (This objective is more specific and precise. It expresses what is to be accomplished, under what conditions it will be certified, and to what degree the results will be obtained.)

In stating a mission (or converting an existing intent), we start by specifying what has to be accomplished: the statement of mission (sometimes in general terms only) is the first step.

Some examples of general starting points might be:

(*1*) Develop each child to her/his capacity.

(*2*) Reduce drop-outs.

(*3*) Eliminate illiteracy in Simstown within ten years.

These, according to our taxonomy of results (see Table 4.3) are simply statements of goals, aims, or purposes. To be useful, our mission objective should be stated in interval or ratio terms (Step 2 of the template in Figures 4.3 and 4.4). Let's see how we might move from the intentional to the precise by supplying performance requirements.

For example, begin by asking, ''If we were to develop each child to her/his own capacity, what would result?'' If we moved to a results-oriented mode, our response might be ''There would be fewer drop-outs and increased completers." (This moves us to the output level.) Continue by asking, "If we reduced drop-outs and increased completers, what would result from that?" A response might be "More jobs for graduates and fewer people would go on welfare."

By continually asking "So what would happen if we did that?" we move up the results chain from inputs, to processes, to products, to outputs, to outcomes. We are rooting our strategic plan in both current and future societal consequences. Continuing our development from the intention to "develop each child to her/his own capacity" we might come to a more complete example of a useful mission objective:

> Decrease by at least ten percent per year each year for the next fifteen years the number of drop-outs of the Jac School District who are not self-sufficient and self-reliant as indicated by: positive credit ratings, no convictions for crimes, no commitments to mental institutions, full employment, less than 3/100 divorces, and no welfare recipients. Accomplishment will be certified by the Superintendent of Schools on the first school day of each new calendar year, and based upon independently verified data. The budget shall increase by no more than five percent per year after adjustment for inflation, and will show positive return on investment.

Notice that this mission objective contains both quantitative and qualitative aspects:

- *Q: What is to be accomplished?* A: Increased self-sufficiency and self-reliance and reduction of drop-outs.
- *Q: Who or what will display it?* A: Learners in the Jac School District.
- *Q: Under what condition(s)?* A: By at least ten percent/year for the next fifteen years within a budget of no greater than five percent per year increase, after adjustment for inflation, and justified positive return on investment.
- *Q: What criteria (how much or how well) will be used?* A: Certification each year by the Superintendent and based upon independently verified data.

A mission objective has to successfully communicate to assure that all educational partners know where they are going (mission statement) and how they determine when they have arrived (performance requirements). Precision and rigor will help assure that reality. Another feature of a measurable mission objective, including its results orientation and precision, is that it must also contain the criteria for evaluation and continuous improvement. Loose or unclear terms such as "quality," "excellence," "appreciate," and "understand" are not meaningful unless they are defined precisely. A mission objective has to be free of terminology that is just qualitative. And let's always keep in focus a learner orientation and her or his ultimate ability to be a contributing, successful member of today's and tomorrow's societies.

Remember, there are four conditions stated in a useful mission objective and together they must show at least three characteristics, as shown in Table 4.6.

DERIVING THE MISSION OBJECTIVE FROM THE IDEAL VISION

As mentioned at the beginning of this chapter, the educational mission objective must identify the results the organization commits to deliver on its way toward fulfilling the ideal vision. If the mission objective does not contribute to the achievement of the ideal vision, the organization may be superfluous. The mission objective is derived from rolling down (see Figure 2.6) from the ideal vision the elements you are taking responsibility for delivering.

In order to relate the mission objective to the ideal vision, accomplish the following:

(1) Identify the elements, including performance criteria, that your educational agency commits to deliver. Of course, your organization cannot be responsible for the entire accomplishment of any one or several parts of the ideal vision, but you can directly impact its accomplishment. For example you could not single-handedly cause everyone in the world to be self-sufficient and self-reliant but you may cause individuals to become so . . . thus contributing to the progress toward achievement of the ideal.

(2) Identify the elements, again including performance criteria, that your organization commits to deliver in cooperation with one or more other agencies (such as social welfare, health and human services, business and industry).

(3) Identify the elements, including performance criteria, which must be accomplished in order for you to deliver on your results, but for

which your agency does not take responsibility, and which will be monitored to assure their delivery.

Following are examples of an ideal vision, and following that, a possible educational mission objective that has been derived from it.

An Ideal Vision

The world will be at peace, and there will be no murders, rapes, starvation, crimes, or disabilities from substance abuse.*** All people will feel secure and move around the state and nation safely without regard to time or place.** It will be free of infectious disease***, and every child brought into the world will be a wanted child.** Poverty will not exist. Every woman and man will earn at least as much as it costs them to live, unless they are going to school and moving toward becoming self-sufficient and self-reliant.* No one will be under the care, custody, or control of another person, agency, or substance.**

No species will become extinct due to unintended human intervention, pollution, or action.** Beaches, cities, towns, and the countryside will be free of litter, graffiti, and defacement.** People who have made their living through and with the environment will continue to do so without depleting the resources that provide their sustenance.*** Accidents will increasingly approach zero, and they will not result in death, disability, and daily living.**

The unlucky and unfortunate among us will be helped to help themselves so that they are increasingly close to being and becoming self-sufficient and self-reliant.** People will take charge of their lives and be responsible for what they use, do, and contribute.** People will form personal, intimate, and loving partnerships that will sustain them.**

Government's contribution will successfully assist people to be happy and self-sustaining,** will reinforce independence and mutual contribution, and will be organized and funded to the extent to which it meets its objectives. Business will earn a profit without bringing harm to its clients and our mutual world.***

Each statement within the ideal vision should be attributable for responsibility to one or more levels:

* indicates a direct responsibility of the educational agency
** indicates a direct concern for education but will be done in cooperation with one or more other agencies or agents
*** indicates a direct concern but no direct responsibility. We will track the progress and results in this area because they are important to us in delivering our results.

Education is probably unique among organizations in that what it uses, does, and delivers is basic to most, if not all, citizens and society. Education is the intersection of everything in our society. For example, we are not directly responsible for every child being a wanted child, but we can model and transfer values for human life, for instance, how to keep healthy, and how to make choices which do not negatively affect one's self and others. Another example is in safety, where the values learners bring to campuses are not directly controlled by the schools, but each school must assure the safety of its learners and staff.

The mission objective is built from the elements in the ideal vision it commits to deliver. Here is an example based upon the above sample ideal vision:

> By the year 2010 and continuously moving thereafter toward the accomplishment of the ideal vision, the following will be accomplished:

> All of those who graduate from our system will enroll in accredited higher educational programs and/or get jobs above minimum wage in their first, second, or third professional or occupational choice. In addition, they will choose to continue their formal and/or informal education and training.

> All graduates will be responsive and responsible citizens who volunteer in, as well as participate in civic activities. They will have come through an educational system that has served them so that they compare favorably on valid and reliable criterion and/or norm-referenced assessments for their general and specific knowledge and abilities. Neighbors and employers will rate them as both ''good neighbors'' and cost-effective associates.

> Their education will take place in a drug-free, crime-free, supportive, environment. All who seek it will have universal access to valid and reliable information and knowledge with validated learning opportunities geared to each learner's diverse characteristics, abilities, and potential. Learners will leave realizing that their higher educational experiences readied them for life, work, and the future.

> The knowledge, skills, abilities, and attitudes they acquire will be based on validated research (published in refereed journals or jury acceptance for the performing and literary arts), and the total educational system will be fully accredited.

> The learners will show no differences in graduation rates, job placements, employer satisfaction, or dropouts on the basis of such variables as location, income adjustments, color, race, creed, sex, sexual orientation, religion, or national origin. Additionally, there will be no decrement in the results levels as every learner and the system moves continuously toward the ideal vision.

There will be no births to learners of children who are is not supported, housed, loved, and maintained, as indicated by children who
do not require welfare, Aid to Dependent Children, or other government transfer payments targeted for socially dependent people.

Note that the above are still in nominal or ordinal scale terms. Strategic
planners would next put all of the elements in measurable performance
terms – interval and ratio indicators – as identified earlier in this chapter.

By using the processes provided in this chapter, your educational
organization will provide:

- a measurable, precise, and rigorous mission objective (which
  includes performance criteria in interval or ratio scale terms)
- a mission objective which links directly to the ideal vision
- identification of the results your educational agency commits to
  deliver as well as those results which it will cooperate with other
  agencies to deliver

Thus, you will have a mission objective which states where you are
headed and provides the precise criteria for assessing your progress and
your accomplishment. It will contribute to achieving the ideal vision.

IDENTIFYING EXISTING POLICIES, RULES, LAWS, AND REGULATIONS AS PART OF THE DETERMINATION OF MISSION

When identifying where your organization is headed, also identify any
current "ground rules" which may be required to operate or accomplish
its goals. As part of determining current mission(s), include the formal
consideration of existing laws, rules, regulations, and policies . . . not
that they will have to be adhered to blindly, but as a logical step for
identifying what currently guides the educational system and its parts as
well as serving as a basis for negotiating required changes. The current
policy for legal limitations are part of "what is" for the system. These
specifications should be considered as part of the performance requirements when developing the organization's mission objective.

During strategic planning, it will likely be noted that one or more
existing rules, regulations, policies, or requirements are not useful – that
is, they do not contribute to the revised mission objective. Based upon
the data collected in the needs assessment and the visions, a rational case

may be made for changes. Even laws can be revised or modified if the reasons are strong enough; but more on that later.

SOME CURRICULUM CONSIDERATIONS

There are some interesting curriculum considerations in this required interaction and facilitation among the various "sub-missions" of an educational organization. For example, the levels in the chain shown in Figure 4.5 should be mutually contributory—each level should contribute to the others.

Assuring that all of the missions (a) are measurable on an interval or ratio scale, and (b) are mutually contributing is the basic design of making everything "fit together" within strategic planning.

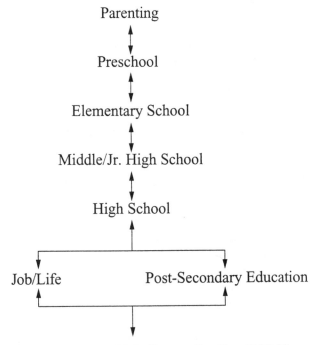

Figure 4.5. An Educational Results Chain. Each Level Should Link and Contribute to Others (© R. Kaufman, 1994).

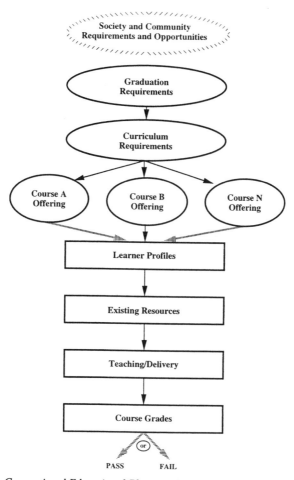

Figure 4.6. *Conventional Educational Planning Framework (© R. Kaufman, 1994).*

When strategic planning commits the organization to continuous improvement in its move toward fulfilling the ideal vision, some transformations are certain to occur. Curriculum, an engine of educational accomplishment, will take new forms as will the learning experiences that flow from it, and will be more effective and efficient. (see Wang et al., 1993). Differences in curriculum which become possible when one shifts from conventional models, shown in Figure 4.6, to this approach to strategic planning, which is provided in Figure 4.7.

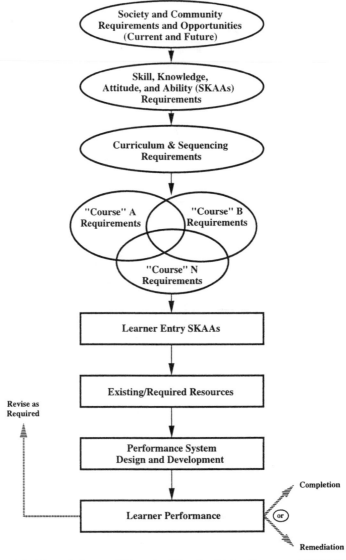

Figure 4.7. *Mega-Referenced Education Planning/Doing Framework (© R. Kaufman, 1994).*

SUMMARY

Strategic planning begins with an ideal vision from which an organizational mission is derived. An organizational mission statement is a general description of purpose, whereas the mission objective identifies, in performance terms, where the organization is headed and how to measure success. A mission objective — as with all objectives — is focused exclusively on ends and not means. It states four things:

- who or what will demonstrate the performance (or accomplishment)
- the performance to be demonstrated
- the conditions under which the performance will be observed
- the criteria (ideally on an interval or ratio scale) used to determine success

Objectives relate only to results. All results can be measured. Not all results are the same, therefore differences exist among the indicators that relate to reliability of the measure.

Frequently, so-called mission objectives for an entire educational organization are no better than mission statements. For strategic planning purposes, such statements must be converted to mission objectives that are measurable on an interval or ratio scale. A series of templates is provided and discussed to assist the planner in this conversion process.

All too often, planning only considers what currently exists. This thinking accepts the validity and usefulness of current objectives, and thereby only improves upon existing consequences. True proactive planning extends such thinking to include the two planning dimensions of "what is" and "what should be."

Remember, the mission objective is that part of the ideal vision which the organization takes on as its responsibility. When determining performance requirements, do not overlook current policies, rules, laws, and regulations. As the plan develops, new possibilities will take form.

CHAPTER 5

Needs Assessment

CHAPTER FRAMEWORK: Needs Assessment Basics—Defining "Need" in Needs Assessment • Needs Assessment, Needs Analysis, and Confusion • Resolving Problems Using Needs Assessment • Opportunity Finding • The Nine Steps of a Needs Assessment • The Basic Steps of Holistic Educational Planning

KEY HIGHLIGHTS: Differences and relationships among ends, means, needs, and wants • Importance of results-oriented needs assessment to the planning process • Differences between needs assessment and needs analysis • Identification of a nine-step needs assessment process • Identification of a six-step problem-solving process

THIS chapter provides the general concepts and tools for performing a needs assessment. Then, in the following chapters we furnish the specifics of how to use a needs assessment in strategic and tactical planning. It is important to first agree on the what, why, and how of a needs assessment and, with those understood, show the steps for doing a needs assessment at the mega-, macro-, and micro-levels as you move from the ideal vision to a mission objective and to the balance of strategic and tactical planning.

NEEDS ASSESSMENT BASICS—DEFINING "NEED" IN NEEDS ASSESSMENT

Planning defines what has to be accomplished to deliver useful and intended results. It is *proactive*. The success of planning depends upon using a results focus. Planning—good results-orientated planning—demands that we define and agree on precise terms and make clear the differences and relationships between ends and means as well as between needs and wants. So, for the purposes of this book in particular and

75

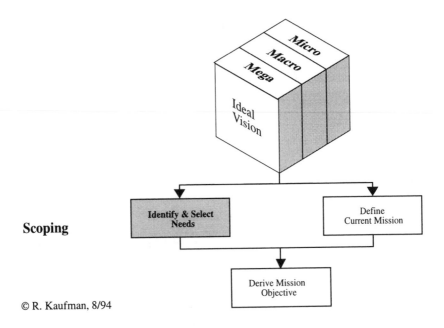

© R. Kaufman, 8/94

planning in general, we will use need only as a noun, and define it as the gap between current results and desired results (not gaps in resources, methods, procedures, or means) (Figure 5.1). *A most important single paradigm shift involved in successful planning, design, development, implementation, and evaluation is the crucial difference and relationship between ends and means.* Using "need" only as a noun—meaning a gap in results—will help us to focus on ends, not means.

The word *need* is all too often used (in both planning and everyday life) as a verb. When we use *need* as a verb, we are prescribing, that is imposing, a solution, method, procedure, or activity. So ingrained in our common language is *need* as a verb that we are always prescribing to others how they should do things, what they should use, and the way they should live their lives—a tactic of disempowerment. We disempower when we dictate to others what to do without involving them and their welfare, in the decision . . . we take away their choices and options.

When planning (and indeed in one's own personal life), using *need* as a noun—a gap between current results and desired ones—can make the difference between success and failure. As we previously noted, many educational reforms have been solutions in search of problems: means prescribed in the hope of delivering useful ends. Just as *Critical Success Factor #2* emphasizes the important difference between ends and means,

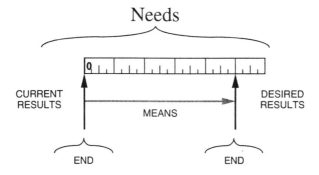

- First select the **Needs**, then (and <u>only</u> then)

- Identify and select the means, solutions, or

   processes to close the gap in results

Figure 5.1. Needs (© R. Kaufman, 1994).

and *Critical Success Factor #3* extends that difference to recognize that there are three levels of ends, or results, the use of *need* to denote a gap in results is also vital to strategic thinking and planning.

Critical Success Factor #6: Need *is a gap between current results and desired or required ones (not a gap in resources, methods, or means).*

By reserving the use of need to signify a gap in results, your strategic thinking and planning will yield a rational basis for identifying and selecting useful ends and then finding and choosing the best means to get there. By so doing, you will avoid rushing from unwarranted assumptions (we ''need'' more computers; we ''need'' more in-service training) to foregone conclusions (''computers will make learners more competent in both school and life''; ''in-service training will make teachers competent and successful''). When we choose to use need as a noun, we benefit by putting *Critical Success Factors #1, #2,* and *#3* to work.

NEEDS ASSESSMENTS, NEEDS ANALYSIS, AND CONFUSION

All that glitters isn't gold, and all that gets called a needs assessment isn't! Earlier we noted the tendency to call things we want, really want,

Table 5.1. A Needs Assessment Audit.

	Yes	No
1. Needs are identified as gaps between current results and desired results (or stated another way, the gap in results between "what is" and "what should be").		
2. There is a clear distinction between ends (results, consequences, payoffs) and means (resources, methods, how-to-do-its).		
3. There are three levels of results identified, one for individual performance (micro-level), one for organizational contributions (macro-level), and another for societal and client contributions (mega-level).		
4. The three levels of results include the mega-level (results, payoffs, consequences) for external (outside of the organization) clients.		
5. Mega-level results are clearly related to an ideal vision for both the organization and society which the organization intends to serve.		
6. The three levels of results include the macro-level (results, payoffs, consequences) for the organization itself.		
7. The macro-level results are clearly related to required results at the mega and ideal vision levels—macro results are "nested" within the ideal vision and the mega-level results and payoffs.		
8. The three levels of results include the micro-level (results, payoffs, consequences) for individuals and/or small groups within the organization.		
9. The micro-level results are clearly related to (and nested within) required results at the ideal vision, mega-, and macro-levels of results.		
10. Any statement of need is free from any indication of how the need will be met (such as training, computers, technology).		
11. Any statement of need is free from any indication of what resources will be used to meet the need (such as personnel, time, money, equipment, etc.).		
12. Needs are prioritized on the basis of what it costs to meet the need versus what it will cost to ignore it.		
13. Needs are listed in priority order.		
14. Interventions are selected on the basis of a costs/results analysis for each need, or cluster of related needs.		
15. Evaluation and continuous improvement criteria are taken directly from the "what should be" dimension of the selected needs.		
16. Evaluation and continuous improvement results report the extent to which needs, or families of related needs, have been reduced or eliminated.		

or really *really* want "needs." Because of this, we often hear "what technology do we 'need,' " not "what performances do we require" . . . the desire (almost, at times, passionate) to get a solution, or "fix," and get it quick. So many things labeled "needs assessment," "training needs assessment," or "needs analysis" really are examining the desires (wishes, wants, demands, fantasies) for a particular solution.

Before picking a particular needs assessment model, ask the questions in Table 5.1.

Needs assessments provide the unvarnished results-based data required to identify the gaps between current and desired (or required) results. It uses both judgment-based and performance-based results. Much of what gets called "needs assessments" and/or "needs analyses" only tends to give part of the story. Many available formulations don't completely deal with the important aspects listed in the Needs Assessment Checklist, questions 1, 2, 3, 5, 6, and 7 (Table 5.1). In addition, most approaches to needs assessment tend to rely on the perceptions of organizational players and do not use performance data.

It is usually easier and less threatening—more comfortable—to ask opinions about means, processes, and resources than it is to find out about gaps in results. Needs assessments are more than just questionnaires. Both "hard"—independently verifiable—and "soft"—personal, not independently verifiable—data must be collected and compared before you can have much confidence in the needs identified and selected.

A *needs analysis* comes after a needs assessment. In order to analyze something (break it down into its constituent component parts) you have to identify what that "something" is. Needs assessments identify the needs to be analyzed. Needs analyses find the causes and reasons behind the existence of the needs. In other words they examine the linkages between adjacent organizational elements such as between processes and products, products and outputs, and/or outputs and outcomes at either the "what is" or "what should be" levels, as shown in Figure 5.2.

NEEDS ASSESSMENTS WILL IDENTIFY AND DOCUMENT PROBLEMS, IDENTIFY WHAT SHOULD AND SHOULDN'T BE CHANGED, AND RECOGNIZE OPPORTUNITIES

In our world of extensive media coverage, where sound-bites are a substitute for reality, it is attention grabbing to criticize every aspect of

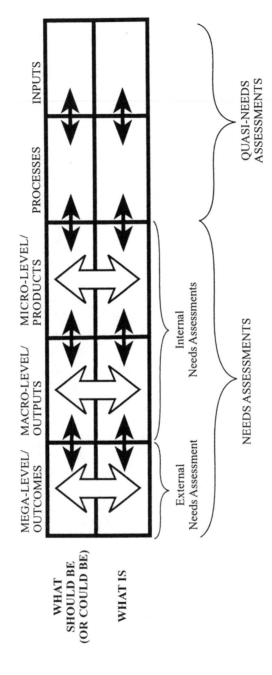

Figure 5.2. *Possible Needs Assessments, Shown by Hollow Lines and Arrows, and Possible Needs Analyses, Shown by Broken Lines and Arrows, Based on the Organizational Elements Model (OEM)* (© *R. Kaufman, 1995*).

education and state that everything must be thrown out and redone. That's nonsense—attention grabbing—but nonsense. Although there is much to change, we should also be careful to (1) maintain what is working and (2) identify future opportunities and directions.

Although most current attention in education is related to reactive actions for fixing, repairing, modifying, and responding to crises, we also have other concerns.

RESOLVING PROBLEMS USING NEEDS ASSESSMENT

Reactive responses to problems are vital when things are going wrong; we have to stop the hemorrhaging before changing the diet. Most educational organizations have plenty of problems that demand immediate attention: low student achievement, vandalism, improperly certified teachers, violence, drug use in the school and on the streets, etc. Where there are problems, both on the surface and hidden, a needs assessment is important to (1) identify the gaps in results, (2) place them in priority order, and (3) select the most important for resolution. Needs selected for reduction or elimination are defined as ''problems.''

Maintaining What's Working

Not everything has to be changed. Remember that there are many things going on in education that should be maintained. Much of education should be preserved by design, not modified while sweeping changes are being made to resolve other problems. Rather than changing what's working, the areas where there are no gaps in performance (needs) should be flagged to (a) make certain that no changes are made to successful means and resources and/or (b) develop methods and means to continue what's working so that needs will not emerge.

OPPORTUNITY FINDING

In addition to identifying needs and associated problems, there is the proactive task of identifying future requirements so that future needs will not develop and/or so that we can identify a new direction in which to steer. This assessment would identify gaps in results between what is and what could be (more discussion on this later in this chapter.)

Table 5.2. The Nine Steps of Needs Assessment.

1. Decide to plan using data from a needs (not wants) assessment.
2. Identify the three needs assessment (and planning) levels to be included (mega, macro, micro) and commit to the mega level as the starting place.
3. Identify the needs assessment and planning partners.
4. Obtain needs assessment partners' participation.
5. Obtain acceptance of the needs assessment frame of reference: Linkages between mega, macro, micro.
6. Collect both hard and soft internal and external needs data.
7. List identified, documented, and agreed-upon needs into a needs assessment matrix.
8. Place needs into priority order and reconcile differences.
9. List problems (selected needs) to be resolved and obtain agreement of partners.

Based on Kaufman, 1992a, 1992b, 1995.

THE NINE STEPS OF A NEEDS ASSESSMENT

The entire needs assessment process may be viewed as nine steps and are described below. Following each of the nine steps are some ways and means for doing them. The exact methods and tools you choose should be based on your particular situation . . . these are but guides. *Needs assessment is a major element in creating the decision making database for planning.*

1. DECIDE TO PLAN USING DATA FROM A NEEDS ASSESSMENT

Choose a Proactive Approach

Performing a needs assessment to identify and document problems seems, at first, more time-consuming than jumping right into a solution. The urge to "look active, and keep moving" is deceptively attractive, but it often turns out that our intuitions don't resolve the real problems. We often act in haste and repent in leisure. Modifying an old axiom, for every problem there is one single solution which is simple, straightforward, understandable, acceptable to everyone . . . and wrong!

A proactive needs assessment identifies and justifies the problems before doing anything. You may decide you don't have the time to do a needs assessment, only later to be forced to go back and repair the damage from not having resolved the basic problem the first time around.

Another consideration is the future. The past is prologue to the future, and planning is an attempt to make positive change and create—even invent—a new tomorrow. But the future is murky, unpredictable, and fickle. Some people view it with awe and trepidation, and seem to want to leave it unaddressed. A needs assessment should look at "futures" in order to identify where the organization is headed, where it could be going, and where it should be headed. Planning that attempts only to improve on solutions that have worked in the past ignores the possibility that these solutions might be the seeds of future failure. The world changes, often in dramatic and systematic ways (Drucker, 1993; Naisbitt and Aburdene, 1990; Toffler, 1990; Marshall and Tucker, 1992). We can choose to be the victims of change or the masters of it. Again, as Drucker reminds us, if we cannot predict the future, we should create it.

2. IDENTIFY THE THREE NEEDS ASSESSMENT (AND PLANNING) LEVELS TO BE INCLUDED AND COMMIT TO THE MEGA LEVEL AS THE STARTING PLACE

All results are not created equal (Tables 2.2 and 2.4). All results are ends, but, as we noted earlier, each organization deals with three kinds of related but distinct results. Realizing and accepting that there are three levels of results is critical. If we blur or confuse the different types of results, we risk not being able to achieve the right enroute results that are required to satisfy clients and to be responsive to the client's world (Rodriguez, 1988; Rojas, 1988).

Warning: If we restrict our needs assessment and improvement to the operational (micro) level, or to the operational plus the organizational (macro) level, we should do so only if we have complete confidence that the results chain will be properly formed. Starting at a macro- or micro-level risks getting here-and-now results that might not make an organizational contribution or have a positive payoff for the client and the society. Starting below the mega-level, or assuming it, is very, very risky. And impractical.

A useful way to keep ends and means related is to use the organizational elements model (OEM) covered in Chapter 2 and shown in Table 5.3.

Successful planning considers both what is and what should be;

Table 5.3. Three Types of Educational Results, the Primary Level of Their Needs Assessment and Planning Focus, and Typical Examples.

Type of Result	Level of Planning and Needs Assessment Focus	Typical Examples of Data Points
Outcomes	Mega	Individual self-sufficiency, self-reliance, collective social payoffs, etc.
Outputs	Macro	Graduate, certificate of completion, licensure, etc.
Products	Micro	Test score, course passed, competence gained, etc.

therefore, planning using the three types of results should be bi-level, as shown in Figure 5.3. The OEM can help us visualize and relate what our educational organization uses, does, delivers, and contributes; we can then compare these against what it should use, do, deliver, and contribute to discover the results gaps between ''what is'' and ''what should (or could) be.'' Use the OEM for your school or system, and you will see how things relate and identify the missing or non-integrating elements.

Each time an entry is made, check to be sure that it is entered at the correct results level and that it is an end, not a means. Also, be certain that all results are linked to the mega-level.

Type of result	Current Results	Desired Results
OUTCOME (Mega)		
OUTPUT (Macro)		
PRODUCT (Micro)		

Figure 5.3. A Needs Assessment Matrix for Tracking the Three Types of Results.

INCLUDE BOTH WHAT IS AND WHAT SHOULD BE IN PLANNING

Planning, after all, intends to create a better future. It aims to get us effectively and efficiently from a current to a better (ultimately ideal) state of affairs. Our planning could focus on improving our current efficiency — making "what is" better — or it can also create a more responsive "what should be." There are two dimensions, or levels, for proactive, responsive, and responsible planning and doing:

- what is (our current results)
- what should (or could) be (an improved or "best" set of results)

Quasi-Needs Are Gaps in Resources or "How-To's"

As noted earlier, we are usually eager to get educational change moving, and quickly. Although it is tempting to talk about "computer needs," "program needs," "financial needs," "in-service training needs," (the deceptive) in-service "training needs assessment," or "facilities needs," doing so confuses means with ends. For example, if we start identifying "facilities needs," when we are anxious to get long lead-time items, such as new buildings, we should first identify the needs — gaps in results — to which they would be responsive. How embarrassing and wasteful to build a new school, only to realize before it opens that it was in the wrong place and/or it would not accommodate the curriculum and methods of tomorrow.

A *quasi-need* is a gap between "what is" and "what should be" for inputs and/or processes. It only makes sense to deal with a quasi-need after we have identified and selected the needs that it will meet. To do otherwise places us in the position of selecting means that might not deliver useful ends. Because of the widespread ends/means confusion, most so-called needs assessments are actually quasi-needs assessments (as shown in Figure 5.4.)

Planning, starting at any level, has direct or indirect impact on all other levels. When selecting any level, there are consequences at all levels . . . it all is part of a system.

Remember, the two-dimensioned OEM serves as a planning guide to remind us that any educational system has both current and desired resources, activities, and results which impact one another. It is often

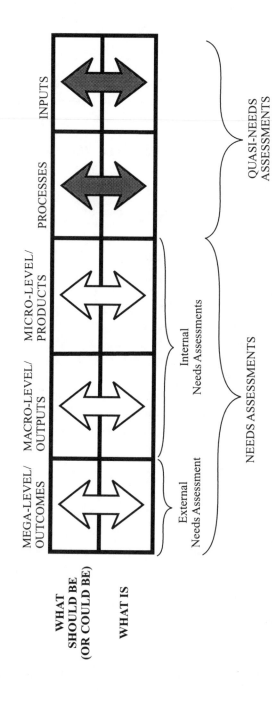

Figure 5.4. Three Varieties of Needs and Two Types of Quasi-Needs (© R. Kaufman, 1995).

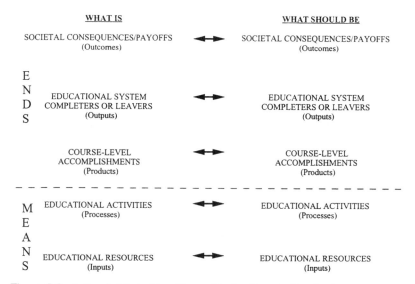

Figure 5.5. *A Result Chain That Shows Needs: Gaps in Results (based in part on Kaufman, 1988a).*

tempting to ignore these dimensions as continuing, important, and worthy of our planning attention.

3. IDENTIFY THE NEEDS ASSESSMENT AND PLANNING PARTNERS

Partners in Planning—Significant Others—Are Critical to Proactive Needs Assessment and Planning Decisions

The people important in making and supporting the results of any plan should be included in this decision. To identify them, list those who:

(*1*) Could and will participate in the planning
(*2*) Approve or support that which comes from the needs assessment and planning
(*3*) Will be influenced by any plans and results

Such ''gatekeepers,'' or stakeholders, could include representative:

• supervisors, managers, and executives who will use the plan
• important and representative community members (or leaders)

- parents, educators, and union leaders
- those who may be influenced or affected by what might be planned
- other educators and professionals (e.g., State Department of Education experts, psychologists, counselors, healthcare specialists, professors, etc.)
- key communicators
- those who could control the success of the effort

Including significant others in the planning process—in proportion to their representation in the total population—makes sense for many reasons:

- They will provide useful perspectives and information which might be otherwise overlooked.
- Their presence reduces the possibility of implementing a quick fix.
- They will likely "own" both the planning process and its results and will tend to become its proponent.

It is important that all planning partners and those who might have authority over its results have a common frame of reference. The rationale in this book could provide them with a shared "North Star": results and payoffs at the mega-level . . . the ideal vision.

It is advisable to involve both a "vertical and a horizontal slice" of all partners, ranging from the sweepers to the board chair, from learners to teachers. By using this representation, you add validity and credibility to the planning partnership and what it produces.

Including people as "planning partners" in the process is done to obtain both useful input and get the significant others involved in both the process and consequences of the resulting identified needs. Representatives of three partner groups (Figure 5.6) include implementors (those developing and who would likely deliver any interventions); recipients (such as teachers, learners, administrators, volunteers, and custodial workers); and society-clients-community (those who will be impacted by outputs external to the system). Also, active and genuine participation will develop critical mass ownership among the partners and their constituencies.

One way to view the planning partnership is a triangle, as shown in Figure 5.6. It emphasizes that the perceptions of the partners relative to the gaps in results between "what is" and "what should be" are all important.

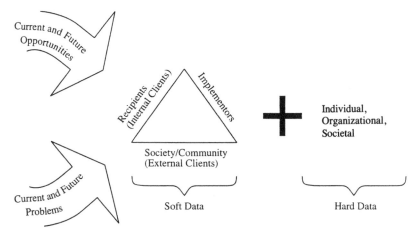

Figure 5.6. The Partners (and Clients) for Planning Include Learners, Educators, and Society/Community Plus Actual or Required Performance. Feeding into the Partnership Are Considerations of Current and Future Opportunities (Including but Not Limited to Educationally Related Ones) (© R. Kaufman, 1995).

4. OBTAIN NEEDS ASSESSMENT PARTNERS' PARTICIPATION (AND COMMITMENT)

When you are do a needs assessment you can do without those who (1) were told to be there, (2) only didn't want to miss anything, and (3) view participation as another opportunity to seek power and influence. There is too much to accomplish without getting tangled up with these types of people . . . useful planning (and needs assessment) depends on the right people doing the right things at the right time.

Get a Commitment and Be Frank

After identifying representatives who should be included, get them involved and committed. Contact each one and follow up in writing with all of the facts and mutual understandings. Tell them definitely what will be provided (such as data, access, materials, human resources, transportation, expenses, payments). Relate exactly what they will have to provide in terms of schedule, travel, and levels of work. Give them information about the form of their participation, who they will be working with, what reports you expect, and target timelines.

Meetings can be face-to-face, or through questionnaires, teleconferences, a Delphi Technique (a method of encouraging group interaction without convening people in face-to-face groups), or computer-networking (refer to Chapter 3 or Chapter 7 for a discussion of this and other consensus-building techniques).

Candidly discuss the implied criticism and threat carried by strategic planning and needs assessment, and provide assurance that there are none intended in this activity. Let everyone know that there will be no blaming, fault-finding, criticism, or scape-goating. The plan and the process is their property, used only so that they may become proactive in identifying which results are useful and which should be changed.

Many people come into a planning situation believing that others will hog the limelight, that a report has already been framed and they are only there to rubber-stamp it, or that they are only being used for window dressing. These are your partners in planning; be clear, precise, accurate, and truthful. Assure each partner that activities will be scheduled based on their requirements, not just yours. Deliver on your promises.

5. OBTAIN ACCEPTANCE (OR CONFIRMATION) OF THE NEEDS ASSESSMENT (AND PLANNING) FRAME OF REFERENCE: THE LINKAGES AMONG MEGA, MACRO, AND MICRO

Agreement on level and scope is both crucial and essential. Let the planning partners know the optional frames of reference. The results chain usually reveals that the success of the organization resides in the linking and integration of all of the means and ends, from mega to macro to micro.

More than likely, one or two partners will want to zero-in on a pet process, solution, or resource. Try not to let this business-as-usual orientation take the day. Revisit the total relationship among organizational efforts, organizational results, and societal and client payoffs. Discuss the importance of creating a better future, not just a more efficient mirror of yesterday.

Choosing the Correct Level for Needs Assessment and Planning

Keep a better future for learners, educators, and the society on center-stage. Recall that there are two dimensions to useful planning: "what is" and "what should be."

If some partners choose to concentrate on inputs (such as funds, facilities, resources, staff) or processes (such as methods, courses, course content, training, scheduling, team-building) ask:

"If we were to implement _____, what results will we get?"

"If we do _____, what are the results we could get with the findings?"

"If we increased the number of teaching assistants, what would be the results and payoffs?"

"Increase of the budget to _____ will bring what kinds of payoffs?"

"If we were to close that school, what would happen to and for learners?"

"If _____ is the solution, then what's the problem?"

Show them where they are in the OEM and results chain, and ask them to describe the path through to the required results. Most educators and planning partners have never considered an organization as being a means to societal ends . . . walk them through the OEM and the results chain so they will get comfortable with the end-means relationship. Be tolerant, enduring, and patient.

Steer clear of the tendency to simply "sweeten the pot" by improving the work environment, adding perks, or working on would-be motivational possibilities. Recall the two dimensions of results ("what is" and "what should be"), self sufficiency-related, and quality of life-related, and ask the partners to make certain that both dimensions are being included, in proper sequence.

If the planning team decides to restrict the effort to less than the mega-level, at least they did so with full knowledge of that which they were excluding or assuming, and that they are publicly taking full responsibility for the consequences.

6. COLLECT NEEDS DATA (BOTH EXTERNAL—OUTSIDE THE ORGANIZATION—AND INTERNAL—WITHIN YOUR ORGANIZATION)

When collecting data, there is information which came from both internal and external scanning. This is the stage where those data are put to work.

Needs assessment data will be important, as we will discuss later, at the mega-level when we will want to know the gaps between what is and what should be based on the ideal vision. The needs at the mega-level will be the basis for an assessment of consequences based on future costs and benefits: the costs to achieve the ideal vision and the costs to ignore it.

Collecting Soft Data

People's perceptions are their reality. What we believe and how we see and filter reality is their paradigm, or frame of reference. There are useful data available from people's perceptions; their informal observations and experiences. This perception information is called "soft data." Keep in mind, however, the notorious unreliability of personal observations when used alone. Soft data are the most trustworthy when they are supported by actual performance results (hard data), or at least by multiple observations or consensus of several different "soft" data sources.

Many sources of perception data exist or may be constructed. Frequently, questionnaires and interviews are used to collect soft data. This data is important so that (1) we take advantage of what is known by our partners, and (2) important partners and opinion leaders will identify with the results—that which Drucker termed "transfer of ownership" from the planners to the partners.

But when you simply ask about needs or suggested solutions (such as resources, methods, support, course titles, etc.), there is not much you can do with the summary of a respondent's wishes or desires. Without knowing the gaps between current and desired results, there is no sensible and justifiable way to establish priorities among the perceived needs. Questionnaires should:

- seek information about gaps in results, not gaps in resources, methods, or processes
- look for gaps in the three levels of results
- communicate clearly and without confusion
- not be biased by including (either directly or implied) solutions, methods, resources, or processes
- be relatable to hard data to be able to find agreements and disagreements between soft and hard data

- be long enough to give reliable results, and short enough to ensure that people will actually complete them

While questionnaires are quick and easy ways to assemble and collect data, and while there are a variety of published so-called "needs assessment" instruments, all seldom provide crucial data for identifying gaps in results. Questionnaires, especially the off-the-shelf variety usually only target wants or wishes about methods, resources, and how-to-do-its . . . listings of desired resources and "fixes." Asked in the conventional manner, most people would speak to favored solutions and not even consider any underlying problems or opportunities.

There are other techniques allowing the planning partners to identify the perceptions and rationales of others, share different views (if not biases) and achieve a sensitivity to other perspectives. The art of facilitation is helpful here, especially if the planning partners first accept a common mega-level "North Star" toward which all may steer. Transformation—the complete shift from one position to another—is more difficult, but can—and should—happen when rationality is in focus within a context of a practical and justifiable results orientation.

Collecting Hard Data

In addition to the ideal vision and the beliefs, and values of the partners there should be a databased "partner" who supplies "hard," performance-based, independently verifiable indicators. Actual results and consequences which can be independently verified must be included in a sensible needs assessment.

Collecting internal organizational performance data is simple. Most schools and systems have a lot of hard data available. Decide what you want and then locate it. Useful variables might include truancy, contact hours, graduation rates, disciplinary actions, problem referrals, audit exceptions, ethics violations, accidents, on-site injuries, grievances, courses completed, certified competencies, sick leave, work samples, promotions, test scores, and rejection rates. Assure the validity and reliability of these data, and use them only when they will supply useful performance information.

If the planning partners have chosen the mega-level needs assessment—and they should—they should first collect external performance data. Some examples include successful graduates/completers, recidivism, civil right adjudications, arrests and convictions, performance and success, job tenure, citizenship, quality-of-life, etc. Possible data points, questions and quantitative indicators are shown in Table 5.4.

7. LIST IDENTIFIED, DOCUMENTED, AND AGREED-UPON NEEDS

Using a Needs Assessment Matrix

After collecting the data, enter it into a form to help assure that it is complete. Enter it into a ''needs assessment matrix'' such as suggested in Figure 5.3.

Keep improving the entries in the matrix until there is agreement about the data. Assure yourselves that entries deal with only results. This might take several repeats. Stay consistent with the linkage to the mega-level. Get agreement among the partners about the needs to be addressed. Assure agreement has been reached about operating at the mega-level, and that the hard and soft data also agree.

Relating the Ideal/Mega-Level to Distant and Closer-In Mission Objectives

As we noted in Chapter 3, first the ideal vision is derived, then those elements which your educational agency commits to deliver become the basis for its mission objective. Based on that mission objective, and linking it to the mega-level ideal vision elements, a needs assessment can be accomplished. This first needs assessment identifies the gaps between current results and those identified in ideal vision.

Based on the ideal vision, a basic organizational mission objective is derived from those elements you commit to deliver. Then, a needs assessment is accomplished to determine gaps between current and desired results. More specifics on this will be found later in this chapter and the next one where the ideal vision is subjected to a needs assessment and the elements of the vision the organization commits to deliver are identified.

Once these initial needs are identified, the planning partners identify the timelines for meeting the needs. Scanning of internal and external environment data will provide specific requirements to be met (trends

Table 5.4. Identification and Collection of Hard Data Elements within the Associate OEM Classification.

	Input	Process	Product (Micro)	Output (Macro)	Outcome (Mega)
Typical actual data point	Social class Color Race Ethnic background Values Primary language Economic level	In-service training Site-based managing Teaching Learning	Truants Grievances Promotion to next grade Standardized test results Criterion-referenced test results Honors and awards	Graduates Drop-outs Push-outs Promotion to: middle school high school Graduation from: high school college	Accidents Parents complaints Lawsuits Unemployment Underemployment Citizenship acts Pay taxes
Typical suggested questions to ID data points for results	What is the distribution of the student population within the school? What is the primary language used within each student's home?	What programs are available for updating teacher performance? What management tactics are in use?	What is the failure and success rate of students in various courses? Do our students get promoted/retained? Which ones?	Do our students get accepted to colleges and universities? Do our nursery school completers do well in the early grades? Do our completers get desired jobs?	What are/is the financial status of completers? For which learners and majors or areas of study? How many employees hold jobs outside of our organization in order to make ends meet?

(continued)

Table 5.4. (continued).

	Input	Process	Product (Micro)	Output (Macro)	Outcome (Mega)
Typical quantitative indicators	Student profiles School population profiles	GPA Retention rate Promotions Delinquency rates State/national/local test rates	Graduation rates Drop-out rates Students in: colleges workforce vocational programs Number of: merit awards scholarship placement rates	Do our students get accepted to colleges and universities? Do our nursery school completers do well in early grades? Do our completers get desired jobs?	Employer satisfaction Incarcerations in: jails mental institutions Parole Citizenship participation Improved quality of life Government subsidies Substance abusers

in funding for education, demographic trends, etc.) and obstacles to be overcome (political activism in the area, support for voucher systems, etc.). Based on this needs assessment, distance and closer-in mission objectives are identified:

IDEAL VISION
↓
BASIC MISSION OBJECTIVE
↓
MISSION FOR THE YEAR 2010
↓
MISSION FOR THE YEAR 2000
↓
MISSION FOR NEXT YEAR
↓
MISSION FOR THIS YEAR

This will provide the time-frame for meeting the selected needs—a sequence for their elimination and/or reduction. This also provides a continuous improvement chain for tracking your progress in moving continuously toward your missions and the accomplishment of the ideal vision.

Dealing with Disagreements

When there is disagreement, either between the "hard" and "soft" data, or among partners (or both), collect more data. To reconcile differences, look at the data in different lights, but don't go ahead until the disparities are resolved. Some sources for disagreements might include:

- incomplete or faulty hard data
- partner(s) still focused on means or resources
- missing hard data
- territoriality

Frustration will be part of the scene at first as you watch some of the partners get back into their comfort zones and become preoccupied with means, solutions, and "the way we have always done it" methods (old paradigms) . . . in spite of data which show that the overall results clearly do not meet the needs. Be patient when a few people become resistant to change, or when they distort reality by calling "means" "ends," or argue that the system cannot be changed, or that the bosses won't "buy it," and every other excuse imaginable. Be patient, remember the integrity of the approach and the importance of continuous improvement toward the ideal vision, and calmly keep reintroducing rationality.

An Integrated Approach: NOM Assessment

A NOM (*Needs, Opportunities, Maintenance*) assessment (Kaufman, 1992b, 1995) also may be done at this juncture. For each "what is" and "what should be," identify (1) those needs that should be closed, (2) those critical areas for which there are no gaps (and there shouldn't be), and (3) areas where there will be gaps in the future if you don't attend to them soon. Also, based upon the ideal vision, identify those areas for which new objectives (even at the mission level) might be considered.

Because it is vital to identify needs, opportunities, and maintenance requirements, all three perspectives are worth including as part of strategic thinking and planning. The basic concepts underlying needs assessments still hold: the nuclei are still results and priorities. A possible format for a NOM assessment, building on the elements of needs assessments, is shown in Table 5.5.

8. PLACE NEEDS IN PRIORITY ORDER AND RECONCILE DISAGREEMENTS

Have the partners rank each need (or related clusters of needs) on the basis of the cost to meet and the cost (both financial and social) to ignore

Table 5.5. NOM Assessment Table. *Note:* In This Format for a NOM Assessment, Needs, Opportunities, and Maintenance Factors Are Included (based on Kaufman, 1992b, 1995).

Current Results	Desired Results	Needs Exists?		Maintenance Required		Future Opportunities	Consequences/ Payoffs or Penalties
		Yes	No	Yes	No		

each. With these rankings, the partners (or their representatives) should derive the priorities.

Agreements on priorities should be based upon what's ''right'' – and useful – and not simply on adding up votes . . . that is why the needs data was collected in the first place. Stay with the methods, rigor, and data that brought you this far. When you have disagreements, don't argue and fight. Recall the usual ends/means confusion and realize that most differences come from people really believing that they are dealing with ends while in actuality mired in means. Pose ''if we accomplished _____, what would be the result? And what would be the result from that? And from that?'' Use the results chain as the basis for tracking results, and for relating ends and means.

Another useful model for understanding why people act the way they do is provided by Greenwald (1973). He advises that people do what they do because they receive payoffs which are important or valued by them, even if we outsiders don't realize or value those consequences. For example, a student might misbehave to get attention, while most of us wouldn't use that method. When someone seems to be acting in an unusual or unorthodox manner, ask yourself ''what payoffs might they be getting for their position and actions?'' If you know what they find rewarding, you might use that information in facilitating their awareness of better consequences for different conduct.

9. LIST PROBLEMS (SELECTED NEEDS) TO BE RESOLVED AND OBTAIN AGREEMENT OF PARTNERS

(Although we include this step here, further in-depth discussion is provided in the next chapter.)

This is the easy part. List the agreed-upon problems (needs selected for resolution) along with their assigned priorities. The problems in priority order provide essential planning information for:

- making revisions to the ideal vision[11]
- preparing a possible new or revised mission objective
- completing a needs analysis . . . to reveal the characteristics, causes, and detailed specifications for eliminating or reducing each

[11]This is usually not required due to the stability of the ideal vision.

- considering optional ways and means for meeting the needs, and then identifying the advantages and disadvantages of each possible methods-means
- selecting the best tactics, tools, and methods
- deriving a management plan
- beginning a sensible, justifiable evaluation and continuous improvement process which uses the needs, problems, and requirements to discover if (a) progress is being made, and (b) we have resolved the problems and met the needs, as we move continuously toward the ideal vision

THE BASIC STEPS OF HOLISTIC EDUCATIONAL PLANNING

We have identified six *Critical Success Factors,* a framework for strategic planning and thinking, and the basic building blocks of objectives and needs assessments. There is one more concept, or tool, that will be useful any time you want to get from your current results to desired ones: a six-step problem identification and resolution model (Kaufman, 1972, 1988a, 1992a, 1992b, 1995). The six steps are shown in Figure 5.7.

Most problem solving is only problem resolution. If we don't first identify and justify a problem, we just might be resolving the wrong problem, or just working on a symptom (Kaufman and Gavora, 1993).

What we are doing in planning is identifying and resolving problems. Part One of this book, Chapters 1–6, deals with identifying and justifying problems. When we get beyond that, we are resolving the problems. The six-step problem-solving model serves as a basis for all planning, designing, developing, implementing, evaluating, and revising. It does have two basic (but related) phases: problem identification and problem resolution.

Problem Identification

(1) *Identify (or verify) problems based on needs.* Function 1 deals with identification or verification of needs—gaps in results—and selects those for reduction or elimination. When a need is selected from resolution or reduction, it is called a "problem"; no gap in results,

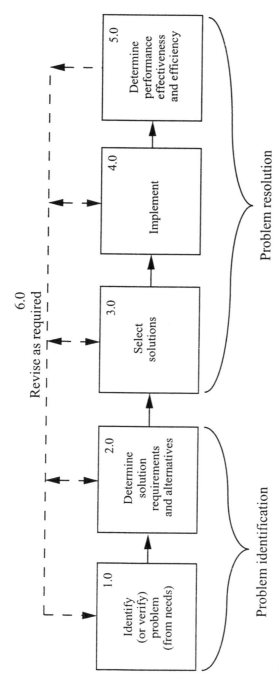

Figure 5.7. *A General Problem-Solving Process. The Last (Revise as Required) Is Indicated by the Broken Lines and May Take Place at Any Problem-Solving Step (© R. Kaufman, 1994).*

no need; no need, no problem. *Critical Success Factors #2, #3, #4, #5,* and *#6* come into play here.

(2) *Determine solution requirements and alternatives.* Function 2 derives detailed objectives and for each one identifies (but does not select) possible ways and means for meeting them. *Critical Success Factors #3* and *#5* and the "ABCD" format are important here. At this step, detailed objectives for resolving the problem selected in Step 1 are prepared, and possible methods and means are identified but not selected—we simply seek to determine whether there is at least one way to meet the objectives. Selection takes place in the next step.

Problem Resolution

(3) *Select solutions (from among alternatives).* In Function 3, the methods and means are selected for each objective or family of related objectives. The selection is based on the cost and consequences for each alternative "how" identified in Step 2.

(4) *Implement.* Function 4 is the management, implementation, and control of resolving the problems and meeting the objectives.

(5) *Determine performance effectiveness and efficiency.* This step is summative evaluation. Based on the criteria in the objectives (from 1 and 2) results are compared with intentions. Decisions are made on what to change and what to continue.

(6) *Revise as required.* Function 6 is really continuous evaluation—continuous improvement—and revision while planning and during implementation. The purpose of this step is to revise as required along the way to resolving the problems. Rather than waiting until Function 5 to make revisions, corrections and changes are to be made mid-course to best assure that the needs will be met and the problem resolved.

Functions 5 and 6 deal with evaluation and continuous improvement: finding out where planning and implementation have failed and where they are working. It is crucial to keep in mind that evaluation data must be used to fix, not blame.

These six problem-solving steps, shown as a flowchart (or management plan in Figure 5.7) may be used each time you want to define and then get from what is to what should be. Further reference regarding this model can be found in Chapter 8 when discussing the mission profile.

SUMMARY OF BASICS OF NEEDS ASSESSMENT

We have come a long way in this chapter. We have identified that needs—gaps in results—and needs assessment—identifying and prioritizing needs—are basic tools for planning. We also noted how needs assessments are conducted and how they form the basis for identifying the building-block mission objectives which will allow us to continuously improve as we move toward our basic mission objective and the ideal vision.

While this approach might, at first, seem to be rigid and hierarchical, it is not. It is based upon a very open agreement among partners about what kind of world we want for society. From that agreement, the roles and functions are defined for organizations and then for their people. Any role, function, and mission is changeable; but because of the nature of an ideal vision, that "guiding star" will be very stable. What might change are the building block objectives which range from the missions themselves down to the requirements for the derived building block roles and functions. The continuous improvement process is in force during this whole process—revise as required any place, any where, any time.

Before going to the next chapter, let's see what is coming based upon the basics of needs assessment.

THE ROLE OF NEEDS ASSESSMENT IN MOVING FROM THE IDEAL VISION TO THE BASIC ORGANIZATIONAL MISSION

In the next chapters we will show you how needs assessment is used to identify and justify your plans as you move from strategic planning to tactical planning and then to operational planning.

Now let's turn to using these needs assessment basics to application in strategic planning and providing the bases for moving from strategic to tactical to operational planning.

The basic mission objective identifies what part of the ideal vision the organization commits to deliver. But how do you get from the ideal vision to a basic mission objective which is sensible and justifiable? It is accomplished by applying needs assessment to the ideal vision.

Needs Assessment at the Mega-Level

After deriving the ideal vision, it is time to do a needs assessment. The identified needs are then assessed on the basis of the costs to close those gaps in results versus the costs to ignore them: a costs/results (or cost/consequences) analysis. Doing this allows you to identify the elements of the ideal vision your organization will commit to deliver.

Figure 5.8 shows the basic steps to be performed to do a needs assessment at the mega-level.

Here is the sequence of steps and products for doing a needs assessment at the mega-level and using it to derive the basic mission objective:

(*1*) Derive a shared ideal vision (see Chapter 3).

(*2*) Perform a needs assessment where you identify the gaps in results between what is and what should be for each element in the ideal vision. Note that the "what should be" portion of the mega-level

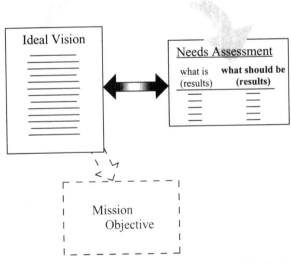

Figure 5.8. *First Step for Deriving the Mission Objective* (© *R. Kaufman, 1995*).

needs assessment contains the elements of the ideal vision (Figure 5.8).

(*3*) Make an estimate of the costs (both financial and social) to meet the needs (close the gaps in results) as compared to the costs to ignore them. At this level of strategic planning, informal estimates (including simply rank ordering) of the cost to meet versus the costs to ignore the needs are made.

Figure 5.9 shows the basic steps for using the needs assessment data and the estimates of costs and results for meeting and not meeting the needs to identify which of the ideal vision elements your organization commits to deliver and move ever-closer to—that is, which ones will be the basis for the basic mission objective.

(*4*) From this costs/consequences analysis (or estimates), identify those elements of the ideal vision in which your organization has interest and/or commits to deliver. As shown in Figure 5.7, identify those ideal vision elements for which you will have primary responsibility with a single asterisk (*). Identify those for which you will have shared responsibility with one or more other agencies with two asterisks (**). Identify those elements that are important for you in moving toward the ideal vision but for which you will not be responsible with a triple asterisk (***).

(*5*) List your ideal vision and those elements marked for those which you will commit to deliver (Figures 5.9 and 5.10) and move toward.

The portion of the ideal vision you select for your basic mission objective is part of the total ideal vision. Seen in this way, your organization is not responsible for the total ideal vision while being able to identify planning and implementation partners (those shown with ** and ***) as you move from strategic to tactical to operational planning.

Now, these data form the basis for the strategic and tactical planning. Figure 5.11 shows the full process for moving from an ideal vision down through the identification of building-block missions, functions, and tasks.

(*6*) Prepare your organization's basic mission objective (see #5 in Figure 5.9).

(*7*) Using the basic needs assessment approaches, do a macro-level

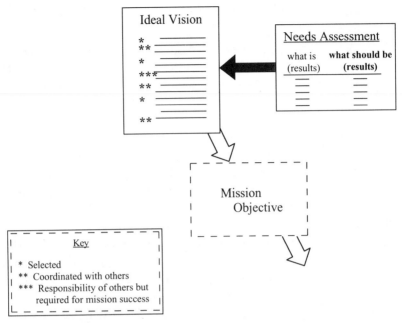

Figure 5.9. The Elements from the Ideal Vision, Based on Needs, Are Selected to Form the Mission Objective (© R. Kaufman, 1995).

needs assessment and identify the gaps between current results and required results (see #6 in Figure 5.11).

(8) Prepare the building-block/continuous improvement missions for distant and closer-in missions (i.e., for the years 2010, 2000, next year, this year) (see #7 in Figure 5.11).

(9) Flesh out the missions to fit functions within your organization, such as vocational schools, high schools, middle schools, elementary schools, etc., and conduct a value-added reality check.

(10) Prepare a management plan—called a mission profile—to identify the functions required to get from "what is" to "what should be" (including the mission objective). This is covered in Chapter 7 as we discuss system analysis in general and mission analysis in particular.

The objectives and functions from these will serve as the basis for identifying detailed functions and tasks, and can then be used to identify and select the methods-means and operational requirements.

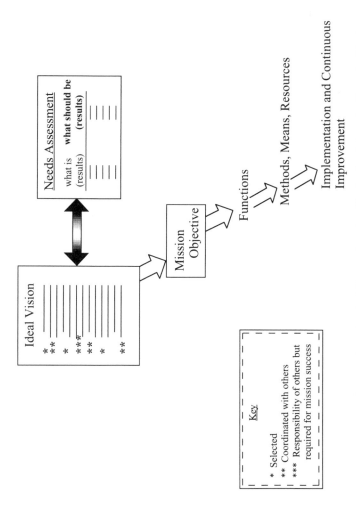

Figure 5.10. *The Elements from the Ideal Vision, Based on Needs, Are Selected to Form the Mission Objective (© R. Kaufman, 1995).*

108

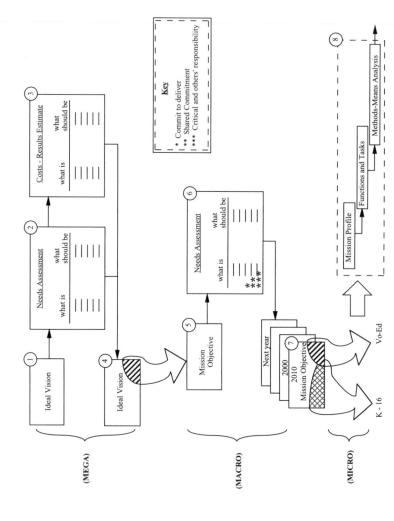

Figure 5.11. *The Complete Process and Functions for Moving from the Ideal Vision through Strategic Planning to Tactical Planning. The Numbers Identify the Recommended Sequence (© R. Kaufman, 1995).*

There is repetition in this top-down[12] (or rolling down) approach of many of the tools and techniques we provide in this book. Needs assessments are conducted at the mega-, macro-, and micro-levels. Objectives are set at the mega-, macro-, and micro-levels as well. And at every level, the six *Critical Success Factors* come into play.

Isn't this all terribly complicated? At first it might seem to be quite complex, but as you apply the processes and tools, the rationality of it will emerge as straightforward and necessary. Why necessary? People are complex and so are the organizations they develop and to which they contribute. If we are not to dehumanize, oversimplify, and artificially make our educational world linear and restricted, it is imperative that we develop our strategic plans based upon the actual realities of our organizations and society—which are complex. If we are to make a contribution to moving ever closer to our shared ideal vision, then we must realize the complexities and interactive nature of the whole enterprise.

If this approach to planning seems overly demanding, just stand back and ask yourself "If the world is rich and complex, don't my paradigms—frames of reference—and tools for strategic planning have to be responsive?" We are providing you with a *system approach* where all the parts of our educational system are to operate both independently and together as they link together to achieve a shared destination. Education is a part of the societal system, and this approach provides the concepts and tools for continuous improvement of our educational system.

We now move to the final phases of strategic planning. The next chapters deal with system analysis and then systems analysis (yes, they are different but related); and mission and function analysis: the definition of what results must be delivered, and in what sequence, in order for us to get from "what is" to "what should be."

---

[12]Top-down here *does not* mean dictatorial or imposed, but only that we are cascading down from the shared ideal vision to rational derivation of other elements.

CHAPTER 6

Transitioning: The Planning Phase

CHAPTER FRAMEWORK: Identify SWOTs: Strengths, Weaknesses, Opportunities, and Threats • Gathering Information to Complete a SWOTs Analysis • Select the Long- and Shorter-Term Missions • The Management Map: Mission and Function Analysis • The Mission Profile: A Management Plan • Using a Discrepancy Analysis to Prepare the Mission Profile • Function Analysis • Every Level of System Analysis Is Related to Every Other Level • Function Analysis and Feasibility • Task Analysis

KEY HIGHLIGHTS: Significance of the planning phase • Integration of SWOTs analysis within the strategic planning process • Suggested indicators and data sources useful in conducting a SWOTs analysis • Relationship of proximal strategic objectives to the ideal vision • Purpose, importance, and relationship of mission and function analysis • Identification of the parts of a mission profile • Significance of the function and task analysis to the mission analysis and mission profile

ONCE we have completed the scoping phase of strategic planning, we are ready to lay the goundwork for action. In the planning phase we chart our course by mapping out identified objectives to accomplish in fulfillment of the ideal vision and mission.

An important and useful way to begin this phase is to conduct a SWOTs Analysis. Based upon our ideal vision, mission objective, and needs assessment, the SWOTs analysis becomes an organization barometer indicating environmental factors beneficial in determining future en route strategies and tactics.

It is important that we continue to work with a results orientation. The planning phase does not focus upon means, but rather ends . . . not solutions, just results. This phase transitions us from scoping to the actual planning. Our first job in planning is the identification of strengths, weaknesses, opportunities, and threats (SWOTs).

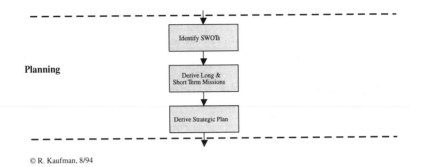

Planning

© R. Kaufman, 8/94

IDENTIFY SWOTs (STRENGTHS, WEAKNESSES, OPPORTUNITIES, AND THREATS)

Based on our ideal vision, basic mission, and needs, we may transform our schools to achieve useful results and payoffs rather than merely tinkering with the status quo.

We now know where we are headed and can justify why we want to get there. We also know that our plan does not begin at ground zero. Every educational agency has positive qualities. There are also many things that can or could get in the way of success (Kaufman and Herman, 1991). Based on where your system is going — its ideal vision-derived mission — and its needs and their priorities, now is the time to identify objectively the system's strengths, weaknesses, opportunities, and threats (SWOTs).

A SWOTs analysis is conducted to determine the strengths and weaknesses, as well as opportunities and threats, that exist both (1) within the organization, and (2) of the external environment variables (support and restraint elements) that exist. The data from both the internal and external SWOTs analyses will allow the planners to identify and select the potential strategies and tactics. These, in turn, will increase the probability of fulfilling the ideal vision and missions.

The SWOTs analysis:

(1) Identifies those supports (strengths) that are available to implement strategies and possible future tactics — not selected now, but later when actually developing the strategic plan — which ultimately will achieve the ideal vision and mission of ''what should be''

(2) Identifies those weaknesses which can or should be corrected or minimized in order to achieve the ideal vision

(*3*) Identifies the opportunities that exist which are not currently or have not been previously utilized

(*4*) Discovers the threats to achieving the ideal vision that exist and which can be avoided, or for which tactics can be developed to diminish the negative impact

For our purpose, the strengths, weaknesses, opportunities, and threats apply to both internal and external environments. Each of these SWOTs factors must be objectively identified, carefully analyzed, and seriously considered when developing future plans.

GATHERING INFORMATION TO COMPLETE A SWOTs ANALYSIS

A strategic planning group for a school district, a school, or a university has many potential sources of information. Types of information to gather may include demographic, political, social, financial, technological, and attitudinal. The planners may obtain such information from documents, state and national databases, experts, or from valid attitude surveys. Make certain that the data is both valid and reliable. It is frequently wise to compare data from among at least two different sources to make certain of their reliability. Some prime sources of information are:

- *Chambers of Commerce:* data related to business and industry status and future plans
- *state and university libraries:* data from historical sources, as well as current study reports dealing with important community, state, and national variables, trends, and values
- *state and federal agencies:* publications and databases
- *financial institutions and major corporations:* demographic projections related to possible future markets, and data related to the financial and corporate markets
- *position statements from associations, political groups, economic groups, and social groups:* directional guidelines that may impact tactics to be utilized by the schools or universities
- *information highway:* information, records and dialogues available through Internet bulletin boards, and related electronic databases and interest groups

- *records of state departments of education (or higher education agencies):* student achievement trends; trends in student population and characteristics; employee staffing trends; financing trends; and construction requirements and financial data by program and school district, community college, or university levels
- *records of the U.S. Department of Education, National Center for Education Statistics:* all types of demographic variables related to school attendance, finance, completion, post-school earnings, etc.
- *records of the U.S. Census Bureau:* all types of demographic variables related to age, sex, race, and other variables beyond education. These data can be retrieved on a single or multiple census tract basis to provide specific information related to the geographical area being served by individual school districts, community or junior colleges, and universities
- strategic plans[13] that have been developed by such organizations as the United Way, and/or regional businesses and/or government agencies, such as local or state Chambers of Commerce
- *real estate associations:* data concerning types of housing and the numbers and categories of adults and children who live in the various types of existing and planned future housing; also demographics of neighborhoods and communities
- *state bar associations:* information related to the impact of recent judicial rulings which may influence the operation of the educational agency
- *business and industry plans:* information related to current and future projected trends, employee skills, organizational mergers, etc.
- *newspapers:* information regarding local, regional, and national trends, obituaries, etc.

Once collected, such data may be placed into a matrix to facilitate its analysis as shown in Figure 6.1.

SWOTs will help guide your decisions, while moving you ever closer to fulfillment of the ideal vision and accomplishing each of the long- and

---

[13]Remember, most conventional "strategic plans" are really tactical plans.

	Strengths	Weaknesses	Opportunities	Threats
Internal data	• Yearly evaluations indicate teachers/administrators are well respected by students, parents, and community • Extensive community volunteerism within district • Student standard test performance at 87th percentile	• Analysis of advanced math and science test data indicates a bi-modal distribution of student performance • The dropout rate has increased over the last five years • There has been an increase in the numbers of students arrested for substance abuse over the last 5 years	• An instructor's spouse is a nationally recognized computer expert • A group of students indicate an interest in establishing a foreign exchange program	• There has been a growing concern over the formation of student gangs within the district community • A conflict has recently developed between the school administration and a small group of parents over 3 students suspended from basketball due to sports code violations
External data	• Local university is interested in supporting community schools • Some prominent politicians live within the area • Business wants to move here if educational quality can be assured	• Except for athletic activities there is low community attendance at district events	• The accrediting association is due to make a visit • A recent survey indicates a community interest to assist the district schools • There is a 21st century council being set up in the community to define and achieve a better quality of life for all	• A new student suspension policy is up for adoption • A no tax increase group has been organized in the district • Crime on campus has increased
Analysis	• Staff can make presentations to local civic organizations to stimulate additional community support • Extensive volunteerism promotes 2-way communication and increased awareness • High student performance increases scholarship potential • University support could increase curriculum offerings • Political awareness and interest could be stimulated			

Figure 6.1. A Partial and Hypothetical SWOT Matrix for Geyser High.

shorter-term mission objectives – the next step within our strategic planning framework.

SELECT THE LONG- AND SHORTER-TERM MISSIONS

Based upon the agreed-upon ideal vision, identified needs, existing missions, and identified SWOTs, select the strategic mission for both the long-term (e.g., the year 2010) and shorter-term, related objectives. Figure 6.2 shows the relationship between an ideal vision and the shorter-term objectives.

From these strategic objectives, tactical objectives may be derived. Therefore, by aligning with an ideal vision, eventual selection of methods, means, and resources may be both sensibly selected and justified.

By relating strategic objectives to our ideal vision we will move systematically and continuously toward creating the world in which we want tomorrow's child to live, as well as creating – transforming – a responsive educational organization. This is a commitment to a defined better future that discourages drifting in the same directions in which we are now heading. Because the basic organizational mission for education rolls down from the ideal vision, it identifies those portions of the ideal vision that it intends to take on, as shown in Figure 6.3.

Ultimately, each of these long- and shorter-term mission objectives should (a) be based upon the now-shared ideal vision, needs, and existing mission, and (b) precisely identify where the educational organization is headed, and how everyone will know when (and if) they have arrived. Because measurable criteria are used, progress toward each of the missions and the ideal may be plotted and reported toward continuous improvement. Appropriate responses, resources, and en route changes may be related.

When developing mission objectives, check to assure that each one will make a contribution to the ideal vision. Figure 6.4 supplies an algorithm for assuring the linkages between objectives and the chain of results from micro to macro to mega to ideal vision.

We have now developed the front-end of strategic planning. We have clearly stated where we are headed and have provided the criteria for measuring our progress. We have further specified our mission objective based on our ideal vision, needs, and our current mission.

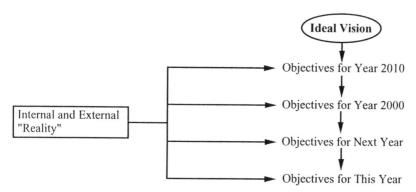

Figure 6.2. Ideal Vision (© R. Kaufman, 1994).

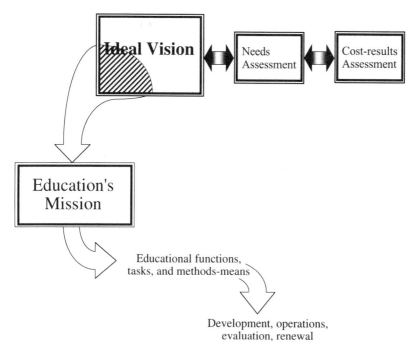

Figure 6.3. Organizational Mission (© R. Kaufman, 1994).

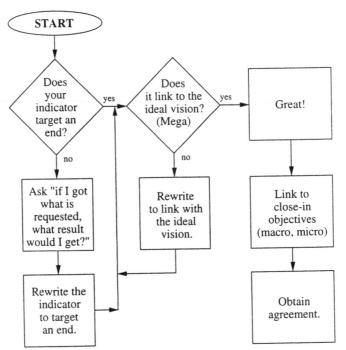

Figure 6.4. *Linkage between Objectives and the Chain of Results (© R. Kaufman, 1995).*

THE MANAGEMENT MAP: MISSION AND FUNCTION ANALYSIS

Determining the requirements for getting from where we are to where we should be is termed *mission* and *function analysis.* Both help us to ascertain *what* is to be accomplished to meet the needs, but not *how* we will meet them.

The mission analysis tells us what is required for overall problem resolution. Function analysis tells about specific detailed aspects of each part of resolving problems; what the building-block results are (again without selecting any how-to's). The use of these tools has been likened to looking through a microscope with lenses of increasing magnification (Corrigan and Kaufman, 1966). The first lens (mission analysis) gives us the big picture, and the second lens (function analysis) shows us a smaller part of the total problem in greater detail.

Mission analysis is one of several tools in a cluster called *system analysis*. When the mission analysis incorporates the outcome level of concern, it is a process for *mega-planning*. When it deals only with the output level, it is a component of *macro-planning*. If it begins at the product level, it is a process of *micro-planning*. The relationships among social requirements, needs, mission, functions, and tasks are shown in Figure 6.5. Rather than being isolated, they are nested. More on each of the system analysis steps and tools follows.

System analysis depends upon valid priority needs and purposes having been identified. Each system analysis process:

- is results-oriented
- identifies functions – building-block results – to be completed in order to meet needs
- differs from other tools in degree, not kind

Mission analysis focuses on the overall result to be accomplished. Function analysis identifies what has to be completed in order to get each element identified in the mission analysis accomplished. Complicated? Not really. Lock-step and linear? No, since it is understood that we are

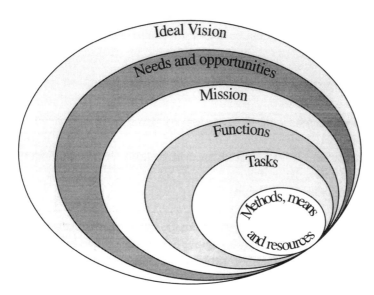

Figure 6.5. *The Relationships among the Ideal Vision, Needs, Mission, Functions, and Tasks (© R. Kaufman, 1995).*

building a complex education system where all parts work both independently and together, and are linked to move continuously closer to the ideal vision.

Mission analysis asks: "Where are we headed and how will we know when we have arrived?" Function analysis asks: "What has to be accomplished in order to get each part of the mission analysis accomplished?" The differences between the two are in degree, not kind.

A system approach to planning, of which mission analysis is part, has several components. In both planning and doing, organization members must recognize that organizations are complex and that all of its parts interact as parts of a whole. We are building a responsive and responsible system which build synergies among its parts.

There are two phases to being successful—planning and doing.

A system approach to planning, not surprisingly, has two major parts (Kaufman, 1988a, 1988b, 1992a, 1992b, 1995):

- planning what to accomplish (results)
- planning how to get from here to there

Useful organizational system planning consists of:

- identifying and justifying problems and opportunities[14]
- identifying what must be accomplished to deliver what is required

MISSION ANALYSIS

Mission analysis is the system analysis step that reveals (1) what is to be achieved, (2) what criteria will be used to determine success, and (3) what the building-block results are and what order of completion will move you toward the desired state of affairs. The steps and tools of mission analysis are in Table 6.1.

Continuing along from the needs assessment, problems delineation, SWOTs analysis, and selection of long- and short-term missions, the mission analysis states the overall identified mission and the measurable performance requirements (criteria) for the achievement of required

---

[14]There are important differences between problems and opportunities. Sometimes they are compatible, and sometimes they are different. In order to simplify the discussion, however, we will use the term "problem" to mean "problem and/or opportunities."

Table 6.1. Steps and Tools of Mission Analysis.

Step	Tool
1. What is the system to accomplish and what criteria will be used to determine success?	1. Mission objective and performance requirements.
2. What are the basic building-block products, or milestone results, required to be completed in order to get from where one is to where one should be? (Management Plan)	2. Mission profile

results. The mission objective and its associated performance requirements state the appropriate specifications for the system being planned and designed.

The next part of mission analysis is the statement of a management plan, called a "mission profile," showing the major milestones, or the central pathway, for the building-block results to be accomplished— moving from "what is" to "what should be" in solving a given problem.

THE MISSION PROFILE: A MANAGEMENT PLAN

The mission profile is a graphic presentation of the management plan. The most basic mission profile is one for identifying and resolving problems (referenced earlier in Figure 5.7).

The planning effort so far has yielded (1) what is to be delivered (the mission objective), and (2) the performance requirements for the mission. Now you want to plan what to accomplish to get from where you are to where you want to be. This step focuses on what is to be accomplished, not how or who (see #2 in Figure 6.6). The importance of keeping this analysis focused exclusively on results cannot be overemphasized!

When the basic and major functions of a mission are identified and placed in a logical sequence, they constitute the mission profile. The mission profile is a results-referenced management plan that shows which results must be accomplished to meet needs.

A mission profile shows the functional path for achievement of a larger end result. The actual number of individual functions that make up a mission profile can vary, from two to n, depending on the complexity of the mission.

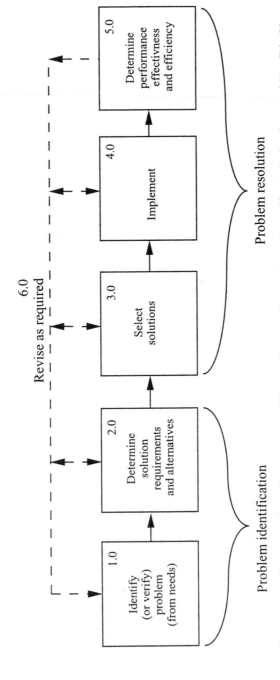

Figure 6.6. A General Problem-Solving Process. The Last (Revise as Required) Is Indicated by the Broken Lines and May Take Place at Any Problem-Solving Step (© R. Kaufman, 1994).

122

USING A DISCREPANCY ANALYSIS TO PREPARE THE MISSION PROFILE

Identifying needs as results discrepancies between "what is" and "what should be" is at the heart of doing a needs assessment as well as a system analysis. Identifying gaps in results is a *discrepancy analysis*. [15] The discrepancy analysis process happens over and over in a system analysis. Planning is used to create a better future; this often involves identifying and eliminating a discrepancy (to meet a need).

A completed needs assessment tells us where we should be in terms of results—which ones provide the mission objective with its performance requirements. Now we can devise the product path for getting from our current results to required ones, and in so doing we derive the mission profile—a management plan—which identifies what is to be completed in order to get us from the "what is" of our needs statement to "what should be." A mission profile displays the orderly progression of products to be completed and delivered. How is a mission profile derived?

Step 1

Obtain the mission objective and those performance requirements that specify where we will be when we have completed the mission. Next describe the current results—the status quo. Develop a mission profile that identifies what products—building block results—are to be completed in order to get us from "what is" to "what is required." The mission profile lists the necessary functions (products, or results) to be completed, and defines the logical order in which the functions are to be completed. Remember to leave out *how* any of the functions will be done. Identify and list the first function to be completed.

Step 2

When the first major function in the mission profile has been identified, ask the question: "What is the next logical product to be delivered?" List it as the next function. Continue this process until you have moved from the first function of the mission profile to the last

---

[15]This is not a deficiency analysis; a gap might be caused by too much as well as too little.

function required to meet and accomplish the mission objective and its performance requirements.[16] The mission profile is graphically presented in a flow chart. Figure 6.7 illustrates the rules for construction of flow charts, including mission profiles.

Step 3

When all the major functions in the mission profile have been identified, it is time to make certain that they are compatible with the needs, the mission objective, and the ideal vision—that they are internally and externally consistent. This rechecking will also ensure that the functions have external validity and usefulness based on the needs.

This process of check and recheck is performed throughout the entire system analysis process. By reviewing the scope and order of the functions—the building-block results—the planner can determine if any have been omitted or if unnecessary ones are included, and the planner can make sure that the functions are in proper sequence. Some functions can be unified under a larger function, so this checking process will help keep things at the same level of detail. While examining the mission profile, check to see if any performance requirements have been overlooked.

Step 4

Once internal and external consistency has been ensured, arrange the functions in a flow chart. This mission profile is an orderly array of rectangles connected with solid lines and arrows that show the flow of the functions from first to last; from "what is" to "what should be."

An example of such a management plan—a possible mission profile for preparing instructional materials (a product-level problem)—is presented in Figure 6.8.

The system analysis process in general, and mission analysis in particular, are dynamic processes. When new data are uncovered, the

---

[16]In performing a mission (and function) analysis, the planner may, if desired, reverse this top-down, front-to-back process and move from the end to the beginning. In this "back-to-front mode," the mission objective defines the end; it states where you will be when you have accomplished the mission, and this becomes a known. Then the analyst begins with the known and works backward until arriving at the beginning, all the time with a results (not means) orientation.

- Functions are related in sequence and joined with solid lines.

- When one or more functions may be completed in any order or at the same time, they are "stacked" and are called "parallel functions."

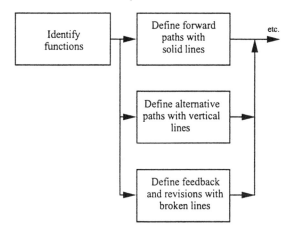

- When there is a choice between two functions, they are shown as an "or" gate (with the "or" placed between the alternate pathways.)

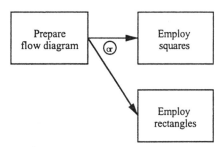

Figure 6.7. Basic Conventions in Preparing Flowcharts (based on Kaufman, 1988a).

- Higher order functions may be broken down into lower order constituent functions.

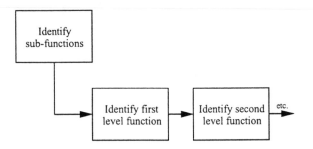

- Revision pathways are shown as broken lines

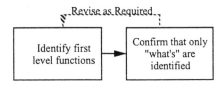

- An open block indicates inputs from another source or place

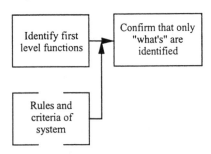

Figure 6.7 (continued). *Basic Conventions in Preparing Flowcharts (based on Kaufman, 1988a).*

126

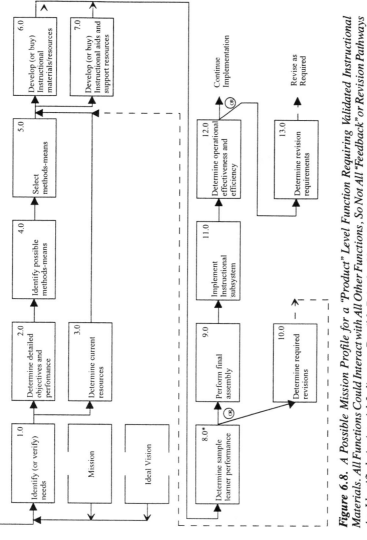

Figure 6.8. *A Possible Mission Profile for a "Product" Level Function Requiring Validated Instructional Materials. All Functions Could Interact with All Other Functions, So Not All "Feedback" or Revision Pathways Are Identified. An Asterisk Indicates a Possible Point for Obtaining Management Approval Before Proceeding* (© R. Kaufman, 1994).

127

mission objective and its performance requirements, and mission profile might change. Be ready and willing to change the profile at any time.

The overall mission analysis process is shown in Figure 6.9 in the form of a mission profile.[17] The major steps are:

(1) State the mission objective (based on needs) as well as the performance requirements in measurable, precise – ideally interval or ratio scale – terms.

(2) Develop the missions profile/management plan, which shows the major functions required to accomplish the mission.

(3) Revise any or all of the previous steps as required along the way to maintain consistency among the original requirements and the products identified by the missions analysis.

The mission profile is a type of road map, which depicts the basic functions involved in getting from what is to what is required.

Not all mission profiles are alike, nor do they have the same number of functions. While all mission profiles provide a management plan displaying the functions to be completed to get from "what is" to "what should be," they are all different. Since each shows the functions required to reduce or eliminate a specific need and complete a mission, and because all needs and missions are different, each mission profile is tailor-made to meet unique needs.

Use the basic six-step model (Figure 6.6) for identifying and resolving problems to develop a mission profile. Every profile (regardless of its level of analysis) should have every one of the six steps represented (Figure 6.9). (Usually, there will be several functions for each of the six steps of the problem-solving process.) Figure 6.10 is a mission profile for a strategic planning effort derived from the mega-level. It also shows the related six steps of the problem-solving process.

A mission profile identifies, in logical sequence, the major functions that must be performed while meeting the performance requirements. This is the major results pathway for meeting the mission objective.

When the mission objective, performance requirements, and mission profile are completed, the mission analysis is finished. The stage is now set for the second phase of system analysis: function analysis.

Figure 6.11 is a checklist of the steps in a mission analysis.

[17]Not all steps discussed in this chapter are shown in Figure 6.7; missing are some of the lower-level functions, or sub-functions (detailed later in this chapter).

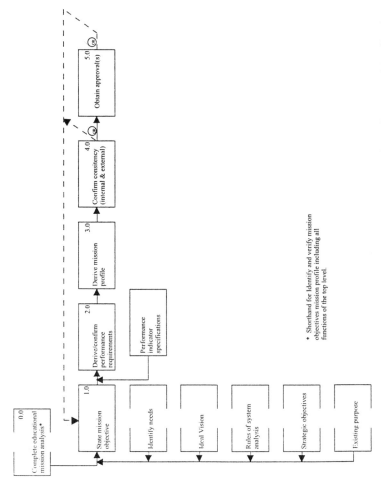

Figure 6.9. *A Mission Profile for the Completion of a Mission Analysis. Revision of Any Previous Function Is Possible; the Dotted or Broken Lines Show Feedback of Data for Use in Revision and Continuous Improvement (© R. Kaufman, 1994; based in part on Kaufman, 1992a).*

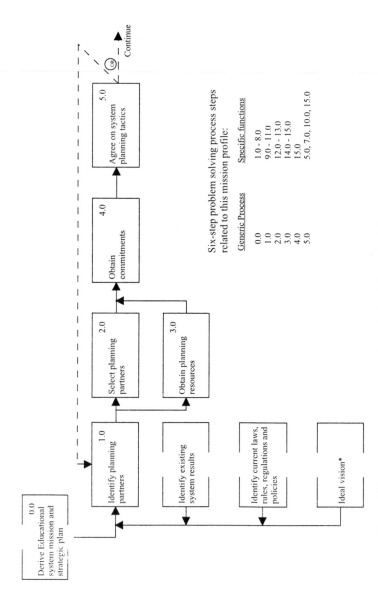

* To remind all planning partners that the mission objective is derived from the ideal vision

Figure 6.10. *A Mission Profile for a Strategic Planning Effort Derived from the Mega-Level* (© R. Kaufman, 1994).

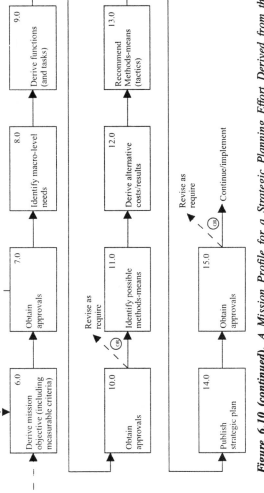

Figure 6.10 (continued). A Mission Profile for a Strategic Planning Effort Derived from the Mega-Level (© R. Kaufman, 1994).

_____ 1. Obtain needs data from needs assessment and select problems (selected needs) to be resolved or reduced.

_____ 2. Derive the mission objective (which includes the performance requirements) so that it is possible to answer, in measurable performance terms, the following questions:
- What result is to be demonstrated?
- By whome or what is the result to be demonstrated?
- Under what conditions is it to be demonstrated?
- What criteria will be used to determine if it has been accomplished?

_____ 3. Make certain how the objective will be reached is <u>not</u> included.

Together, the mission objective and the performance requirements answer the questions:
"Where are we headed?"
"How will we know when we have arrived?"

_____ 4. Verify that the mission objective (and the performance requirements) accurately represent the problem selected based on the documented needs.

_____ 5. Prepare a mission profile which shows the major functions required to get from what is to what should be. The mission profile is a management plan displaying the functions (or products) that will, when completed, eliminate the discrepancy that constitutes the problem. Each function identified will:
a. Identify a result (product) to be delivered.
b. Show its relative independence from the other functions in the mission profile.
c. Be numbered in sequence to show the relationships among all functions.
d. Be joined by arrows to show the flow and the relationships among each function and all other functions.

_____ 6. Assure that all six steps of the problem-solving process are represented.

_____ 7. Check the mission analysis to make sure that:
a. All functions are present
b. They are in the correct order
c. They are consistent with the mission objective and the performance requirements (and will contribute to achieving the Ideal Vision)
d. They are consistent with the needs selected and the associated problem.

_____ 8. Make any necessary changes based on the Ideal Vision, the strategic plan and/or the needs assessment data.

Figure 6.11. A Mission Analysis Checklist.

132

FUNCTION ANALYSIS[18]

A function is a building-block result, or product, to be delivered. A function is a product that, along with other products, contributes to a larger one. It is a collection of delivered results necessary to accomplish an objective. Each function integrates with other functions to accomplish the mission.

Analysis breaks something down into its parts. Analysis identifies what each part of a system contributes and shows how the parts interact. Function analysis identifies the building-block results, the interactions among the parts, and the order in which the results must be accomplished so that a larger objective will be met.

The function analysis builds on what has gone before. It proceeds from the original statement of purpose [obtained from the strategic planning, needs assessment, and mission analysis (including the mission objective and its performance requirements, and the mission profile)].

Function analysis defines the whats that must be completed in order to achieve the mission objective and its performance requirements. Function analysis, like mission analysis, identifies what has to be delivered as well as the order in which the products are to be completed. Function analysis is *not* work breakdown structures, making computer flow charts, PERT diagrams, or process charts.

Some examples of functions as they might be stated in a function analysis are:

(*1*) Identify functions

(*2*) Complete function analysis

(*3*) Deliver budget

(*4*) Obtain resources

(*5*) Validate in-service training programs

(*6*) Collect data

(*7*) Summarize data

(*8*) Derive ideal vision

Function analysis proceeds from the top-level (mission profile) functions and breaks them down into lower-level, building-block functions.

---

[18]In popular language, ''function'' is often (inappropriately) used to indicate a process. We use it precisely as a result, as do system engineers.

This process continues until it has identified all the functions, down to the lowest level of importance, at each level, and has determined the interrelations required to achieve the mission.

It is absolutely essential that each function be identified (regardless of level):

- State a product (result) to be delivered; not the means, methods, or resources.
- Be precise and clear about what is to be delivered.
- Have measurable performance requirements for each function or group of functions (this works best on an interval or ratio scale).
- Be linked to the ideal vision.

The function analysis process analyzes what should be accomplished and gives the proper order of subordinate, lower-order products (e.g., jobs or tasks), required to achieve the mission objective and its performance requirements. Function analysis:

- analyzes
- identifies
- orders

LEVELS OF FUNCTION ANALYSIS

Because a function is one of a group of results or products contributing to a larger result, a key to the levels of function analysis may be found in the term "larger result." Larger results (outputs or outcomes) are called higher-level functions. The highest-level function for a system analysis is the mission itself, and all other functions are derived from that overall function while contribution to the ideal vision.

Try viewing the relationship between the mission analysis and the function analysis as a matrix, with the mission analysis forming the "width" of the matrix and the function analysis making up the "depth." In performing a function analysis, we are filling in the depth of the mission analysis. Figure 6.12 provides a simplified version of such a relationship.

The function analysis is a vertical expansion of the mission analysis. Each element in the mission profile is composed of functions, and it is the role of the function analyst to identify, for each function in the mission profile, all the subordinate functions and their interrelations.

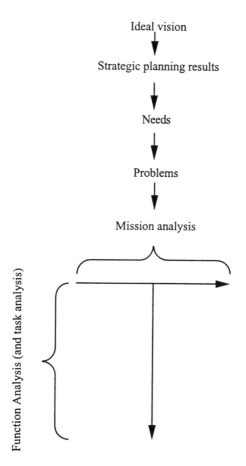

Figure 6.12. *Function Analysis (and Task Analysis) May Be Seen as a Vertical Break-out of the Mission Profile Functions, Which Are Based on Needs and Selected Problems (© R. Kaufman, 1994).*

The function analysis puts flesh on the bones of the mission analysis. It specifies the requirements and interrelations among the sub-functions for each product in the mission profile.

INTERACTIONS

An important contribution of function analysis is the identification of the ways functions interrelate with each other. These interrelationships are called interactions. All systems have interactions, so a vital element of system analysis is identifying interactions and planning for and assuring the successful meshing of parts. Rather than being a rigid, structural, and linear approach, this really defines and applies a dynamic system network that moves continuously closer to completing its mission.

Figure 6.13 shows the numbering format. In a function analysis flow diagram, each function block contains the statement of the function and the appropriate reference number. Since the overall function is the mission objective, it is labeled 0.0.

WHEN IS ENOUGH ENOUGH?

Function analysis continues to break down the functions until there are several ''layers'' or levels to the function analysis. The process continues until you are confident that functions are defined with enough clarity, precision, and scope to ensure getting the required results; any further breakdown requires the identifying of processes, or means.

FUNCTIONS ARE PRODUCTS, NOT PROCESSES OR MEANS

When a planner first performs a function analysis, it is tempting (because we are trained to be ''doers,'' not planners) to list the means for performing the function instead of first showing the end product or result. Throughout an analysis, when you find solutions ''creeping in,'' ask yourself; ''What is it that this method or means will give me when I am through?'' or, ''Why do I want to use that particular method or

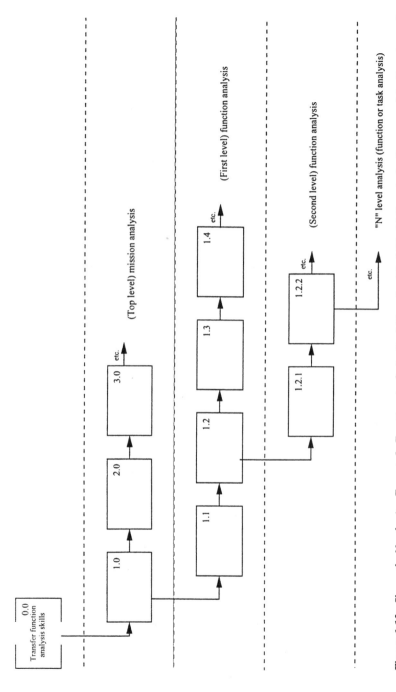

Figure 6.13. *Shows the Numbering Format. In Function Analysis, Each Function Block Would Contain the Statement of the Function and the Appropriate Reference Number. Since the Overall Function Is the Mission Objective, It Is Labeled 0.0 in a Flow Diagram.*

137

approach? Will accomplishment of this move us closer to the ideal vision?'' By asking these questions you will be able to determine the product you require and avoid locking yourself into a less than optimal process or solution.

A critical reason for performing a system analysis in general and a function analysis in particular is to free ourselves to identify and consider new, responsive, responsible, and better ways of doing things. (Remember to apply *Critical Success Factor #1:* Shift your paradigm to be larger and more inclusive—focus at the mega-level, and think globally as you act locally.)

The system analysis process is dynamic . . . especially vital in our world where cycle time is rapidly reduced. Quick—yet valid—planning and doing are imperative.

EVERY LEVEL OF SYSTEM ANALYSIS IS RELATED TO EVERY OTHER LEVEL

The process of system analysis starts with the statement of the ideal vision and continues with the assessment of needs. What is required is the core of the mission objective and the bridge between needs assessment and mission analysis, as illustrated in Figure 6.14.

Recall that the mission analysis identifies the mission objective, (including the performance requirements), and the mission profile and interrelates the levels of analysis in a logical, internally consistent manner. The mission profile—the top level of function analysis—thus bridges, or links, mission analysis and function analysis.

Function analysis continues until all the functions have been identified for all the top-level (mission profile) functions. This tells *what* must be accomplished and delivered to achieve each top-level function.

All the functions and sub-functions are revealed until vertical expansion of the mission profile is complete. Then all the functions which describe *what* has to be accomplished to meet the mission objective and its performance requirements are specified.

Each time a function is identified, performance requirements for it must be specified. That is, one must identify in precise, measurable terms, what must be delivered in order to accomplish a given function. This performance requirement identification for each function resembles that which is accomplished in identifying the performance

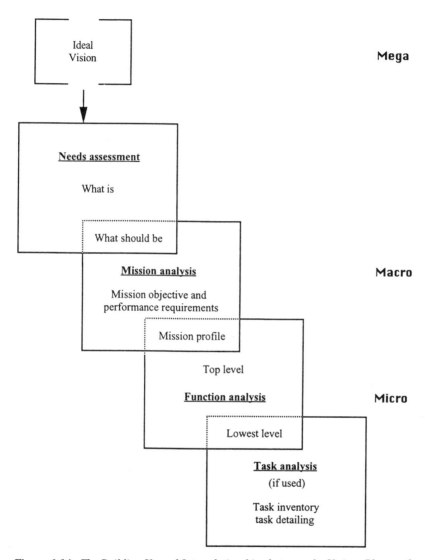

Figure 6.14. *The Building Up and Interrelationships between the Various Phases of a System Analysis.*

requirements for the mission except that it occurs at each lower-level function. Preparing a function is similar to preparing a mission objective, only at a more narrowly defined level: it states both the product to be delivered and the specifications for determining the quality of the product—as if we are to do acceptance testing. There is a continuous process of determining *what* must be accomplished, as well as the criteria for accomplishment and the kinds of lower-order products that make up the function.

Try to remember that the differences among the analyses at the various levels are a matter of degree rather than kind; there really is no difference in approach or tools used for a mission analysis that includes a mission profile and the function analysis or any one of its functions. That is, the process is exactly the same, only the actual levels of function differ. Miniature or subordinate "missions" are identified each time a function is "broken out." Performance requirements must be set for each function even if it is the very first one—performance requirements of the mission—or the very last function that can be broken out.

In function analysis, as in mission analysis, the planner's job is to identify the major milestones for completing a function and to know when a function has been successfully performed or delivered.

FUNCTION ANALYSIS AND FEASIBILITY

A Preview of Methods-Means Analysis

Each time a function (or a family of functions) and its performance requirements are identified, it is time to check to see if one or more reasonable methods-means or "how-to's" exist for achieving those requirements.

It is necessary to keep checking back through previous functions and requirements of the needs statement and the ideal vision to conform that the "whats" (functions) are both internally consistent and externally valid. All the functions must be compatible with one another as well as the need and the selected problem.

If there is one or more possible methods-means (there should be), we may continue the function analysis to the next level. However, if there is not at least one possible methods-means, we have a constraint that must be reconciled before going on to the next level.

DECIDING WHEN TO STOP DOING A SYSTEM ANALYSIS

The planner continues a system analysis only to the extent required to answer basic questions. If the analysis relates to strategic planning, then it may suffice to identify the mission objective, mission profile, and performance requirements. If the planner wants to determine specific product design objectives—micro-level concerns—it may be necessary to carry the function analysis through two or more levels.

For a planner who wants to advise on specific projects, curriculum, course content, programs, or the design and development of interventions, task analysis is necessary.

TASK ANALYSIS

Task analysis is the (depending on your purposes) lowest level of a system analysis; it is derived from a mission analysis and the related function analysis. It yields the most discrete level of detail required to identify all the "whats" for problem resolution (as shown in Table 6.2).

Task analysis can consist of two parts: (1) the identification and ordering of the steps to be taken (task inventory), and (2) the description of the salient characteristics and requirements of successful job and/or task accomplishment (detailed task analysis, or task description). Together, they reveal the units of performance and performance requirements for each task. Frequently, the task listing, along with its performance requirements, will give you all the necessary information.

By and large, task description charts are prepared for task analysis. Many and varied task analysis formats may be used, and selection

Table 6.2. The Starting Places for the Phases of System Analysis.

Starting System Analysis Phase	Assumed or On-Hand Data
Mission analysis	Ideal vision-related needs
Function analysis	Ideal vision-related needs
	Mission objectives (and performance requirements)
Task analysis	Ideal vision-related needs
	Mission objectives (and performance requirements)
	Functions (and performance requirements)

depends on the required results of the analysis. Such formats vary from a basic and simple one suggested by Mager and Beach (1987), which utilizes four columns—(1) task number, (2) steps in performing the task, (3) type of performance, and (4) learning difficulty—to quite complex machine interaction formats used in the aerospace field, which might include detailed physiological and psychological considerations and relationships.

The steps for performing such a task analysis description are as follows.

Step 1

List all the tasks and sub-tasks necessary to accomplish the function being analyzed. This is the same derivation process employed in the break-out of the mission profile and the function analysis. The tasks identified are placed in sequence, the order in which they will occur. In identifying the tasks, we want to make them independent, so there will be minimal or no overlap. This is the *task-listing* process.

Step 2

List, by tasks, the stimulus requirements (if relevant). These are the "input" requirements, the data required by the "operator"—learner, teacher, developer (or "doer" of the task when it is assigned)—to perform the tasks. State what form the data will or must be in to be usable.

Step 3

List the response requirements (the action requirements). These are the operations, the number of times each will occur, and the time necessary to perform the operation, if time is a real consideration.

Step 4

By task, list the support requirements. These are the kinds of materials and equipment necessary to support the operation of the task and the types of personnel or equipment required as "operators."

Step 5

List the performance criteria. Here is the specification of the product of the task. Just as a mission will produce a product, and a function will produce a product, so will the task produce a product, that is, a performance result. The performance requirements may be such items as (1) there will be no errors, (2) the list must contain all items, (3) copy must be smudge-free and readable, and (4) the form must have adequate space for teacher notations; all as certified by the project manager (or other valid performance assessment).

Step 6

Specify the prerequisite knowledge and/or skills the operator must have in order to be able to perform a given task. If, for example, in the preparation of a proposal there is a necessity for a high skill level of artwork, then advanced art capability may be a critical requirement, and as such, is a prerequisite that must be noted.

Table 6.3 presents a hypothetical task description for an administrative function. It represents an arbitrary selection of a task-analysis format.

As a matter of practice, the lowest-level sub-function that is being analyzed at the task level is always identified by the function number from which it derives. This function number (e.g., 4.1.1) is usually placed in the upper left-hand corner of the task analysis form. Failure to identify the function being analyzed will serve to confuse just about everyone.

The task analysis format selected by the planner should be only as complex as is necessary to supply the data required in the planning process itself. The important thing to remember and include in the task description is that it must specify the total requirements for accomplishing the task. Remember that the purpose of performing a system analysis is to identify the requirements for the accomplishment of a given mission. The system analysis process indicates all the parts and the relations between the parts for accomplishing a given mission.

SUMMARY

A SWOTs analysis is done to identify the strengths, weaknesses, opportunities, and threats both internal and external to the organization.

Table 6.3. An Example of a Task Analysis.

	Function 4.1.1		Response (Action) Requirements			Administrative Tasks			
Task (in performance or "doing" terms)	Input (Stimulus) Requirements	Prerequisite Knowledge or Skill Requirement				Support Requirements			Performance Criteria
	Data Form		Operation	No.	Time	Materials	Equipment	Personnel	
Obtain list of items	Items from 2.0	None	Physically pick-up	1				Clerk	None
Sequence items	Items on last cumulative folder sequence	None	Note relevant cumulative sequence; list items in order	1		Paper, pencil		Clerk	Include all items Sequence follows Cumulative sequence
Design format	Sequence of items	Basic drafting skill	Locate name column; count items; measure paper; divide space available by items; locate item columns	1		Paper, pencil		Illustrator	Space for all items; adequate notation space in each column

Table 6.3. (continued).

| | Function 4.1.1 | | | | | Administrative Tasks | | | |
| Task (in per-formance or "doing" terms) | Input (Stimulus) Requirements | Prerequisite Knowledge or Skill Requirement | Response (Action) Requirements | No. | Time | Support Requirements | | | Performance Criteria |
	Data Form		Operation			Materials	Equipment	Personnel	
Prepare reproducible	Data form with items	Knowledge of word-processing software	Select reproduc-ible, adjust and align; prepare rule columns	1		Micro-computer	Word-processor	Entry-clerk	No errors
Reproduce data form	Reproducible	Skill in operation of offset press	Obtain paper	1		Paper	Offset printer	Offset printer operator	Readable, non-smudged copy
Store on shelf			Run press	1					

In a sense, it becomes an organizational barometer by indicating environmental factors beneficial in determining the future strategies and tactics to be used in fulfilling the ideal vision.

Once completed, en route objectives are identified. They are the stepping stones or results markers as the organization moves toward the ideal vision.

The tools for determining the requirements for getting from where we are to where we should be are termed mission and function analyses. Likened to a lens on a microscope, the mission analysis provides a broader overview, whereas the function analysis magnifies a smaller piece within the overall problem.

All of these pieces are nested, interrelated parts of what is called a system analysis. A system analysis depends upon priority needs having been identified and selected. It is results-oriented; identifying the functions necessary to be completed to meet the needs.

Once the priority functions have been identified within the mission, each function is logically sequenced and becomes a map or management plan. Such a management plan is called a mission profile and only delineates *what* is to be accomplished. It does *not* define *how* the functions will be accomplished.

A function analysis builds upon this graphic picture. It further, or more closely, identifies steps (results) to be accomplished within each priority function. Task analysis yields the most discrete level of detail required to identify all the ''whats'' for problem resolution.

System analysis reveals, in layers, the sub-systems involved in mission analysis. The performance requirements for each task or task element provide the detailed information and criteria to further assure that the most relevant and practical possibilities (methods and means) are being used to accomplish the function being task analyzed. The results of a task analysis are useful in system design and development, providing direct input into learning specifications as well as techniques for management and continuous improvement.

PART TWO

TACTICAL PLANNING

CHAPTER 7

Tactical Planning

CHAPTER FRAMEWORK: How to Get from Here to There • Prerequisites for Methods-Means Analysis • When Does Methods-Means Analysis Begin? • Uncovering Methods-Means Information • Match Methods and Means to Each Function (and Task) • Compiling and Storing the Methods-Means Data • Procedure for Performing a Methods-Means Analysis • From System to Systems Analysis • Approaches to Systems Analysis • Methods and Means Selection

KEY HIGHLIGHTS: The focus of a methods-means analysis • Methods-means analysis can take place at any point • The advantages and disadvantages to conducting a methods-means analysis concurrently with each step of the needs assessment • The significance of a methods-means analysis for each performance requirement • Understanding the clear-cut form and protocol for organizing each element of the methods-means analysis as it enables objective consideration and choice between alternatives • The relationship of system analysis techniques to system analysis elements (mission, function, task, and methods-means analysis) • The importance of a cost-results/cost-consequences analysis to the selection of methods and means

HOW TO GET FROM HERE TO THERE

SYSTEM analysis is a dynamic process. It identifies where to go and details the requirements for getting there. The bridge between planning and doing is the methods-means analysis, the system analysis step that allows you to:

- determine if there are any ways and means to get the mission and functions accomplished
- do a feasibility study, which will tell you when there is no possible way of getting where you have to go
- identify the advantages and disadvantages of each of the optional methods and means

149

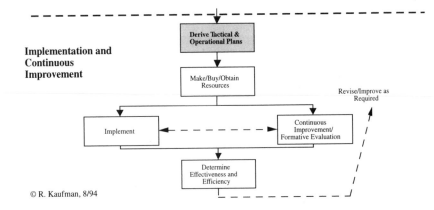

© R. Kaufman, 8/94

The identification of ways and means for getting required results is based upon the previous system analysis data. Mission and function analyses (and task analysis) are used to identify and justify the products to be completed in order to reach a mission objective. Once required products have been identified, it is time to find out whether there are one or more methods and means (solutions, tactics, or processes) to achieve each product or group of products. You want to know not only what to accomplish, but the feasible ways and means to deliver the necessary results.

In order to make the best selection of ways and means (inputs and processes) for each function, the planning partners should compile a list of possible solutions and the advantages and disadvantages of each. This tally serves as a databank for selection and further design and development. The process by which the databank is produced is called *methods-means analysis*.

Before we choose how to meet our mission objective (and accomplish all of the related functions), we should have a databank of the possible techniques and tools (methods and means) for achieving them. This is what a methods-means analysis provides. It lets us know if there are any tactics and tools (or ways and means) available to meet our performance requirements. As part of this analysis we also identify the advantages and disadvantages of each option. Methods-means analysis not only identifies what methods and means are available, but also provides a feasibility study, so that we don't try to move ahead if we can't get from here to there (Kaufman 1988a, 1988b, 1992a, 1992b, 1995).

Methods-means analysis identifies *what* — what how-to's are available to meet our objectives. The methods-means analysis *does not select how* the performance requirements will be met; it only identifies the possible ways and means for getting them done. This analysis compiles the necessary data and criteria for actually selecting how we will do the job.

PREREQUISITES FOR METHODS-MEANS ANALYSIS

Before starting a methods-means analysis, you should have on hand:

- mission objective, including performance requirements, based on the ideal vision
- mission profile
- functions and their performance requirements
- tasks and their performance requirements (if you have done a task analysis)

With this system analysis data, you are now ready to:

- identify possible ways and means to accomplish each function and task
- identify advantages and disadvantages of each possible methods and means available to get the job done
- identify constraints and eliminate them if possible

Constraints: Is the Mission, Function, or Task Feasible?

As obstacles (weaknesses, threats, or constraints—anything which will keep you from meeting one or more performance requirements) are identified during the mission analysis, it is useful to view them as actually being performance requirements. When viewed as a type of performance requirement, they provide criteria for the characteristics or conditions under which the mission must be completed. If, for instance, it is given that "no additional funds may be spent," this "obstacle" becomes one of the ground rules—a requirement. Even if a performance requirement is seen to be unachievable (a constraint exists), the troublesome requirement must be specified and addressed before quitting or changing the mission.[19] Thus, a constraint arises when it seems

[19]To further an understanding in this area, additional reading on force field theory and force field analysis developed by Kurt Lewin should be done.

that a mission objective, a performance requirement, or a set of performance requirements is not achievable.

A constraint is a condition that makes it impossible to meet one or more performance requirements.

Identifying a constraint requires planners to (1) change the mission objective and/or its performance requirements (and risk not meeting the needs); (2) be creative—develop a new methods-means or combine two or more methods-means that alone could not get the job done; or (3) stop, because it does not make sense to address a problem if you now know that the effort will fail. Once a constraint has been identified, we know then that blindly plowing ahead will present an unacceptable risk.

If a performance requirement can be delivered by one or a combination of methods-means, the system analysis continues. If not, then you have a constraint that must be reconciled before you continue.

WHEN DOES METHODS-MEANS ANALYSIS BEGIN?

A methods-means analysis can begin whenever you choose. It can be done each time a function, including the ideal vision, is identified, or it can be delayed until all the mission, function, and task analyses are complete. At the planner's option, methods-means analysis may be done at any stage of the system analysis process.

Experienced planners usually prefer to start the methods-means analysis as soon as ideal vision and the mission objective and its performance requirements have been identified. As the system analysis continues, the methods-means analysis portion may be done in parallel with each step, with continuous checking to make sure that the mission can be accomplished. Thus, continually identifying possible *hows* and the relative advantages and disadvantages of each means provides that an ongoing feasibility study is being conducted, as shown in Figure 7.1.

If there are no possible methods-means (or tactics and tools), STOP! If you cannot get there from here, why push on? If there are some possible ways and means, then go ahead with the assurance, at least at this point in your analysis, that what you want to accomplish is feasible.

For less experienced planners, choosing to conduct the methods-means analysis after all the functions and tasks have been identified and

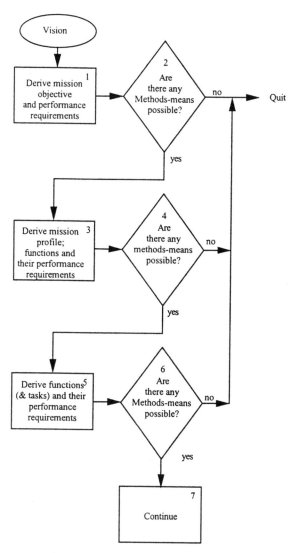

Figure 7.1. *The Ways in Which a Methods-Means Analysis May Be Used at Each System Analysis Step (based on Kaufman, 1992a).*

the performance requirements for each have been determined and listed can have several advantages:

(*1*) There is less distraction from the process of identifying what is to be accomplished.

(*2*) It avoids the all too common temptation to ''cheat'' the process by prematurely selecting the how. To avoid this risk, or to avoid the problem of possibly mixing ''whats'' and ''hows,'' the methods-means analysis may be delayed until all functions and tasks and performance requirements have been identified.

(*3*) As part of a greater system, each function and its associated methods-means have impact on one another. In the methods-means analysis, a constraint may arise which may have implications for other functions.

However, waiting to do the methods-means analysis until the last part of the system analysis also carries with it these unacceptable risks:

(*1*) You unwittingly may have let premature methods-means slip into the objectives.

(*2*) You missed an earlier constraint which had to be reconciled before moving further.

A methods-means analysis provides an ongoing feasibility check. We recommend the parallel conducting of methods-means analyses as shown in Figure 7.2. The figure shows the progression of the overall system analysis $(1-2-3-4)$ and the possible starting places for methods-means analysis (A, B, or C).

With experience, you will identify the methods and means and their relative advantages and disadvantages.

UNCOVERING METHODS-MEANS INFORMATION

Methods-means information is found wherever useful data may be located. If you are concerned about the methods and means of successful instruction, several texts and journals, especially those focusing on educational technology, discuss means at great length and great detail. If you are interested in other areas (such as facilities construction and management of human resources), you can consult specialists, vendors,

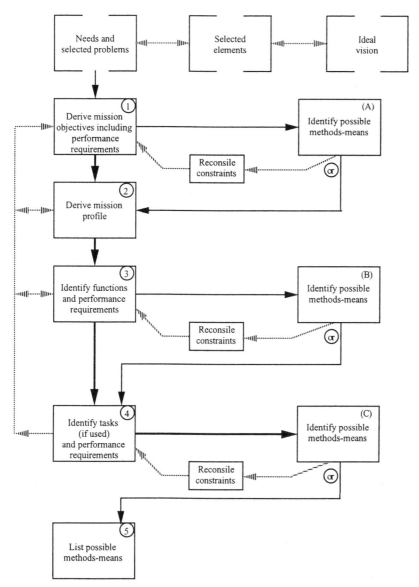

Figure 7.2. *Algorithm of Methods-Means Analysis (© R. Kaufman, 1995; based in part on Kaufman, 1988b).*

education texts, and books and articles in those fields. Libraries and document search services are good sources for methods-means information. This step of the identification of appropriate tools and tactics is the chance to "brainstorm" and be creative. Here we are not fettered by "the way it's always been done," and we can explore ideas that might seem extreme so as to determine if a vehicle and/or a tactic might work to meet the performance requirements. When you have completed your research, list all the possible methods-means for each requirement, and list the advantages and disadvantages of each.

MATCH METHODS AND MEANS TO EACH FUNCTION (AND TASK)

Each performance requirement should be matched with possible methods-means; each and every requirement must be met. Often, performance requirements that are related can be pooled into "families."

COMPILING AND STORING THE METHODS-MEANS DATA

In a function-flow block diagram each function has a unique number: 0.0 for the mission; 1.0 for the first function in the mission profile; 1.1 for a function derived from block 1.0; and so on.

Record the function-flow block diagram number for each function, and list the performance requirements for each function on a methods-means form (Table 7.1). Give each performance requirement a letter (e.g., 1.1A, 1.1B, or 3.1A). For each alphanumerically identified performance requirement, list the methods and means that could be used to meet the requirement.

These data will be entered for each functional unit as the analysis continues. Record-keeping will provide a summary of possible methods-means combinations for each function performance requirement (or performance requirement family). Table 7.1 is an example of the methods-means analysis format.

After completing the system analysis, identifying performance requirements at each level, and identifying possible methods-means possibilities for each function, prepare a methods-means summary to use during the design, development, and implementation phases.

Table 7.1. A Methods-Means Identification Summary Form (© R. Kaufman, 1994).

| Need* | Identify Possible Ways and Means to Close the Gaps in Results | | | Cost/Results Analysis | |
	Current Performer Skills, Knowledge & Abilities	Required Performer Skills, Knowledge & Abilities	Possible Interventions	Advantages	Disadvantages

*Needs may be clustered; several might deal with some common gaps in results.

To make the methods-means summary, arrange performance requirements and the associated methods-means possibilities into families. Such families are related by the top-level function from which they derive and by sub-functions that may be traced to the top-level functions.

PROCEDURE FOR PERFORMING A METHODS-MEANS ANALYSIS

To perform a methods-means analysis, use the following steps:

(*1*) On a methods-means identification form, like the one shown in Table 7.1, record the function number of the function with which you are dealing.

(*2*) Under the "Performance Requirements" column, list the performance requirements that any methods-means combination must meet. Label these requirements alphanumerically to link them with their appropriate functions.

(*3*) Under the "Possible Methods-Means" column, list any methods-means combinations meeting the requirements in the previous list. Number these to match the requirements list.

You should have at least two methods-means possibilities for each performance requirement. This encourages you and your planning partners to consider all the possibilities, not just those that have been used before.

(*4*) List the advantages for each methods-means possibility, such as availability, cost, time, reliability, transportability, and ease of use.

(*5*) List the disadvantages for each methods-means combination, such as cost, time, or policy/law changes.

(*6*) After completing the methods-means analysis for each function, summarize and integrate them into functional families as they relate to top-level (mission profile) functions or as they might relate with other functions from different top-level functions.

REQUIREMENTS FOR METHODS-MEANS ANALYSIS

Creativity, innovation, objectivity, results-orientation and methods-means analysis should all go together. For each performance requirement or group of related performance requirements, at least two alternative methods-means should be listed; this will force you to consider new and innovative possibilities. Some of us are frequently tempted to pick a familiar method or solution that has been successful in the past. Sticking with the comfortable and familiar discourages finding better ways to do things and deliver useful results.

The formality of this process encourages you to be bold, innovative, and creative. Indeed, innovation and creativity are encouraged by a system analysis in general and a methods-means analysis in particular.

The methods-means analysis answers the question: "What how-to's are possible, and what are the advantages and disadvantages for each?"

When you have completed the lowest level of function or task analysis and the final methods-means analysis, there are two products:

- a database of feasible *whats* for problem resolution
- a database of possible *hows* and the advantages and disadvantages for each.

FROM SYSTEM TO SYSTEMS ANALYSIS

The next step is to select the best ways and means to get from "what is" to "what should be." This marks the transition from planning to doing—from functions 1.0 and 2.0 in the problem-solving process to 3.0. Oddly, this is exactly the point at which most people start their work—they believe they already know the needs and problems and can jump right to a solution! Too many planners leap from unwarranted assumptions to foregone conclusions.

Systems analysis is not the same as system analysis. Both are very useful. Fortunately, there are many books and articles on systems analysis that show how to choose methods, solutions, and interventions. There are several different (and often confusing) labels for this process but a convenient name is *systems analysis.* This is not the same as *system analysis.*

System analysis focuses on finding out *what* to accomplish in the first place, while *systems analysis* focuses on *procedures* for selecting the most effective and efficient ways and means. Systems analysis draws upon the products of system analysis (Table 7.2).

Too often, planners choose methods, means, tools, techniques, inter-

Table 7.2. Comparison of System Analysis and Systems Analysis.

Tool	Focus
System analysis	Identifying and justifying WHAT should be accomplished; results-oriented.
Systems analysis	Identifies the most effective and efficient ways and means to get the required results; solutions and tactics oriented.

ventions, and solutions on the basis of biases, past experience, conventional wisdom ("everyone else does it that way . . ."), and hunch. Unfortunately, the likelihood is that the quick fix of the week or the most "mainstream" solution will be picked.

It does not have to be that way. You are better off using the appropriate tools and doing the job right the first time. Investing time in systems analysis is wise.

Worthwhile procedures for rationally choosing among alternative methods and means have been available for many years. These include (but are not limited to) such systems analysis methods as operations research; simulating; planning, programming, budgeting system (PPBS); queuing; relevance trees; decision theory; strategic market planning; portfolio analysis; market attractiveness assessment; operational gaming; game theory; Delphi Technique; nominal group technique; pooling; and cross-impact analysis. Discussion of such methods can be found later in this chapter.

Following are brief summaries of some of the most straightforward tools and techniques. When you attempt to select methods and means, these will be worth exploring.

APPROACHES TO SYSTEMS ANALYSIS

Systems analysis is a way to choose the most effective and efficient solution, or intervention, from alternative possibilities. Cleland and King (1968) define it as:

(1) The systematic examination and comparison of the alternative actions related to the accomplishment of desired objectives
(2) The comparison of alternatives on the basis of the resource cost and the benefit associated with each alternative
(3) The explicit consideration of uncertainty

Systems analysis is useful and appropriate when you have already identified objectives and requirements (ideally based on needs and an ideal vision) and when you are ready to ferret out and appraise possible optional methods and means. Systems analysis is best used after you have finished the phases of system analysis – mission, function, task, and methods-means analysis.

Systems analysis is the generic name for selecting solution strategies from among alternative possibilities. Following are some systems analysis tools, divided into two general groups: (1) those oriented primarily to numbers and facts, and (2) those oriented primarily to people and judgments.

TECHNIQUES ORIENTED PRIMARILY TO NUMBERS AND FACTS

Operations Research

When we know our goals, objectives, mission, and requirements, operations research can be useful. This approach seeks to find optimum solutions to specific problems where relationships among the variables are known and evaluation criteria are tangible. One representative definition is provided by Alkin and Bruno (1970):

> [Operations research] may be considered a method of obtaining optimum solutions to problems in which relationships are specified and criteria for evaluating effectiveness are known. Operations research summarizes alternatives into mathematical expressions and models. It then identifies the set of alternatives that maximizes or minimizes the desired criterion for evaluating effectiveness.

After completing a needs assessment and a system analysis, planners can use operations research to choose the methods-means that will most effectively and efficiently meet requirements.

Planning, Programming, Budgeting System (PPBS)

Most authors agree that PPBS is best used for identifying alternative courses of action required to meet the objectives of an organization, project, activity, or intervention and ranking the alternatives (sometimes called *systems*) in terms of their respective costs and benefits. This allows planners to choose among the alternatives on a rational basis and to derive a budget based on the cost of achieving objectives.

Although it makes sense to base the budget on what is planned, the budget is sometimes made up before the planning has been accomplished. After the budget is set, organization members often scurry around to find out what they might do with the dollars they have been allocated. *Too often, budgeting systems seem to be more important than planning; this is a serious and usually fatal flaw.* Many, if not most, operations are weakened by being driven by dollars alone and forced to fit their objectives, functions, and purposes to the money available. Before problems are defined, needs should be identified; then planners can move on to detailing objectives, identifying functions, finding the possible methods and means, and selecting the best tactics and tools. Only then should attention turn to programming and budgeting.

The usefulness of PPBS depends on the validity of the original objectives chosen.

Simulation and Gaming

We use simulation daily. We "anticipate" such future events as a request for a raise and try out various approaches in our heads. If there is to be an important briefing or meeting, we rehearse the pitch and try out simulated responses in order to shape our final offering. Whenever we set up a representation of the world and try out something before the fact, we are simulating.

Simulation constructs and tries out a model of a predicted or actual event or situation. Simulations range from making a mock-up of a multimedia training room to see how it will accommodate a dress rehearsal of a play, to running complex, multi-variate mathematical models of city traffic through a computer.

Queuing

Queuing uses a mathematical method to optimize waiting time in a crowding situation (such as customers waiting to be served food, standing in line for refunds, registering an automobile, or scheduling a rock concert). Frustration and cost are the variables most often studied.

Relevance Trees

Relevance trees (Martino, 1983) are used to identify hierarchies, the various levels of complexity of events. Consider the manufacturing of an intricate product such as an automobile, where successively lower levels of a complex process emerge like the branches of a tree from a common trunk, each more detailed and/or distinctive. By breaking down a series of sequential components of a system into the approaches, tasks, jobs, or actions where problems or opportunities might occur, planners can identify the associated difficulties and distinguish the best pathways or alternatives.

Decision Theory

Decision theory (Rappaport, 1986) determines optimum strategies for reaching a specific goal based upon probabilities for alternative pathways and methods. Probabilities are assigned to each option, and the options are examined as branching possibilities (as in relevance trees) and alternative anticipated consequences. Points where decisions are to be made, or the operation of chance could determine consequences, are also included. This approach allows the identification of alternative branch pathways by computing the probabilities of reaching the goal through each action/option.

Market Planning

Many so-called strategic planning approaches have evolved that provide useful ways to choose among alternative market plans (Abell and Hammond, 1979). *Market planning* views a business as a system in which different parts (including possible product lines) interact and contribute to or detract from corporate health. Various techniques for selecting mixes of businesses (or products and outputs) have been offered. One useful tool, *portfolio analysis,* appraises an organization's products and their differential strengths (plotted as circles of various sizes) relative to the two dimensions of relative market share and sales growth rate. From such an assessment, planners can consider differential expansion, reduction, change, and divestment.

A related tool (Abell and Hammond, 1979) is *market-attractiveness—business position assessment*. This technique uses a two-dimensional matrix (market attractiveness and business position) in which an organization's market size is graphically depicted. By examining present and future market possibilities, planners can simulate alternative change strategies in terms of return-on-investment payoffs and penalties.

Kaufman, Stith, and Kaufman (1992) have proposed a marketing model which relates to the mega-level.

TECHNIQUES ORIENTED PRIMARILY TO PEOPLE AND JUDGMENT

Operational Gaming

A variation on simulation and model building is *operational gaming*. Here, people play such roles in specific situations as customers or opponents in a political debate. For instance, suppose we faced a court appearance in a lawsuit over our liability due to alleged poor training of technicians in a nuclear plant. We might set up a ''game'' in which people played the different roles of judge, jury members, opposition attorney, witnesses, and spectators. The mock trial will help us determine what could happen on hearing day.

Gaming, as well as simulation, can be used during implementation. An executive, manager, or planning team can stage a simulation or game before moving to the next phase of operations to test whether it will deliver desired results. If the simulation indicates some possible surprises, planners have the opportunity to change the approach.

Game Theory

In *game theory*, ''players'' with opposite interests who are equally knowledgeable and informed and have a known number of options are asked to complete their task in a limited time frame (Bell and Coplans, 1976). Game motivations include payoffs (not necessarily monetary), differing value sets, and a desire to correctly predict the best course of action. Both operational gaming and game theory attempt to simulate actual, real-world happenings before the fact.

Delphi Technique

The *Delphi Technique* stimulates group responses and achieves consensus without getting the groups together face-to-face. Delphi uses the opinions of expert panelists in a round of questions targeted to future events and consequences. For each question (e.g., "When will all countries work toward the progressive documented elimination of environmental pollution?", or "When will AIDS be controlled?"), the respondents provide their expectations. After each set of responses, the manager reports the median response and the ranges of responses (usually the center fifty percent) along with, when appropriate, actual comments made by the panelists.

By the end of several rounds (usually three or four are sufficient), responses are clustered into groups that reflect the built-up and integrated considerations of the panelists as they reply both individually and with knowledge of the responses of other panelists.

Nominal Group Technique

This is a structured problem-resolving process (Van de Ven and Delbecq, 1971) staged to generate ideas and produce group consensus. This technique encourages the participation of everyone in the group, focuses concentration on a specific question, and reaches consensus through voting.

Usually the leader clarifies objectives, illustrates what is desired in terms of the scope and concreteness of the responses, prepares the room and environment to encourage participation, and begins. Participants are asked to generate ideas in writing and then share them with the group. Without responding to requests for clarification (in order not to get bogged down in detail), the leader simplifies these inputs in brief phrases or statements. Nominal group protocol provides adequate time for thinking, avoids interrupting others, reduces premature focusing on a single idea or solution, eliminates aggressiveness and prevents "bosses" from taking over.

Next there is a round-robin translation of ideas in order to cluster the group's thinking. Each idea is considered, in turn, by each group member, and duplicates are eliminated. Discussion is discouraged until the end of the process. When the process is completed, the group will have reached a consensus of judgments. One potential problem which may arise from this technique is that "outlying" positions are eliminated even though they might be correct.

Polling

Polling entails questioning representative members of a group about their preferences or predications. Sampling methods are crucial. It is important that respondents represent at least a stratified random sample of the group to which the results are to be generalized.

Agreement is not validity. One danger in using consensus-building approaches lies in forcing agreement among participants by leveling responses towards an agreed-upon central position. The risk is that the group might not be correct, and an outlying (out of the mainstream) viewpoint that might be correct will be eliminated because it is not popular or in accord with conventional wisdom.

Cross-Impact Analysis

Our world is not linear. Events happen together—as parts of a system—rather than in isolation from other events. Prediction would be easier if things happened in isolation, but we have to choose alternatives on the basis of the whole, not just a part. Cross-impact analysis tries to account for potential interaction effects. In cross-impact analysis, each event is assigned a probability of occurrence and a time frame for likely occurrence. Prior incidents (experience) are used to "guesstimate" the probability of future events happening or not happening. For example, as scientific knowledge increases, so does the influence of fundamentalist religions; the pressure not to use nuclear power increases while the concern over the greenhouse effect demands lower use of fossil fuels; and homelessness becomes widespread in the midst of demands for tax reductions. Given important events, times, and probabilities, a cross-impact analysis examines possible arrays of changes in timing potentials, and modifies each of the predicted variables to determine optional possibilities (Martino, 1983; Phi Delta Kappa, 1984).

Hybrid Techniques

Many of the available tools and techniques overlap and complement each other. One such "hybrid" technique—harnessing and using both hard performance data and personal perceptions and insights—is *quality management.*

Methods and Means Selection

Part of being strategic is selecting the best ways and means to move continuously closer to the ideal vision. A *cost/results analysis* will simultaneously ask two questions: "What do you give?" and "What do you get?" of each possible how-to (or cluster of methods and means).

Figure 7.2 provides an algorithm for methods and means selection on the basis of a cost/results analysis.

Costs/results (or cost/consequences) analysis relates ends and means by identifying "what we get compared to what we give." Sometimes "systems" analysis tools also speak to alternative means and possible consequences.

The selected methods and means will identify what programs, projects, activities, classes, courses, and interventions are working; which ones are missing; and which should be dropped. Remember, the identification of functions, possible methods and means, and the selected methods and means are the basis for getting from current results to the accomplishment of the missions.

SUMMARY

System analysis enables planners to purposefully and logically move from an ideal vision and mission to developing operational plans. This is done through a determination of alternative ways to achieve the mission and functions, completion of feasibility studies to ensure there are one or more avenues, and identification of the advantages and disadvantages of each method and means. In performing a methods-means analysis, the mission objective should already be in place, along with a mission profile, a listing of functions and their performance requirements, and even task analysis information (if one has been completed).

System analysis will provide an assessment of the advantages and disadvantages of each possible method and means, and it will provide a description of the constraints that could interfere with fulfilling the mission.

Methods-means analysis can take place at any point, but conducting the analysis during mission description can lead to the temptation to seek solutions and processes before all possible alternatives have been evaluated. Each performance requirement must be paired with methods-means through the use of organized structures such as charting and linking each proposed methods-means with the appropriate function and performance requirement.

Systems analysis techniques can be used after mission definition, functional, task, and methods-means analyses have been completed. Systems analysis techniques move into the descriptive phase of doing the activities that will reduce the gaps in results.

We have reviewed several models, methods, techniques, and procedures for selecting the most effective and efficient tactics and tools. They form, loosely, two groups: one that is oriented to facts and one that is oriented to judgment. As both quantitative and qualitative data are important, both approaches are useful. If you have performed the analyses explained in previous chapters, the basic inputs for using these tools are at hand.

These approaches all relate cost and consequences. Several tools have been only superficially covered. They take us from planning to achievement. The resources cited here will allow you to make the transition to ''doer.'' It is when you choose the actual ways and means for getting required results that the shift from ends-orientation to means-orientation takes place. All our planning and analyses are simply a prologue to doing—where the most energy is spent and the most work occurs.

Planning—it seems like it takes forever. If you have followed the precepts described in this book, you have by now:

- identified where you are headed
- clarified why you and your organization want to get there
- identified the functions necessary to get from here to there and detailed their requirements
- selected the best methods and means to get from here to there.

You are now ready to put the plan into action. At last! But, if it is worth doing, it is worth doing well—planning provides this quality assurance!

DESIGNING A RESPONSE

Putting the strategic plan to work involves (1) developing structures within the organization that will achieve the strategies decided upon; (2)

monitoring the activities and evaluating the activities and the strategies; (3) developing an integrated management information system (MIS) to aid those responsible for management of the strategic plan; (4) making in-process adjustments in strategies, tactics, or activities when the monitored data indicate that a change is required; and (5) ensuring the effectiveness of the activities and the success of the strategies employed. More about this will be discussed in the next chapter.

LOOKING AHEAD

Now that the various elements of strategic and tactical planning have been thoroughly discussed, the next two chapters will speak to applications of what has preceded: implementation.

PART THREE

IMPLEMENTATION

CHAPTER 8

Integrating Strategic Planning, Quality Management, and Needs Assessment

CHAPTER FRAMEWORK: Capturing the Power of Knowing Where to Head • Definitions (and Some Review) • Quality Management (QM): A Discussion • Quality Management Is Appropriate for Education • Making QM a Reality in Your Organization • Putting Principles to Work in Education • Doing a Needs Assessment for Quality Management Initiatives • Planning: Where Should We Be Headed? • The Strategic Planning Framework and How It Relates to Quality Management • Shifting the QM Paradigm: Quality Management Plus (QM +) • Do Most Total Quality Programs Go Far Enough? We Think Not • Quality Management "Plus" (QM +) • What's to Be Gained by Using QM + ? • Relating Planning and Quality Management • Delivering the Synergy • QM + , SP + , and Continuous Improvement

KEY HIGHLIGHTS: The importance of quality management • The critical relationship and usefulness of applying both quality management and strategic planning • An understanding of quality management • Quality management's importance for educational organizations • Identification of some key issues for organizations when building quality management teams • Application of quality management principles for education • The significance of a needs assessment and evaluation • The value of using Quality Management Plus as opposed to using the conventional quality management vision • The ultimate contributions to the organization using both Strategic Planning Plus and Quality Management Plus • The significance of the mega-level vision to quality management and strategic planning for the organization

CAPTURING THE POWER OF KNOWING WHERE TO HEAD

STRATEGIC planning and quality management are two useful processes when applied consistently and correctly. They can and should be integrated. When combined, and operated from the same database and with the same partners, they are much more powerful than when used

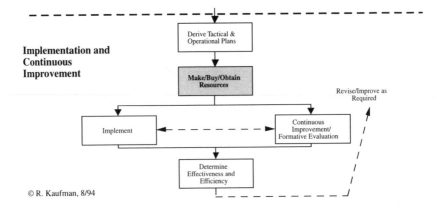

© R. Kaufman, 8/94

independently. Quality management (QM)[20] is recognized as a vital means for achieving organizational success (U.S. General Accounting Office, 1991). Strategic planning (SP), as described in this book, defines the right organizational direction. This chapter briefly reviews the basics of strategic planning (SP) and Strategic Planning Plus (SP+) and defines quality management. We then identify how (and why) they should be used together rather than as individual processes.

Unfortunately, many organizations are not getting maximum power from SP and QM because they (1) employ incomplete approaches which don't target big picture societal (ideal) visions and purposes, and/or (2) view QM and SP as distinct efforts and run them on parallel tracks. To get the best return on investment from both, apply them fully and together. It is a story that sociologists have known for a long time: the whole is more than the sum of its parts. Let's define each, and then relate how SP and QM can work together while using the same needs assessment database.

DEFINITIONS (AND SOME REVIEW)

We will build upon what we have provided in earlier chapters, and talk more about quality management.

[20]We use quality management and *Total Quality Management* interchangeably here. We defer to reports that Deming did not like the TQM term (preferring "profound knowledge"). Quality management communicates that there is a formal and continuous improvement process to be realized.

Strategic planning plus (SP+): (discussed in Chapters 1 – 6) defines where to head and justifies why you want to get there. With strategic planning, new objectives may be set and old ones modified or thrown out. It is direction finding.

Tactical planning: (discussed in detail in Chapter 7) identifies and selects the best ways and means to achieve existing or already selected objectives. It is direction achieving. After all, if you want to get some-place, it's rational to find the most effective and efficient ways to get there. Naturally, if you don't have the right objectives, achieving efficiency and effectiveness is a waste of time.

Quality management (and continuous improvement) (QM): enrolling all organizational members – everyone – to deliver total client satisfaction and quality. Each person in the organization strives to continuously improve everything they use, do, and deliver. Individuals and organizations learn from mistakes, and use performance data to improve, not blame.

The quest to achieve quality is prudent and timely. While businesses are pursuing quality management programs, attention has now turned to do likewise in our schools. The basic principles are the same, regardless of whether we are speaking of schools or a factory floor: both enlist people to continuously improve and deliver the things to external clients that satisfy them.

Quality management (QM) is a continuous process which intends to deliver to clients what they want when they should have it.[21] When QM is successful, the client will be satisfied with what is delivered. Quality may be defined as providing what is required as judged by the client. It is accomplished through (1) everyone in the organization committing to achieve useful results; (2) a shared passion for quality; and (3) decisions based on performance data.

Quality management (QM) programs are increasingly popular in education. Not only do organizations realize that they have to define and achieve quality, there must be continuous improvement in what organizations use, do, produce, and deliver. Deming's advice (Deming, 1982; Joiner, 1985 and 1986) was prudent, and we are now realizing that defining and achieving quality are, for both us and others, a partnership for quality.

---

[21]For a more complete explanation of this, please see Kaufman and Zahn, 1993; Kaufman, 1992c, 1994c.

QUALITY MANAGEMENT (QM): A DISCUSSION

QM Is a "People" Process

QM is an ongoing and never completed process. Quality and client satisfaction constitute the continuing QM goal. QM relies on all of the factors of production, including the most valuable one of all—people. Quality-focused people "do it right, the first time and every time," so much so that the client is satisfied. QM operates as if each person in the organization were the actual customer, making things the way they would make them for themselves.

Properly used, QM creates an organizational climate which provides continuous improvement towards perfection. It encourages, but doesn't demand, all employees to constructively participate in the process. QM provides each employee with the opportunity to become a full partner in defining and creating success. QM enlists everyone to achieve, minute by minute, day by day, week by week, total quality and client satisfaction. Everyone is supported, aided, encouraged, and empowered to make a unique contribution to the total quality effort.

Quality management cannot be delegated. All top people must serve as both active participants in, and role models for, quality. It is better to continue operations as usual than it is to "fake" total quality by having the executives and/or school board "looking down" on the quality process without being fully committed players. System-wide commitment and action is vital if an organization is to define and consistently deliver quality.

The more the system-wide commitment to quality, the better it will be achieved: QM is best done at the system or district level and extended into all schools and operations. If that is not possible, it should be initiated wherever it will find a friendly host. It should be pointed out that an educational organization should be a total system where all the parts operate independently and together to achieve useful results. While it is important that each school achieve quality, remember that the outputs of a middle school will be the inputs of a high school . . . there should be a seamless flow of quality and a value-added quality dimension from one part of the system to the next.

The Basic Elements of QM

Let's take a brief look at the components of QM in the private sector and see if there are some lessons to be learned for our unique and vital educational enterprise.

Assuring that the resources, methods, products, and deliverables are of consistent high quality makes sense. Without QM, ordinary organizations don't have a future. How can any organization not realize that external clients must be satisfied? Client satisfaction comes from delivering a quality output time after time after time.

For QM to work, everyone—from mailperson to chief executive officer—must act with the same goal: providing total quality to the customer. They must also be competent in how to identify and deliver quality . . . which often requires extensive education and training.[22]

Good intentions, slogans, and glittering generalities are not enough, nor even desirable. We have to be specific: define quality objectives, develop criteria for measuring and tracking accomplishments, and identify what has to be done to get us from where we are to our success vision.

QM works in business and industry. The U.S. Commerce Department's Malcolm Baldridge Award is coveted, and organizations compete to win one. By earning one, each employee can take pride in being distinguished for delivering total quality—for achieving client

Customer Satisfaction

Quality Outputs

Quality Products

Organizational Processes

Quality Inputs and Resources

Figure 8.1. *The Linked Elements in a Conventional Total Quality Management Program (© R. Kaufman, 1992).*

[22]Training is for specific and known identified skills, knowledges, attitudes, and abilities; education is for transfer of skills, knowledges, attitudes, and abilities which are not yet identified or known. Education is more about transfer and generalization to unknown situations.

satisfaction. The Deming award, usually only awarded in Japan, is seriously and proudly proclaimed. International quality standards, such as the ISO9000 series, are being actively sought by both public and private sector organizations. *USA Today* and Rochester Tech present a quality award for groups, and many states have initiated quality awards for exemplary school districts and individual schools.

Quality doesn't stop with an award, or even a happy customer. It requires that quality improvement and client satisfaction be continuous. This year's excellent organization can be next year's also-ran. The world changes, and a successful QM process must be continually responsive.

QM Involves the Entire Organization, Not Just a Part of It

QM is a process of continuous improvement. But what is to be improved? In order to successfully apply QM, we first have to understand the total organization, its elements, and then consider the whats and hows of successful QM.

Quality management involves all of the organizational elements – inputs, processes, products, outputs, and outcomes – meshing and melding to deliver client satisfaction. A QM process includes the integration of ingredients, processes, and organizational results. The Organizational Elements Model (OEM) framework, extensively discussed in Chapter 2, identifies organizational resources, efforts, results, and consequences.

Frequently missing from usual QM applications are (1) an understanding of the total system to which QM is to be applied, and (2) a balance in application of statistical quality control and decision making, motivation, and a shared ideal vision.

Defining the "Q" in QM

Usually, client satisfaction, or dissatisfaction, is based on the degree to which outputs meet specifications . . . perceived quality (cf. Caplan, 1990). If enough customers believe the ''Imperial'' is the finest auto they have ever owned, then that Division gets about one-third of the total points for winning a Malcolm Baldridge Award. Output quality and customer satisfaction are the ''vision'' targets for QM. And satisfaction comes from everyone in the organization working constantly to achieve customer satisfaction.

QM emphasizes that it is important for all elements to fit together.

They should integrate, mesh, and combine to smoothly turn raw materials, through competent and caring processes, into the products and deliverables which satisfy clients. QM enlists and enrolls everyone in the partnership for quality—suppliers and workers, sellers and buyers—in defining and achieving the vision of delivering total quality.

The QM Process: Rolling Up to Achieve Client Satisfaction

Figure 8.2 shows the elements of the typical QM process. It starts with the best ingredients, and then turns those into products and outputs which meet or exceed customer expectations.

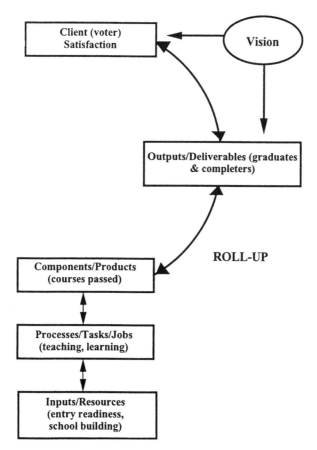

Figure 8.2. *A Typical Total Quality Management Process, Including the Basic Elements and Their Roll-Up Sequence (© R. Kaufman, 1994).*

Ordinarily, a general purpose of "a satisfied client" is consecrated, and then a sample of clients are asked to define what they like and don't like about the outputs that are currently delivered them. Based upon the satisfaction surveys, changes in the inputs, processes, products, and outputs are determined. Doing so is reactive . . . there is little consideration of new and different goods, services and deliverables. The typical QM approach intends to improve the quality of what the organization already makes or delivers.

QUALITY MANAGEMENT IS APPROPRIATE FOR EDUCATION

Educational agencies, regardless of their level, must not only change how they do business, they also have to re-invent—transform themselves, actually—if they expect to survive into the next century. Sensing this urgency, education is applying quality management.

Education, like other organizations, uses resources, develops products, and delivers outputs to external clients. It links ends and means to help learners become competent in the worlds of today and tomorrow. Although educators tend to use more delicate words for our concerns and activities than do business people, we deliver an output which is paid for, and judged by, society.

Unquestionably, educational agencies are not mills cranking out identical contrivances from standardized raw ingredients. Without doubt, our inputs (learners) are splendidly distinctive. They possess diverse backgrounds in health, values, experiences, and readiness to begin school. Regardless of the diversity, we promise to deliver a useful output . . . useful to both our learners (who will become our future neighbors), as well as to the society which pays for the graduates as they take their place in our communities. Education performs a vital function in a changing world. Each year, the demands shift and grow more complex. Quality management and continuous improvement are important enterprises for educators.

The success of QM depends on a balance among the three clusters of Deming's fourteen points: (1) a passion for quality, (2) everyone on one team, and (3) data-based decision making (Joiner, 1985 and 1986; Kaufman and Zahn, 1993). A way for QM to disappoint us is to allow it to only focus efforts on winning an award.

QM is essential if we are to transform education and move, continuously, toward achieving our mission and fulfilling the "vision." QM can become the engine of continuous improvement. As such it will be most successfully implemented when the correct objectives are identified and become our targets. That is why it is most powerfully linked to and integrated with strategic planning.

MAKING QM A REALITY IN YOUR ORGANIZATION

Basic Steps

First, get commitment. Start right away to build the total quality partnership. Successful partnerships have the following characteristics:

(*1*) Everyone cooperates toward a common end.

(*2*) Everyone is important. Each person makes a contribution toward the shared effort and destination.

(*3*) Each person provides support and assistance to the others.

(*4*) Everyone is honest with themselves and each other.

(*5*) Everyone is committed to improving, and never in showing up someone else as wrong.

(*6*) Objectives are stated clearly, concisely, measurably, and without confusion.

(*7*) Evaluation and feedback are used for continuous improvement, never for blaming. Everyone learns from mistakes and experiences. A quality system collects and uses performance data and provides it to all so they may identify what works and what doesn't.

(*8*) Means and resources are selected based upon the results to be obtained, not the other way around.

(*9*) There is no limit to what can be accomplished if one doesn't have to get credit for one's ideas.

(*10*) Constant progress and cooperation characterizes everyone's day-to-day efforts and contributions. Everyone looks for opportunities for action.

(*11*) There is constant management and monitoring of performance, and the results are used for improvement.

Building the Team

A total quality effort builds a partnership with common destinations; it is a cooperative effort, and shared ownership of quality results. A quality venture is also built upon data-based decision making; not upon biases, prejudices, and doing things "the way we have always done it." Provide each member of the organization with the attributes of a successful partnership, and ask them if that is the way they would like to work. Also, share with them that not everyone will like every decision, but convince them that their common destination is worth the required give-and-take.

Schedule the team members, and set up the meeting so that people may interact: a circle or arrangement where people can look directly at each other is the best, but sometimes the group gets too large for that. Let everyone know that this is a meeting of equals, and that the choice is optional. Reveal to the educational partners what's involved, and what will be the payoff. This will demonstrate a change in the usual "culture" of planning and doing—from leaders, followers, and hitchhikers—to a full partnership among equals.

The rationale for wanting to form a QM effort varies. If it is a school which is already performing well, note that success is already achieved, and that we want to make it better, day-by-day. If the organization is in crisis (layoffs, poor test scores, cut budgets, lawsuits, etc.) then the realities should be frankly revealed—without blame—to let everyone know that they can make a future shift from desperation to success.

Using Deming's Fourteen Points

Explain the characteristics of QM and the QM process. Deming's fourteen points (quoted in Joiner, 1985; Galagan, June, 1991) are useful and appropriate (after all, he is the father—along with Juran—of QM). As you review them with the educational partners, remember that these points, in their original form, are aimed at private sector organizations . . . the guidelines should be tailored to education (as we will do later in this chapter).

Deming's fourteen points for quality and client satisfaction are:

(1) Create constancy of purpose.
(2) Adopt a new philosophy.

(*3*) Cease dependence on mass inspection to achieve quality.

(*4*) End the practice of awarding business on price alone. Instead minimize total cost, often accomplishing by working with a single supplier.

(*5*) Improve constantly the system of production and service.

(*6*) Institute training on the job.

(*7*) Institute leadership.

(*8*) Drive out fear.

(*9*) Break down barriers between departments.

(*10*) Eliminate slogans, exhortations, and numerical targets.

(*11*) Eliminate work standards (quotas) and management by objective.

(*12*) Remove barriers that rob workers, engineers, and managers of their right to pride of workmanship.

(*13*) Institute a vigorous program of education and self-improvement.

(*14*) Put everyone in the company to work to accomplish the transformation.

Encourage the planning partners at your school and/or district to realize the payoffs for forming a QM team. Discuss the basics and furnish some additional readings on the topic.

The Three Clusters of Deming's Fourteen Points: Joiner's Triangle

Joiner (1985, 1986) summarizes and clusters Deming's fourteen points into the three angles of a triangle:

- quality (an obsession[23] with it)
- scientific approach (data-based decision making)
- all one team

By clustering in this way, it is key to realize that (1) everyone has to define and continuously pursue quality, with every act and decision moving towards its achievement; (2) quality flows from improving the processes, not relying on inspection; and (3) QM takes a total team spirit with everyone acting individually and together to achieve total quality.

There are unique initiatives involved in moving from Deming's principles to an operational quality process:

[23]Kaufman and Zahn (1993) prefer "passion" over "obsession."

(*1*) The quality of what gets delivered outside the organization is paramount. No excuses. No deviations.

(*2*) The realization that about eighty-five or ninety percent of all problems flow from ten to fifteen percent of the activities (based upon a ''Pareto analysis'').[24] Fixing the processes—making the work right—is essential to delivering quality. Decisions on what to keep and what to change must be made on the basis of valid data and analysis of results, not based upon bias, intuition, or power: scientific decision making.

(*3*) Everyone must be headed for the same destination. If everyone is not committed to a common definition of quality and a shared destination, then the results will suffer. Everyone must, continuously and consistently, act on the basis of a shared destiny. Everyone must be on the same team.

(*4*) A quality system—the collection and display of data—has to provide the database for management and continuous improvement: tracking performance—accomplishment, successes, short-falls—to provide the rational basis for change, continuation, and discontinuation.

PUTTING QM PRINCIPLES TO WORK IN EDUCATION

A tailoring of Deming's points—with a special emphasis upon results, payoffs, and contributions—to educational actions and payoffs include (Kaufman, 1992):

(*1*) Create constancy of purpose: the performance and success of learners in school and in later life should be in clear central focus.

(*2*) Adopt a new philosophy: transform your organization and move from school-centered education to learner success-centered; from teaching subjects to teaching learners; from budget driven strategies to strategy driven budgets.

(*3*) Cease dependence on mass inspection to achieve quality: don't evaluate learners and teachers on the basis of constant grading,

---

[24]A Pareto analysis, usually shown in diagram form, indicates which of several problems is most severe and shows the relative severity of all of the problems (Kaufman and Zahn, 1993).

testing, and compliance with scheduling. Shift to data-based self-evaluation and self-pacing of learning based upon an overall mission of success in and beyond school; have learners continuously improve their methods and performance. Provide learners with continuing data on their performance and progress so that they may calibrate their progress and appropriately modify their processes.

(*4*) End the practice of rewarding individual learner classroom performance alone (passing tests, answering oral questions), but instead reward total understanding and overall accomplishments with others.[25] Instead of focusing on course performance alone, look at holistic accomplishments in and beyond schooling. Deal with educational partners who make the most contribution and not with ones who do it cheapest—put an emphasis on results, not on inputs and processes.

(*5*) Constantly improve the systems and processes of teaching, learning, educational support, and service.

(*6*) Institute training on the job. Provide and encourage in-services in topics and areas which are useful. Realize that competence and confidence are central to meaningful empowerment, growth, and self-development.

(*7*) Institute leadership—substitute hierarchical levels of reporting and supervision—while defining and moving constantly towards partnership-derived shared destinations.

(*8*) Drive out fear—reasonable risks are to be rewarded (with or without success) if they were taken to achieve organizational objectives and payoffs. Failure is a friend in disguise . . . the results of failure are opportunities for learning and fixing, not for blaming.

(*9*) Break down barriers between departments.

(*10*) Eliminate slogans, exhortations, and numerical targets (which frequently limit continuous improvement and individual initiative).

(*11*) Eliminate work standards (quotas) and management by objective—mastery and competence is more important than learning (a

---

[25]As some contemporary researchers point out, we teach and reward individual, private, work and accomplishment and ignore the fact that most jobs and social activities require working successfully with others. This cooperative activity is more often punished than facilitated in today's education.

process), and learning is more important than attendance or compliance. Eliminate rigid, inflexible, and arbitrary curriculum guides, rules, standards, and scheduling. Collect, analyze, and provide data for self-evaluation of progress and problems.[26]

(12) Remove barriers that rob educators, administrators, learners, and parents of their right to take pride in their accomplishment and contribution to self and others.

(13) Institute a vigorous program of results-referenced in-service education and self-improvement of all staff members—use evaluation for improving and developing, not for blaming.

(14) Put everyone in the system to work to accomplish the transformation—everyone makes a unique contribution to the shared vision and mission.

After accepting the fourteen points (and Joiner's three clusters of "all one team," "scientific approach" (data-based decision making), and "an obsession[27] with quality")—or revising them before accepting them—get all of the educational partners to identify:

(1) What defines client satisfaction, and how will we measure it.

(2) What would be the characteristics of the outputs (graduates, completers, etc.) of the educational system, and how would we measure it.

(3) What are the building-block results (mastery in courses, abilities, skills, knowledge, etc.) which would deliver #2 and #1, and how we would measure each.

(4) What are the activities (courses, programs, activities, etc.) which would deliver the building-block results identified in #3, and what are the specifications for each.

(5) What resources, including people, facilities, funds, learner entry characteristics, etc. are required to do what is identified in #4 in order to deliver the results in #3.

(6) What must each person do, continuously, to make certain that #5,

[26]This guideline is sometimes seen as contradictory to some of Deming's other steps. It is not. The caveats here enable the QM process to (1) not move away from continuous improvement by settling for a minimum standard, and (2) stop employing minute and unimportant criteria which might actually interfere with the continuous accomplishment of useful results and payoffs.

[27]Again, Kaufman and Zahn (1993), prefer the term "passion" for quality.

#4, #3, #2, and #1 happen effectively, efficiently, and in a timely fashion.

(7) What would be the quality system—how will we track and display our progress, results, and problems on an ongoing basis, being sure to use the results for improving what we use, do, and deliver.[28]

Notice that each of these items requires that measurable objectives be set and used. After setting the specifications, then the gaps between current and desired results—needs—may be identified.

DOING A NEEDS ASSESSMENT FOR QUALITY MANAGEMENT INITIATIVES

Any scientific approach requires that decisions be made on the basis of performance data, not upon biases, hunches, popularly held stereotypes, or quick fixes. A useful tool for determining what works and what doesn't is needs assessment (Kaufman, 1992a, 1995; Kaufman and Herman, 1991; Kaufman, Rojas, and Mayer, 1993). Needs, for the sake of QM as well as planning, are most usefully defined as gaps between current results and desired ones (see our extensive discussion of needs assessment in Chapter 5). For each element in a quality management process, the gaps in results between "what is" and "what should be" are determined so that useful ways and means for meeting the needs can be selected. A general (but not complete) format is shown in Table 8.1.

Selecting the Methods and Means for Delivering Total Quality

Rather than rushing to use old and familiar methods (including ones we bench mark because others are employing them), we can be creative and select techniques and means on the basis of the costs and consequences of what they will deliver.

Take selected gaps in results and identify possible methods and means for closing them. Don't use any tool, technique, or procedure unless it will close the gaps in results, and will do so efficiently. When doing the

[28]As part of continuous improvement, it is important to realize that there will be variability in our results. When we track and use this phenomenon, it provides us with information for constant improvement. The collection of performance data is important for moving from concept to application. Helpful here are the works of Caplan (1990); Imai (1986); Ishikawa (1986); and Shewhart (1931).

Table 8.1. A Needs (and Quasi-Needs—Inputs and Processes) Assessment Format and Some Examples of Educational Total Quality Management (© R. Kaufman, 1994).

	Current Results	Current Consequences	Desired Results	Desired Consequences
Mega-Level (Partial) Board member satisfaction Employer satisfaction Learner income level on jobs Etc.				
Macro-Level Number of graduates Vocational licenses earned Job placements Number accepted to college Etc.				
Micro-Level Course grades Absences Standardization test norms Volleyball win/loss record Etc.				
Process-Level (Quasi-Needs) Computers in use Classroom contact hours Outcome-based education Quality management Etc.				
Input-Level (Quasi-Needs) Quality of teacher credentials Funding availability Availability of human resources Facilities Equipment Clarity of objectives Attitude/motivation Etc.				

methods-means analysis, you might consider possible synergies with other organizational activities. Table 7.1 in Chapter 7 provides a methods-means analysis format.

Evaluating Your Results and Payoffs

Evaluation is finding out what worked and what didn't — seeing which of the objectives were met. Based upon the evaluation results, we can tell what to change and what to keep, and how to continuously improve. The criteria for evaluation comes directly from the ''what should be'' column of the needs assessment form. When applying the Deming principles of continuous improvement, the evaluation data are used for fixing and improving and never for finger-pointing. So, needs assessment not only provides the objectives for the methods and means of education, teaching, activities, and learning, it also produces the data-based criteria for evaluation and continuous improvement.

QM is not isolated from the organization and planning. Strategic Planning Plus (SP+) has an overlap with a rational extension of QM: adding the mega-level. In order to get extra power from conventional QM, let's review SP+ and then show what's to be gained from Quality Management Plus (QM+).

PLANNING: WHERE SHOULD WE BE HEADED? A BRIEF REVIEW

Our ideal vision and derived mission (see Chapters 3 and 4) provides the front-end alignment for the organization. Everything the organization uses, does, and delivers, depends upon heading for the right destination. Defining the correct destination is far too important to leave to a loose or even inspirational philosophy.

Missions and Objectives

Any objective, including a mission objective states where we are headed and how we can tell when we have arrived. Objectives may deal with all of these: an entire organization, the mission, functions, and/or tasks. There are three levels, or scopes, for objectives, depending upon who is to be the basic client and beneficiary of your SP and QM efforts.

The basic questions any organization has to ask and answer (unless we choose the short-term "comfortable" deception of ignoring one or more of them) are shown in Table 2.2.

THE STRATEGIC PLANNING FRAMEWORK—HOW IT RELATES TO QUALITY MANAGEMENT

A three-phase framework which includes (1) scoping, (2) planning, and (3) implementation, evaluation, and continuous improvement, was shown in Figure 1.2. The three phases are provided in detail in Chapter 1.[29] Quality management and continuous improvement is the primary driver, or vehicle, for assuring the strategic plan becomes a reality.

Scoping

The first phase requires making a choice among the first three questions in Table 2.2 to determine the scope of planning. When we elect to start with Question #1, then the conventional strategic planning scope, which usually limits itself to starting with question #2, is expanded to become *Strategic Planning Plus* (*SP+*). SP+ integrates the mega-level into direction-finding. It factors in client good and payoffs—both pleasing clients and serving them well.

The first phase requires that an ideal vision be derived which will shape and drive everything that follows.

Remember, an ideal vision best identifies the overall specifications for our shared world. An ideal vision should only identify ends, not means. Because we seek to define the future, knowing that if we don't someone else will, preparing an ideal vision can be seen as *practical dreaming* (Kaufman, 1992b, 1995; Roberts, 1993). From the ideal vision, next identify the portion, as shown in Figure 4.1, you commit to deliver. No single organization is expected to accomplish the whole ideal, but each should contribute to it.

By selecting the portion of the ideal vision they commit to deliver, an organization may also (1) identify synergies and redundancies with other organizations, and (2) reveal blank spaces in the ideal vision that are

---

[29]The complete list of components within each phase are detailed in Chapter 1. Only key components are discussed here.

currently unattended, in order to identify possible niches for new business or contributions.

Identify current mission(s). Most organizational purposes are mission statements: they state the direction in which the organization is heading, but they don't provide the planning and evaluation criteria for knowing when they've arrived. Mission statements are more inspirational than measurable. As previously discussed in Chapter 4, turn mission statements into mission objectives by changing "How do we know when we've arrived?" to "Where are we headed?" Provide both direction and measurable criteria for accomplishment:

MISSION STATEMENT + MEASURABLE CRITERIA   = MISSION OBJECTIVE

   ↑   ↑   ↗

(Intention)   (Specifics)   (Success Statement)

Identify needs. Need (Chapter 5) is best defined as a gap between current results and desired (or required) ones. Problems are needs selected for resolution or reduction, i.e., no needs, no problems. A needs assessment identifies gaps in results and places them in priority order based on what it costs to meet a need, compared to the costs for ignoring them. Defining needs as gaps in results is critical for sensible planning, and for the "data-based decision making" part of QM (and, as we will note in a moment, QM+).

Planning

The second strategic planning phase uses the products from scoping to map a strategic plan. This phase is results-oriented, transitioning from the scoping phase to the implementation and evaluation/continuous improvement phase.

First, within this phase, the identification of strengths, weaknesses, opportunities, and threats (SWOTs) serves as an indicator of the environment within which the organization is situated.

Once the SWOTs are identified, then the long- and short-term missions are derived. Determining short- and longer-term missions is based on the ideal vision, needs, and current system results. The short- and long-term missions identify how close to achieving the ideal vision in future years you commit.

By arraying subsequent years' objectives in terms of moving ever closer to the ideal vision, you are entering into continuous improvement, an essential ingredient of QM.

The strategic plan itself is next derived. We know where we are headed, can justify why we want to get there, and now can plot the building-block objectives and possible resources and methods required to get from here to there.

Implementation and Evaluation/Continuous Improvement

Now it is time to put it all to work. The responses and resources have been designed and developed—*tactical planning*. Then the tactics are scheduled and put into action based on our *operational plans,* and we *formatively evaluate* (track our progress and revise as required), and then *summatively evaluate* (compare our accomplishments with our objectives).

Finally we determine what to keep and what to change and revise as required. The process of formative evaluation is identical to the quality management thrust of continuous improvement. Based upon the gaps we identify as we move toward fulfilling our mission, we change and improve right then and there—not anticipating a disaster but improving while in-process to assure that we are successful.

The SP+ process identifies where we should be headed, justifies why we should go there, and provides the criteria for planning, designing, developing, implementing and evaluating. It is rational, systemic, and systematic. It also delivers an even greater contribution: it forms the basis of strategic thinking—the way in which we run our lives and make day-to-day decisions. SP+ also provides the basic database required of QM+. Let's see.

SHIFTING THE QM PARADIGM: QUALITY MANAGEMENT PLUS (QM+)

QM, like strategic planning, can benefit from integrating the mega-level—societal and client good—into the process. When you do, you get QM+. Not only will you do continuous improvement, you will assure yourself that your continuous improvement will lead toward meeting your mission and bringing you ever closer to the achievement of the ideal vision.

Adding Societal Payoffs to the Definition of Quality

The definition of quality when applying QM+ is not only to deliver to clients what they want when they should have it, but also to deliver something which is useful to both them and to society. This definition includes both satisfaction and usefulness.

Why QM+?

If we only adopt the conventional QM approach, we could miss being both helpful and ethical. Without the full mega focus, we could delight our clients while doing things which are not useful for them and our shared world. For example we could win a Baldridge Award while making asbestos insulation. We might qualify for an ISO9000 certification (or Deming Prize) even while building a polluting tractor or a gene-destroying chemical.

QM+ adds the societal consequences and payoffs to conventional quality processes. We live in a shared world, and we are better off when we all continuously act in the interests of the common good. Organizations which do, adhere to Drucker's advice that doing what's right is more important than doing things right.

DO MOST TOTAL QUALITY PROGRAMS GO FAR ENOUGH? WE THINK NOT

When Client Satisfaction Is Good, but Not Good Enough

All organizations are means to societal ends, and they all have external clients. Education's client list is a long one, and includes just about everyone in our society: learners, parents, teachers, administrators, board members, governments, businesses, media, taxpayers, and neighbors; and now, more than ever in our history, the actions of these players may have a world-wide impact.

Some of these are internal clients—they work and operate within the educational system. Other clients are external to the system—they pay for education, and become the employers and neighbors of our educational outputs. All clients are important, all are stakeholders, and all must be satisfied with what we use, do, and deliver. Tall order! Usually, the most vocal clients, and those with the most political clout, are the external ones: board members; governments; businesses; media; tax-payers; neighbors.

To keep the external clients satisfied, organizations must deliver value-added outputs and services – a continuing positive return on investment. External clients have to be assured that they are at least getting what they pay for, if not more. Keep in mind that what organizations use, do, develop, and deliver to customers, is evaluated on the basis of both customer satisfaction and the usefulness of what is delivered.

Conventional total quality approaches focus primarily on only one part of the mega/outcomes level: client satisfaction. More often than not, the specifications of client satisfaction are informally or loosely defined. Figure 8.2 shows the general rolling up of the typical (total) quality management program's elements, as it moves from quality resources ("We don't have to inspect it, we know it's right.") to processes ("Everyone knows his or her job and assures it is done right.") to results ("The product is right the first time and every time."). The conventional (T)QM vision, "where we want to be," is focused at the macro/output level shown in Table 8.2, (Question 2) and the satisfied customer levels.

The "vision"[30] for a conventional educational (T)QM effort might be:

> To achieve total acceptance of the quality of education's graduates and completers; everyone will get a job or get accepted into a post-secondary accredited school; there will be no student who fails to graduate or complete. Clients will show their satisfaction by the continued financial support of the school and system.

Of course, satisfied clients are crucial to a viable organization. But is that enough? Isn't there more?

QUALITY MANAGEMENT "PLUS" (QM +)

Beyond Client Satisfaction

Peter Drucker reminds us that doing things right is not as important as doing the right things. (Total) quality management, as usually practiced, concentrates on doing things right.

---

[30]Note that this is an intention at the macro-level and thus is not an ideal (mega) vision.

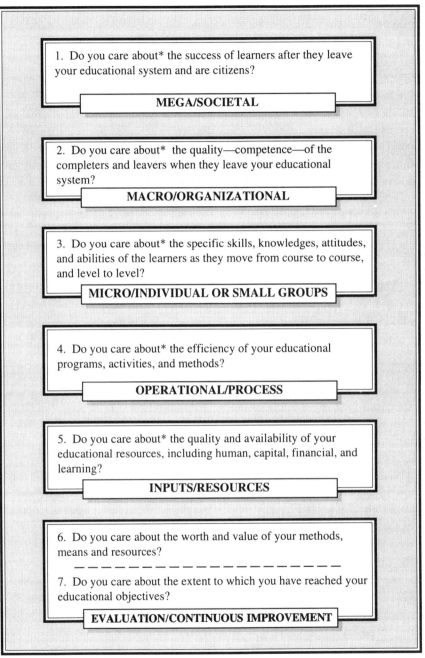

1. Do you care about* the success of learners after they leave your educational system and are citizens?

MEGA/SOCIETAL

2. Do you care about* the quality—competence—of the completers and leavers when they leave your educational system?

MACRO/ORGANIZATIONAL

3. Do you care about* the specific skills, knowledges, attitudes, and abilities of the learners as they move from course to course, and level to level?

MICRO/INDIVIDUAL OR SMALL GROUPS

4. Do you care about* the efficiency of your educational programs, activities, and methods?

OPERATIONAL/PROCESS

5. Do you care about* the quality and availability of your educational resources, including human, capital, financial, and learning?

INPUTS/RESOURCES

6. Do you care about the worth and value of your methods, means and resources?

7. Do you care about the extent to which you have reached your educational objectives?

EVALUATION/CONTINUOUS IMPROVEMENT

* and commit to deliver

195

But what about the contributions and usefulness of what satisfies the clients? We can think of many client-pleasing things which might not be helpful, or even safe. A few items in the private sector resulted in client satisfaction (along with high sales and profits) but turned out to be unacceptable, if not downright unhealthy, including such things as plastic bags, styrofoam cups, plastic packaging and utensils—which are not really biodegradable; toxic chemicals (DDT, Chlordane, red food dye); cigarettes/tobacco products; and asbestos insulation. Unacceptable products of the education sector include graduates of programs for which there are no jobs; completers and graduates who go directly on welfare; completers and graduates who go to jail or mental institutions, etc.

Each of these items above could be the subject of a QM program . . . and each would bring client satisfaction without "quality usefulness" to the client and society. We could be pleased by students graduating from high school, but not if they fail to get jobs, go on welfare, drop out of college, or become social deviants.

The missing quality consideration in conventional QM is delivering results that are good for society and which define and create an exemplary world. An educational mission objective identifies those elements of the shared ideal vision in which there is a commitment to deliver.

An ideal vision defines a shared vision of not just a successful company, an educational system, and/or a satisfied client, but of a successful society and community. Nor should it be simply an extrinsic vision intending to compete with another agency or organization, (the highest test scores, the lowest percentage of drop-outs), but rather identify an ideal—even perfect—condition or world (Senge, 1990).

A practical and effective ideal vision defines a safe and satisfying world where everyone is self-sufficient, self-reliant, and mutually contributing. An ideal vision provides the basis of deriving what elements of that ideal vision the educational agency—through its mission—will be responsible for providing. The organizational mission rolls down from the ideal vision, as shown in Figure 8.3.

An extended, or useful QM will link the ideal vision with conventional QM by adding the mega-level. Figure 8.4 provides a *Quality Management Plus (QM+)* framework. The QM+ process begins outside the organization by identifying what is required for societal usefulness (the mega-level again), rolls down to create what should be delivered to the client, and then meets with the roll-up contributions of conventional total

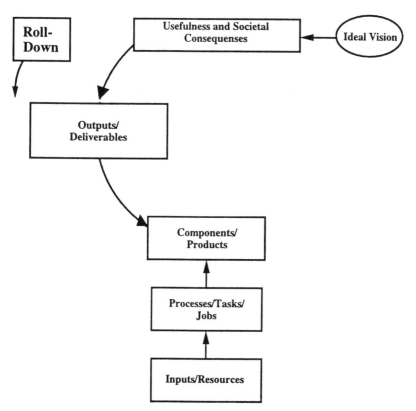

Figure 8.3. The Ideal Vision Provides the Basis for Determining What Education Will
Contribute (© R. Kaufman, 1994).

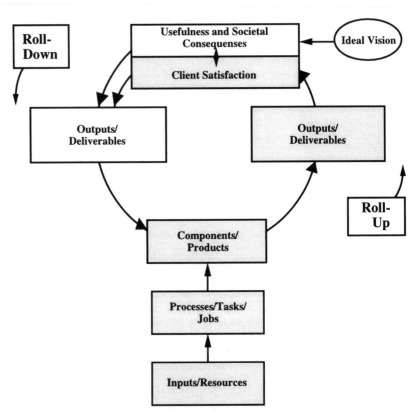

Figure 8.4. The Total Quality Management Plus Cycle. Conventional Total Quality Management (TQM) Elements Are Shaded (© R. Kaufman, 1994).

quality management. QM+ integrates with conventional total quality management . . . it takes a good idea and extends it.

QM+ in Education

A QM+-linked mission objective for a school system might be:

To achieve total acceptance of the quality of education's graduates and completers, everyone will get and keep a job (for at least six months) or get accepted into and complete a post-secondary accredited school; there will be no student who fails to graduate or complete; completers and graduates will be self-sufficient, self-reliant, and not under the care, custody, or control of another person, agency, or substance. There will be continuing necessary financial support of the school and system.

Certainly, this is an idealistic mission, and thus might not get achieved in our lifetime. But we owe it to ourselves and tomorrow's children to set our future direction based upon the ideal and not make ourselves self-limiting. When we restrict our visions and related mission to what we believe can be accomplished, our reach will be the same as our grasp, and we will forfeit our dreams. (There will be those who cry out for us to be politically oriented and give up dreams.) There are probably those who deride Martin Luther King, Jr.'s "I have a dream." They would probably sneer at Walt Disney's belief that if you can dream it, you can do it.

Adding mega-level considerations to classical QM can make it more realistic and practical; adding mega to "bench marking" and "re-engineering" make those more useful. Again, only attending to organizational objectives could only increase your ability to be a solution to the wrong problem.

The statement of a mega-level ideal vision and related mission is real and practical. In fact, its absence from educational strategic planning (Kaufman, 1992a, 1992b, 1995; Kaufman and Herman, 1991; Kaufman and Zahn, 1993) is probably why many so-called educational innovations and change initiatives have not worked . . . they haven't been linked to current and future societal payoffs.

QM+ is responsive to *all* the basic questions most educational organizations ask and answer.

Aren't QM+ and the mega-level hypothetical and academic? Aren't organizations interested only in their own survival? Before rejecting the concept of formally and specifically including societal well-being as a logical extension of QM because that would not be "practical," consider some recent episodes. First, how many companies who were in the Fortune 500 ten years ago are not there anymore? What happened to the Exxon *Valdez*, the old Ford Pinto, or baby apple "juice" which turns out to be only flavored water? Would you want to be part of a company going into the cigarette business? Would you like to be heading up a new school district and announce at the outset that you are going to fail to graduate at least one-third of all learners who come to school? Delivering things which provide societal good is, increasingly, both profitable and ethical. Some authors suggest that any organization that doesn't, is self-limiting, and will probably falter (Senge, 1990; Kaufman, 1992a, 1992b, 1995; Drucker, 1992, 1993; Popcorn, 1991).

What can I *do?* Educational planners and administrators are often the first to realize that something is missing from organizational missions, capabilities, and methods. They see the link between people, productivity, and organizational success, but take a reactive posture, and, in the name of "safety," become interested only in their piece of the total system (Senge, 1990).

When developing a QM program, open the dialogue with all educational partners about going beyond the conventional framework, the comfort-zone related paradigm, by adding societal payoffs to the usual QM vision of just client satisfaction. By deriving an ideal vision, and adding that to the standard QM focus, your educational system will likely reap a richer harvest . . . you will more likely deliver total quality and demonstrate positive societal return on investment to learners and taxpayers.

Doing a Needs Assessment for a QM+ Activity

When applying QM+, the information from a conventional needs assessment, as shown in Table 8.1, is augmented with the identification of needs—the gaps in results—at the mega-level, such as the additional elements shown in Table 8.3.

Action Steps for Implementing QM+

Following are the steps for doing QM+:

(*1*) Define the ideal vision: the world in which we want tomorrow's children to live. Identify only results and conditions, and do not

Table 8.3. Additional Mega-Level Variables, Such as These, May Be Added to the Needs Assessment Format Provided in Table 8.1 for an Educational Total Quality Management Plus Activity (© R. Kaufman, 1995).

	Current Results	Current Consequences	Desired Results	Desired Consequences
MEGA-LEVEL				
Self-sufficient & Self-reliant Completers				
Environmental State/Condition				
Murder Rate				
Health & Well-being of Completers				
Quality of Life of Completers				
Former Students in Who's Who				
Image/Reputation				
Board Member Satisfaction				
Employer Satisfaction				
Etc...				
MACRO-LEVEL				
Graduates/Completers				
Licensures				
Accreditation				
Etc...				

201

include processes, resources, or methods. The extent to which the planning partners make this speak to results, not to favored initiatives or methods, is the degree to which the product of this step will be useful.

(2) Agree to create and use a quality system which will collect performance data and provide it — feedback — to the QM+ partners so that they can clearly and continuously determine the progress of improvement, problems, and opportunities. Partners should understand and accept the concepts of using performance data for continuous improvement.

(3) Determine gaps between current results and the ideal vision specifications.

(4) Based on the ideal vision, obtain agreement with the planning partners on what would deliver client satisfaction for the distant and not so distant future (2010, 2000, next year), and agree on how would we measure it.

(5) Define the characteristics of the outputs of the educational system which would lead to client satisfaction *and* the meeting of societal requirements, and define the criteria we would use to measure it.

(6) Define the building-block results (mastery in courses, abilities, skills, knowledge . . .) which would deliver items (1) and (4), and how we would measure each.

(7) Identify the activities (courses, programs, initiatives, interventions . . .) which would deliver the building-block results, and define the specifications for each.

(8) Identify what resources (including variables such as people, facilities, funds, and learner entry characteristics) are required to do the activities in order to deliver the required results.

(9) Specify together with the QM+ team what each person must do and accomplish, continuously, to make certain that quality results and activities happen effectively and efficiently.

(10) Continue to use a data-referenced quality system which would objectively and accurately track and report progress, problems, and opportunities; and revise as required.

Opportunities and the maintaining of what is already working should be considered at each step. We want the educational system to improve steadily without sacrificing any successful activities and resources already in place.

Isn't adding a focus on results, especially mega-level results, going counter to the basic principles of quality management? No, there must be an interplay between results and processes. When you decide what to continuously improve, you have to identify if there is an important gap between your current results and desired ones—identify needs. Based upon the needs, you decide what to continuously improve and then select how to improve the process.

Extending this ends/means relationship further, it is important to know that your destination is correct and useful before continuously improving. For example we could continuously improve an asbestos insulation production, or even do it for a pharmaceutical product which is hazardous. Likewise, in education we could improve the processes of an operation which has incomplete and possibly wrong objectives. By adding the mega-level to our QM process, we better assure that we will continuously improve toward delivering an output which is useful as well as pleasing.

Bench Marks and Bench Marking

While it is useful to set *bench marks*—measurable mileposts along the way from current results to desired ones—another related method called *bench marking* has been attracting attention. Bench marking is often defined as "comparing your process with another leading organization to identify their processes so you may incorporate them as part of your way of doing business." This might hold some interesting and subtle traps.

If you bench mark another organization you should first assure yourself of the following:

(*1*) They have the right objectives (and are not heading in a direction which is not appropriate for your organization and learners).

(*2*) Their processes which you intend to incorporate are, in fact, the most effective and efficient ones.

(*3*) They themselves are not also continuously improving; you are not just copying an old and less effective process.[31]

The most sensible form of bench marking is to calibrate yourself

---

[31]In the private sector, bench marking a competitor has some additional traps, including the fact that you will always be playing catch-up with your competition . . . they will always be out in front unless they make a mistake. To pass your competition you should do something quite different from them.

against the ideal vision, and continuously improve toward "bench marking plus." Thus, you don't have to copy unless you can justify that someone else's processes will be the best choice for moving you continuously toward your mission and the ideal vision.

WHAT'S TO BE GAINED BY USING QM + ?

Not only do organizations have to be competitive, they also must contribute to our future societal well-being. Futurists (cf. Naisbitt and Aburdene, 1990; Toffler, 1990; Popcorn, 1991) agree that, ready or not, a new world is coming our way. To be responsive to that new reality, we should become active players in creating the kind of world in which we (1) want our children to live, (2) can make a contribution, (3) will get a return on our investment for what we do and deliver, and (4) can (and will) be accountable for useful results.

By using a societal-payoffs dimension when setting our targets— moving beyond just client satisfaction to also include client and societal well-being—we can not only be responsive to our coming world, we can also be the masters of it. A happy client is not enough. A continuingly healthy, safe *and* satisfied one is better.

RELATING PLANNING AND QUALITY MANAGEMENT

When our SP+ reveals where to go and how to get there, we must make certain we commit to the plan, and continuously improve as we deliver on our promises. QM+ provides the "glue" for achieving our strategic plan. Strategic planning and quality management, even used in isolation, are powerful. When combined and integrated, a synergy is developed which makes the organization correctly focused and energized to deliver on its promises.

Integrating the Planning and Quality Partnerships

By integrating planning and quality management, we may, simultaneously, define the right place to head as well as build the team and commitment to get there. Strategic planning best involves the partners who will be responsible for carrying it out. Strategic planning develops the specifications—measurable criteria—for defining where to head.

Quality management also utilizes this data to define what to improve, what to change, and what to eliminate. Both intend to achieve organizational success and contribution. Both use data. Both have a common purpose.

Strategic planning identifies where to head. Quality management provides the engine for change and continuous improvement. They are synergistic, not isolated individual processes. They should be combined and integrated.

Merge the planning team and the quality team: everyone will all be on one team to both plan and deliver quality. By having the planners and the quality partners being the same, we get both buy-in and commitment from their having defined the ideal vision and the mission. Merging the team delivers two critical quality ingredients: all on one team, and a passion for (and measurable definition of) quality.

As the partners do the planning, they will begin the data-based decision-making process—another vital QM+ element—by (1) collecting needs (gaps in results) data, and (2) preparing all objectives (including mission objectives) which target ends and not means. This data-based planning and results-referenced decision making will provide the rational and practical basis for planning what has to be accomplished to get results. Data-based decisioning will also provide the basis for evaluation of progress as the organization continuously improves and moves towards the close-in objectives and the ideal vision.

DELIVERING THE SYNERGY

What makes more sense than to continuously improve and develop a strategic plan that defines where to go? What makes more sense than everyone in the organization enrolling in and constantly contributing to delivering on the plan's vision and missions? What makes more sense than making decisions on the basis of performance data, not on just hunches, intuitions, and biases? QM+ allows everyone to participate in contributing to both serving the clients and satisfying them. Further, by agreeing on the mega-level for the ideal vision and mission, the planned effort is not only profitable, but ethical and socially responsible as well.

When we use SP+ and QM+, we provide the essential human element to organizational effectiveness and efficiency. A great plan is useless if people don't want to make it a reality. Only people can make an ideal vision come true.

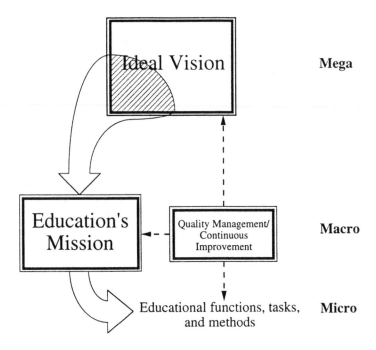

Figure 8.5. SP+ and QM+ Integration (© R. Kaufman, 1994).

Figure 8.5 shows how SP+ and QM+ integrate. Under this integration, QM+ becomes the driver for the smooth transition from strategic planning, to tactical planning, to operational effectiveness.

SUMMARY

Continuous improvement of everything we do and deliver is central to achieving total quality as well as a basic focus of strategic planning. While we move closer and closer to our ideal vision, we assure improvement in every way on every day. By adding ideal vision and mega-level objectives to the core, we add more ingredients for growth and improvement into the mix.

Conventional (and useful) strategic planning (cf. Cook, 1990; Kanter, 1989; Pfeiffer, Goodstein, and Nolan, 1989) starts below the mega-level, and uses visions aimed at what is important for an organization to be successful. Visions developed in these approaches (if done at all) tend to be either macro-level and/or competitive (or extrinsic, for example): achieve the highest test scores in the state, win the teaching excellence award, etc. (Senge, 1990; Kaufman and Herman, 1991).

Strategic Planning Plus (SP+) (Kaufman, 1992a, 1992b, 1995; Kaufman and Herman, 1991) and QM+ add an ideal vision—defining the world in which we want tomorrow's children to live—to the dimension of mega-level planning. It should be emphasized that QM and classical strategic planning are not wrong . . . only that they become more powerful when the mega-level concerns are added.

Our world has a global economy and a shared destiny, and simple appeals to be competitive will not suffice. We have to define and create an ideal, and develop leaders, thinkers, integrators, and contributors who can and will lead us there. To do this, we have to be creative, innovative, and inventive, for what must be done is not currently on the drawing boards. We have to add to the current models, techniques, and approaches that will identify and create what will be required.

As educators we have a choice. We can concentrate on process and resources and do what we are already doing more efficiently. Or we may define quality management to include the "plus" factor; and define and create that which will be useful today and in tomorrow's world. Toffler (1990) and Naisbitt and Aburdene (1990) are only three futurists demonstrating that our world has changed, and that extending today's realities will once again leave us playing catch-up. If tomorrow's world is going to be closer to ideal, then today's education has to define new horizons and new ways to get from here to there.

CHAPTER 9

Delivering on the Strategic Plan

CHAPTER FRAMEWORK: The Strategic Plan Report • The Elements of the Strategic Plan Report • Putting the Strategic Plan to Work • Selecting the Methods and Means—The How-To's to Meet the Objectives • Making, Buying, and Obtaining the Methods and Means • Management and Continuous Improvement • What Will Look Different as a Result of Mega-Level Strategic Planning? • Making Operational Decisions Which Will Be Compatible with the Strategic Plan

KEY HIGHLIGHTS: Making the strategic plan transform from a paper partnership into reality—from plans to results • What is in the strategic plan report?: preparing a document which delivers common understanding and shared commitment • Using the strategic plan to decide and justify what, who, when, and where we use, do and deliver; methods and means selection as the bridge between what we plan and what we accomplish • After selecting the how-to's, what it takes to make, buy, and/or obtain them • The management of the strategic plan: making continuous improvement the process for success • What will look and be different as a result of applying the strategic plan? ... Not the same old thing • A guide for making decisions when applying SP + : making certain that everything you use, do, and deliver will move ever-closer to the ideal vision and your educational missions

IMPLEMENTATION

ANY strategic plan is only as good as the results it delivers. All too often a strategic plan is developed and ''sits on a coffee table'' to impress visitors. Such a coffee-table strategic plan does not meet the basic criteria for usefulness: ''When decisions are made, is the strategic plan pulled out and used?'' If the plan is not used, then it has failed the ''usefulness test.''

The strategic plan, if developed as suggested here, provides the criteria for successful implementation. As an old adage tells us, ''a problem well-defined is more than half solved.'' In a strategic plan there are measurable criteria—written objectives—for educational implemen-

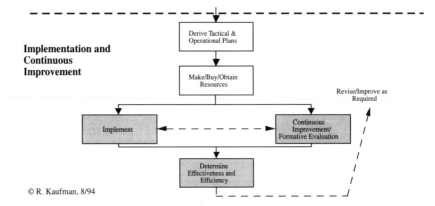

© R. Kaufman, 8/94

tation and evaluation, and because each objective is linked to the ideal vision, educational missions, and functions, implementation is made clearer and more justifiable.

In order to use the results of the strategic planning process, a report must be made. The report is basically a communications document which provides decision makers, including the school board,[32] with the rationale and information to move forward. The following are suggested elements of a strategic plan report.[33]

THE STRATEGIC PLAN REPORT

When the strategic planning has been completed, the report is prepared. It should:

- provide a guide to implementation to move continuously to the ideal vision
- allow the educational partners – learners, teachers, parents, administrators, employers, neighbors, legislators, politicians – to understand what is to be accomplished and what are the basic building blocks for getting from ''what is'' to ''what should be''
- provide the basis for evaluation and continuous improvement

---

[32]We urge that the school board, along with other major stakeholders in education, be represented as active partners *during* the strategic planning process. If they are, then the approval of the strategic plan will be more of a formality than it will be a revisiting of all of the understandings and work done by well-informed educational partners.
[33]Other formats and content are possible, depending upon the audience.

The final report should be extensive enough to provide guidance on what to change and what to continue. It should be concise enough to encourage its actual use. Its length may vary, but certainly less than twenty pages makes this document usable. One litmus test of a strategic plan's usefulness is the extent to which it is pulled out and used when decisions are made. If the strategic plan is not used, then it must be revised.

THE ELEMENTS OF THE STRATEGIC PLAN REPORT

As previously stated, the products that the planning partners create are fashioned into a communications document – the actual strategic plan (Kaufman, 1995). The suggested sections for the strategic plan report are:

(*1*) *Introduction:* this should include the title of the report, the agency (school district, agency, consortium), names of the authors and their positions, and the date of the document.

(*2*) *The ideal vision:* the statement of the ideal vision describes the kind of world the planning partners wish to create with others for future generations. The ideal vision should include indicators of success. An option is to provide the ideal vision on the title page, perhaps boxed.

(*3*) *The mission objective:* the mission objective, including all performance indicators, is provided. An option, if the nature of the readership seems more responsive to tangible purposes first, is to provide the mission objective before the ideal vision in the report. In this "tangible option" the closer-in educational mission objective provides for a more familiar concrete direction before requiring the audience to consider the bigger picture. The mission objective(s) describes the overall agency (school, system, and so on) statement of where it is going and how it will measure (with valid indicators) when it has arrived. The mega-level mission – the ideal vision – has already been stated (including all measurable criteria). This is to be followed by closer-in missions. Recall *Critical Success Factor #4* and make certain that rigorous performance indicators/criteria are included for the mission objective.

(*4*) *Needs:* the gaps in results selected for closure (and anticipated gaps in results and opportunities) are listed. These provide hard data concerning the realities of current results and desired/required ones. The needs at the outcome/mega, output/macro, and product/micro levels provide the rationale for the mission objective. Because they identify gaps between current and desired results, the needs allow:

- criteria for planning to get from ''what is'' to ''what should be''
- tangible criteria for selecting how to get from ''what is'' to ''what should be''
- the basis for evaluation and continuous improvement
- the foundation for justifying what is to be done and spent on the basis of ''what it costs to meet versus not to meet the needs''

Keep in mind that the detailed databases for the needs might be too extensive for most readers. If the data concerning the gaps in results are quite extensive they should be provided in the appendix.

(5) *Policies:* policies identify the decision rules which should be used as the strategic plan is being implemented. The decision criteria that are to be used are listed in this section. Each time a decision is to be made, these policies should guide the decision. Policies should be provided for the mega-, macro-, and micro-levels.

(6) *Roles, responsibilities, budgets, and time lines:* individual and group responsibilities for each of the results and missions are provided. These are based upon the functions identified during system analysis. This section could include specific programs, projects, and activities as well as when they begin and end.

For each function or role, a precise measurable objective (in interval or ratio scale terms) should be prepared and provided. Timelines, perhaps using Gantt Charts, for the accomplishment of major functions should be reported. Budgets for each mission objective element, program, or activity are provided.

Other elements to be addressed in this section include management and continuous improvement. How will all of the projects, programs, courses, classes, and support activities be monitored? What will be done with the performance results? This management plan may be shown by using organization charts and flow diagrams.

(*7*) *Continuous improvement/evaluation plan:* this plan describes what will be evaluated and the criteria to be used for continuously moving toward the mission objectives and the ideal vision. Remember, the criteria has already been identified in the ideal vision. It is now used to move closer toward the ideal vision. A continuous improvement/evaluation plan should include both ''hard'' and ''soft'' data points and proper assurances that the results and recommendations will be objective and will be used for fixing and never for blaming.

(*8*) *Appendix:* any required justifications and rationale for the ideal vision, the mission objectives, and each of the unique interventions or programs, may be provided here. Also frequently useful may be the detailed presentation of the data-based needs (gaps in results) to show the magnitude of the discrepancies between current status and desired condition. Graphics are very helpful. If approval of the plan is required, additional elements should be included:

- the cost to meet each identified need
- the cost not to meet each need
- alternative costs and benefits for the mission objectives and programs, all related to the ideal vision

PUTTING THE STRATEGIC PLAN TO WORK[34]

Selecting the Methods and Means — The How-To's — To Meet the Objectives

Based on the alternative methods and means identified in the methods-means analysis (Chapter 7), the selections of methods, means, resources, programs, projects, activities, and initiatives all are made on the basis of costs/consequences analysis: ''What does it cost to meet versus ignore the need?'' Remember, it will be a challenge to prevent your educational partners from pushing to use a particular favorite solution without (1) using the measurable objectives derived from the needs (what should be); or (2) identifying alternative methods and means

[34]The major focus of this book is on strategic and tactical planning. This section provides only a brief introduction to the delivery of education based on these plans since there are a number of excellent books on educational management and administration. We will not attempt to duplicate these resources but only provide the basic data to be used by them. Of course, the successful implementation of what the strategic plan has identified is the basic purpose of it all.

for meeting the objectives. Once again, the planning partners' group ensures that the most initial selection of representative wholistic thinking has been considered.

MAKING, BUYING, OR OBTAINING THE METHODS-MEANS

Based on the specifications of what each methods-means must deliver, decisions are made concerning who is to do what, and when, as outlined in the strategic plan report. Allocations should be made objectively on the basis of competence to deliver, rather than on historical relationships. In addition, those who will make and/or deliver the methods-means should be integrated into the continuous improvement team of the educational system. A "seamless" development, from inputs to outcomes, forms what is an imperative pursuit. It is vital to recognize that the organizational chain orientation used in planning is not forgotten in the implementation/continuous improvement phase.

When making any decision concerning a program, project, activity, course, course element, or curriculum, reference to the results chain (Figure 2.2) will help the usefulness of what is selected and what that contributes. For example, Table 9.1 provides a form which might be used.

By using this type of "check with results requirements at all levels" approach, any changes to methods and means will more likely have a contribution to what the system commits to deliver. For example, if an educational partner suggests implementing a "total quality management" process, the educational planning partners might go through the following steps (as they apply in Table 9.1).

(*1*) Determine if the suggestion (entered in Column 1) is a means or an end.

(2) If it is an end, it may be compared to the strategic plan's objectives (Column 3 and/or 4) to determine if it is a new objective or will replace an old one. If it is a new objective, then it should be determined if the objective would successfully move the learners and the organization measurably closer to the ideal vision (Column 2). If it is a means (as a quality management process is) then the question asked is "If this process were successful, what results would it deliver at the mega/ideal vision level (Column 2), and at

Table 9.1. A Form for Linking Possible Activities to Strategic Planning Intentions.

[1] Item Being Considered	[2] Ideal Vision Element to Which Related	[3] Basic Mission Element to Which Related	[4] Function to Which Related	[5] Alternative Methods-Means Considered
1. Quality management plus process				
2. Continuous progress				
3. Peer tutoring				
4. Authentic assessment				
5. Outcome-based education				
6. Computer-assisted education				
7. Distance learning				
8. Etc.				

the mission and functions levels (Columns 3 and 4)?'' This question should be asked and answered until a clear set of results and consequences are provided.

(*3*) Assure that if adopted and implemented, positive results — continuous progress toward the ideal vision and derived educational missions and functions — will occur.

(*4*) Define alternative methods and means (Column 5) and determine the advantages and disadvantages of each.

(*5*) Recommend the new item if it meets all of the criteria of continuous improvement toward the ideal vision.

By always checking to assure that any means, process, activity, or program will make a contribution in terms of moving the organization toward the ideal vision and its missions, there will be an increase in effectiveness and efficiency. One detractor from organizations is their tendency to select solutions to no known problems. Linking means to useful ends in this formal way will pay excellent dividends in terms of costs and consequences. Little is more wasteful than implementing a solution that does not deliver useful results.

MANAGEMENT AND CONTINUOUS IMPROVEMENT

Management Is a Do-It-Yourself Kit

Remember, build an educational team which will continuously improve what the system uses, does, and delivers. Each team member should have the opportunity to develop or buy-in to the ideal vision and the educational missions. If someone does not want to be part of the adventure, don't force them, but don't allow them to sabotage or undermine it. If they don't want to be included in a successful endeavor, don't allow them to get in the way.

Encourage and model continuous improvement where everyone is on the same team, has a commitment (passion, even) to the ideal vision and missions, and makes data-based decisions (on the basis of the gaps between current and required results). Thus, the process of Quality Management Plus (Chapter 8) provides the best bases for humane and rational management. Each one of us, really, is our own manager.

Report progress and results, and ask teams to identify what should be changed and what should be continued. Decisions should be made by those who are doing the work.

Evaluation and continuous improvement use performance data to compare results with intentions and decide what to continue, what to modify, and what to discontinue. Evaluation, in its conventional use, is retrospective, or reactive. It is an important, yet after-the-fact, determination of successful accomplishment. By comparing accomplishments with intentions (results with objectives) the implementors are able to determine whether or not the methods-means and resources are appropriate. Unlike strategic planning and its questions (Table 2.2) that are before-the-fact questions, evaluation and continuous improvement are done only after interventions have been put into action. Using a results orientation — including defining needs as gaps in results — evaluation and continuous improvement are both easier and more rational because the criteria have already been derived as part of strategic planning.

Managing the educational system is not telling people what to do or how to do it. It is not closely supervising them. Management is leader-ship/stewardship (Block, 1993) getting closer together. It is moving from supervising to networking, from directing to finding a common destination with everyone contributing (Bennis and Nannus, 1985; Drucker, 1973, 1985, 1988; Deming, 1986, 1990: May 10; Kanter, 1989; Naisbitt and Aburdene, 1990; Joiner, 1985, 1986; Peters, 1987; Popcorn, 1991; Roberts, 1987; Senge, 1990; Toffler, 1990; Kaufman and Zahn, 1993; Block, 1993).

As previously stated, an advantage of being strategic is that everyone knows and uses:

(*1*) The ideal vision in terms of the society we want for tomorrow's children

(*2*) The mission objectives and the performance indicators for telling both direction and destination

(*3*) The policies for decisions

(*4*) What each person and group within the educational system has committed to deliver

The elements of leadership and management include commitment to a common destination and to contributing to getting there. *Management may be done by exception:* tracking progress toward known and agreed-upon objectives, identifying where and when needs appear or might occur, and knowing precisely where and when to make responsive and responsible changes.

Leaders identify where to go. Managers assure that we get there (Bennis and Nannus, 1985; Drucker, 1973). Stewards look after everyone in the organization as they move to a shared destination (Block, 1993).[35] The new paradigm for education is a shared ideal vision that serves as a "North Star," shared missions for education that span from the distant future to close-in ones, and ways in which each individual may make a unique contribution — all toward shared worthy (mega-level) ends.

Under this shared-destination/teamwork approach, "accountability" now is redefined as agreeing on common destinations and measurable results; developing the most effective and efficient ways of getting the

[35]Stewardship, as defined by Block (1993), is very powerful. We encourage the extension of Block's suggestions to the mega-level of thinking and doing. Block seems to stop at the macro-level.

required results; finding what works and what doesn't, fixing it without blame, and getting continuously closer to the missions and ideal vision.

Quality Management Plus (Chapter 8) is the basic implementation "engine" which drives the move from current results and consequences to desired results and consequences. Using a Quality Management Plus approach as part of a strategic approach to education is sensible and practical. Doing so will initially, for some, require a shift in our paradigms and perceptions about organizations—the corporate culture.

Many management experts argue for dramatic changes of our organizational cultures (e.g., Deal and Kennedy, 1982; Drucker, 1973; Kanter, 1989; Kaufman, 1992, 1995; Peters, 1987; Roberts, 1987; Senge, 1990). The world of education has been laboring in a rapidly changing world, a world in fast-forward. Not only have the learners changed dramatically, the world in which they live and work has been dramatically transformed. Some educational decision makers still use the "nuclear family" paradigm. Education and educational partners must shift their views of the world, clients, environment, and purposes as well as how it defines, delivers, and evaluates its services, roles, and responsibilities. The education system must rethink how its organizational culture must change. The TQM+ framework, process, and concepts are keys to success (Kaufman, 1994c).

The elements of quality management as applied to education are provided in Chapter 2. Their use can make the difference between good intentions and useful results.

WHAT WILL LOOK DIFFERENT AS A RESULT OF MEGA-LEVEL STRATEGIC PLANNING?

Very little, on the surface will seem different. One likely result will be learners who are performing with enthusiasm work they enjoy and will see such as useful to them in school and life. It is likely that schools will become places of enjoyment and challenge for greater numbers of students and faculty. Satisfied clients—learners and educators—within the system will provide a different and positive environment.

Curriculum will be different (see discussion in Chapter 4 and Figures 4.6 and 4.7) when based on rolling down from the ideal vision to the missions for education. Courses could yield to structured experiences, and the schoolroom could more readily be seen as extending beyond the walls of a building. Teachers could be learning case managers as they work with learners to apply the basics and expand their competence and confidence. The learning environment could use distance learning principles to provide the basis for allowing students to learn at a time and place convenient to them.

Record-keeping will probably become a computer-based learning resource, and this will release teachers from being clerks. Learners will be taking control of their learning and mastery, and be tracking their own performance and accomplishments. We will transition from teacher-centered education to learner-centered education. Testing will slowly recede while performance products will be developed by learners that will provide the basis for deciding with the learners what the learners might do next and how they should be doing it.

MAKING OPERATIONAL DECISIONS WHICH WILL BE COMPATIBLE WITH THE STRATEGIC PLAN

Each school, program, activity, and operation was provided with the strategic plan. Each person and group decided how they would—applying their unique expertise, knowledge, and experience—move increasingly closer to the mission objective and the ideal vision.

Each time a decision was to be made, they referenced the elements of the strategic plan, and used the objectives for guidance.

Each individual and group may use Table 9.2 to help assure that the sum total of educational activities, resources, and methods would contribute, synergistically, to the total effort and payoffs. By using the format (Table 9.2) at the mega-, macro- and micro-levels, ends can then be linked to useful means.

SUMMARY

Creating Success

Strategic and tactical planning, as we suggest it in this book, can help you define and then create, operationally, a better world. Education is a key to that better world, and the application of the concepts and tools we have just provided will help you and your partners to create success.

Table 9.2. Relating Mega-, Macro-, and Micro-Objectives to Learner Objectives and Educational Activities.

Mega/Outcome Objectives (Societal and Community)
Macro-Output Objective (Organizational)
Micro/Product/School Objectives
Learner Objectives
Activities/Programs/Projects
Alternatives Considered

The journey has not been an easy one. If there were one or two simple steps for instant educational success we would have provided them. Education is not simple, nor are the individual learners we work with every day. Multiply the complexity of individual human difference together—be they learners, educators, parents, legislators and community members—and then congratulate all who dare to help learners be successful in today's and tomorrow's world. Human beings are complex and to be responsive so too will be the methods of education planning. Who among us would say we ourselves are simple and easy to understand? Why then, should anyone insist on simplistic methods for education . . . that would be self-delusion.

For the creating of educational success, it is important to set ourselves in the context of the larger world in which we all would live. To create educational success we must first define the world we wish to help create and then align everything we deliver, do, and use to that ideal place. We can take our lead from environmentalists who advise ''think globally and act locally.'' For creating success, we will do best to ''plan globally and then act locally.''

The line between fact-oriented and judgment-oriented approaches is not clear. You will notice that, regardless of the approach, model, or technique used, human judgment plays an important role. There is no clear line between facts and opinions in planning, management, and evaluation. There is no substitute for rational, sensible human contribution. Ideally, methods and techniques are as much a way of thinking as they are rules and procedures. Use any tool as a guide, never as your master. Mega-planning focuses on the big picture of creating, continuously, a better world for all.

A School District Develops a Strategic Plan: A Hypothetical and Partial Example

INTRODUCTION

LEARNERS and practitioners gain insight in different ways. For some, the chapters, which provided a strategic planning framework and tactical planning guidance, may be exactly what you require to move forward and begin implementation.

Others may best understand through a partially worked example. This Appendix will accommodate that orientation.

A SCHOOL DISTRICT DEVELOPS A STRATEGIC PLAN: A HYPOTHETICAL EXAMPLE

The *New Paradigm School District* is a 13,500 learner suburban school district with two high schools, four middle schools, and eight elementary schools. The district's population can be described as a mixture of well-paid blue collar employees, a large number of white collar employees, and about four percent of business owners and professionals. A wide variety of light industry and service organizations are located in the school district.

The school district has a ten percent student drop-out rate, and the total student body scores a little above the national average on nationally normed standardized tests. Eighty-five percent of the student body participates in some variety of co-curricular activity. The community is also brought into its schools, because the school district offers broad-based community and adult education programs.

Most of the community perceives the school district as doing a reasonable job; yet many feel that the school district could do a much better job of educating the youngsters and expending the district's funds.

This past year the district's operating budget was in excess of seventy-two million dollars ($72M).

Recently, those community members who felt that the school district could do a better job have been active in electing six of the seven members of the school board. The new members are mainly from the professional and managerial ranks, although one parent/union official was also elected. These recently elected school board members felt that the school district must improve its planning methods. Thus, a discussion about strategic planning began, and the decision was made to implement a strategic planning process in the New Paradigm School District.

GETTING STARTED

School districts become interested in strategic planning in one of four major ways:

(*1*) The critics of the current educational system demand systemic restructuring of what is being done.

(*2*) Parents and community members become concerned and sometimes even emotional about the level of the student product that is graduated.

(*3*) High visibility governmental, industrial, political, or business leaders use strategic planning in their operations and they pressure the school board and superintendent of schools to institute it.

(*4*) Knowledgeable and concerned board members and administrative leaders insist that strategic planning is important to the district, and they begin the process.

Once the key school district decision makers at the New Paradigm School District decide to think and plan strategically, they are faced with a series of initial questions that must be answered (as displayed in Table 2.2). In addition, the board drafted some operational/applications questions (as shown in Table A.1).

Policy Matters

The New Paradigm School District's Board of Education, after two readings and discussions at open board of education meetings, adopted the following directional policy:

Table A.1. Strategic Planning Questions for School Districts.

1. What policy or policies are required to implement strategic planning?
2. Who should be involved in the planning effort?
3. What forms of communication can be effectively utilized to inform the community and the employees?
4. What human, temporal, and financial resources have to be allocated to the planning process?
5. What primary focus (outside-in) or (inside-out) should be utilized?
6. What kind of society do we wish to help create?

The New Paradigm School District shall plan to create a better future in a manner that shall make the district, the students, the employees, and the educational contributions the best that they can become to be good neighbors and successful citizens. To accomplish this future, the Board directs that the administration initiate and maintain a continuous system of strategic planning that (1) will include representative stakeholders in the planning process, (2) will establish an ideal vision of what the school district should help create and contribute to, (3) will conduct a comprehensive needs assessment, and (4) will allocate, with approval of the budgetary allocations by the board, the required amount of human, temporal, and financial resources to accomplish the continuous strategic planning process.

Planning Stakeholders

Arriving at the numbers and types of planning stakeholders to include in the planning process will be determined by the following.

* Include a stratified random sample of all district residents and businesses to ensure that there will be broad ownership of the plans that are developed.
* Select stakeholders from internal groups, including teachers, support personnel, and learners to assure that any plans will be acceptable to those who will implement it.

Before selecting the planning stakeholders, a committee charge should be developed, published in writing, and widely distributed in order that all that are to be involved will clearly understand their commitment. Also, this charge and the Board's decision to conduct continuous strategic planning should be communicated through all media avenues. It is important that all community members, community organizations, and employees and employee groups know exactly what is going on throughout the entire planning process.

The charge that was approved by the school board for the New Paradigm School District's Strategic Planning Committee follows:

Since there is no endpoint for the current strategic planning effort, the New Paradigm School District's Strategic Planning Committee's membership and charge will be for one year, with yearly Board-appointed renewals as well as any modifications in the committee's charge to be determined as is necessary. The specific charges of the committee follow:

- The committee members will agree to undergo training on team planning and will receive a knowledge base about strategic planning from an expert prior to beginning the actual strategic planning process.
- The committee members shall develop an ideal vision to be used to then define the mission for the school district. The mission objectives will be in measurable results terms. They will conduct—or cause to be conducted—a comprehensive needs assessment.
- The committee shall be provided with technical assistance and resources as required to complete its charge. All requests should be made through the administrator assigned as liaison to the committee.
- The committee shall make decisions on the basis of consensus after full information is received and full discussion is conducted. All discussions will focus first on results before considering means and resources.
- The committee shall be comprised of about fifty members representative of the wide variety of community members and employees. A quorum of sixty percent of the community members shall be present in order to assure that the final decisions represent the community at large. In addition, a member of the board of education and the superintendent or the superintendent's appointee shall serve as ex officio members of the committee.
- The committee shall meet at least once monthly, the meetings shall be announced in advance and open to any interested persons. Minutes shall be kept of the committee's deliberations and decisions.
- The committee members shall elect a chair, an assistant chair, an administrative liaison, a faculty liaison, a board liaison, and an employee group liaison. The committee can break into sub-committees to accomplish a wide variety of planning tasks related to the ideal vision and mission. However, all decisions have to be officially made by the full committee. The committee may obtain expert help, when required, by directing those requests through the school district's officially appointed administrative liaison. All

financial matters, all taking and distribution of minutes, and all housekeeping matters shall be arranged for by the school district's official liaison—so that all the committee members may spend their time on important planning tasks, discussions, and decisions. Finally, the committee should fill vacancies by (1) asking the groups to nominate replacement member(s)—each group was asked to nominate two members who could substitute in case one member could not make a called meeting, and (2) recommending to the board select replacements required to fill existing vacancies.

* The committee shall make an oral and written quarterly progress report at open special board of education meetings, and the committee shall make an oral and written summary end of year report at a specially called board meeting. At this time, any required changes in the charter shall be discussed, and the extension of the committee members' appointments shall be extended when necessary. Following the quarterly progress reports and the yearly summary report, all important matters shall be released to the press; and the details of the reports shall be distributed throughout the community and to all employees through *The Future,* the district's monthly bulletin.

Once the charge is developed, the selection of the stakeholder group is determined. The school district's decision makers decided that fifty percent of the strategic planning committee members from the community and fifty percent of the strategic planning committee members from the employees would be nominated by their organizations (businesses, civic groups, PTAs, employee unions, and other established and identifiable formal organizations). The school district also decided that the other 50% of each group would be selected, at random, from volunteers, and that the district highly and frequently publicized the method of volunteering for the strategic planning committee. The random selection procedure was highly publicized because the decision makers did not want to be accused of bias in selecting the specific members.

Effective Communication Channels

Throughout the planning process, it is crucial to gain the support of a critical mass of representative persons in order to define support, and then defining and meeting the needs of the school district, in order to support the allocation of resources to the planning process, and develop ownership of the ideal vision. The New Paradigm School District's stakeholder group decided upon a variety of methods for delivering the ideal vision's message and the related needs. They also decided that frequently reporting the progress of the planning effort was crucial to success.

The decisions were to use the following methods of communication:

- to publish a monthly bulletin, entitled *The Future,* distribute it to all employees, and mail it to all residents of the school district
- to publicly announce that all meeting minutes of the New Paradigm School District's Strategic Planning Committee will be available in every school's office, in every school's library/media center, and in every public library in the district
- to invite the radio and TV stations to provide time for a district spokesperson to respond to a radio or TV station employee's questions, and/or to have community call-in shows on the topic of the district's strategic planning
- to ask the area newspapers to cover the progress of the district's planning efforts; and to have the school district's publicist work with the strategic planning committee, the board of education, and the administration to develop interesting news releases
- to publicly announce that members of the strategic planning committee, the board of education, and the administration will make themselves available to talk to Koffee Klatches about the purposes and progress of the school district's strategic planning operation
- finally, to encourage any student, employee, or citizen to phone the district's "hot line" to receive a progress update, or to ask any question, or express any concerns (It was publicly advertised that the repetitive questions and concerns will be addressed in the monthly bulletin that is distributed throughout the district.)

Required Resources: Human, Temporal, and Financial

It is quite obvious that the New Paradigm School District's strategic planning efforts will require resources: *time, people,* and *money.* To neglect the necessity of adequate resources is to create a resultant failure; to have hard-working, dedicated committee members disillusioned, to have community critics complain about the wasted money, and to ensure that the district will not be able to start a similar planning process any

Table A.2. A Summary of First Year's Cost Related Items Typically Encountered in the Strategic Planning Project.

Meeting-related food and beverages	$ ——
Employees' reimbursements	$ ——
District's liaison cost	$ ——
Cost of secretarial services	$ ——
Cost of district's publicists services	$ ——
Cost of employing experts	$ ——
Cost of supplies and equipment	$ ——
Planned contingency cost	$ ——

time in the near future. Table A.2 shows examples of items typically encountered.

It is crucial that the district's decision makers realize, when they initiate the strategic planning process, that an adequate amount of human, temporal, and financial resources be allocated to the process in order to ensure the ultimate success of the planning effort. If the dedication to the process is only in the wish stage, without the allocation of adequate resources, the district is better served by not starting the strategic planning process. It can go on its mediocre way, neglecting the identified needs of society and learners and the criticisms of community members and employees who are not at all satisfied with the status quo.

Deciding on the Primary Focus of the Planning Efforts

After undergoing the knowledge base training sessions given by an expert in strategic planning about the three related foci (mega, macro, and micro results) to be utilized in strategic planning; and after undergoing some simulation experiences related to determining the strategic planning focus; the New Paradigm School District's Strategic Planning Committee reached consensus on their primary focus – the mega (societal) level. Realizing that eventually the macro (total district) and micro (sub-district) levels have to be articulated within the mega-vision, the committee's membership was unanimous in agreement that the statement of an ideal vision must start with a societal orientation.

The ideal (mega) vision developed by the stakeholders included, among others, the following desired ends (Table A.3).

Some who do not understand the importance of it, may initially deride this ideal vision; but it is important that all understand the direction in

Table A.3.

People will take complete responsibility for their lives, and they will accept responsibility for what they do, use, contribute, and become self-sufficient and self-reliant as individuals and members of society. No person on welfare, relief, unemployment, AFCD. . . . All are employed at a wage level above subsistence. All have adequate health; all vital health signs at normal or better. No crime exists. Strong nuclear families become the norm, there will be no abuse. All children born will be wanted and cared-for children, with no instance of abuse, neglect, or poverty. No debilitating drug addiction exists.

which we have to continuously move to plot their progress and to identify what is working and what is not working. This ideal vision and its sub-components should be the guiding light toward which they set building-block strategic objectives that will get the district from its current results ever closer to the results specified in the ideal vision.

The achievement of the en route results on the way to the New Paradigm School District's ideal vision will take time. *Micro* results might start to appear in the initial year, *macro* results might appear at different times over the next several years, *mega* results may not appear for four to ten years, and the *ideal vision* may not be even partially achieved until twenty or more years into the future.

Taking the goal of "everyone obtaining and keeping a job that allows a lifestyle for the person and her/his family at above subsistence or without government support," the school district could commit to taking actions that would assist its graduates to achieve that by the year 2010. The building-block results would have at least ninety-five percent of the graduates mastering the requisite skills, knowledge, attitudes, and abilities by the year 2000; and the building-block competencies will start to be demonstrated by the students during the first year of operation under the strategic plan.

Table 3.2 (Educational Strategic Planning Agreement) provides a prototype that could be used to achieve and register agreements by all stakeholders and all planners involved in the strategic planning process about basic planning purposes. A locally developed modification of this table was developed and utilized by the New Paradigm School District's Strategic Planning Committee. It would be helpful if any school or school district would develop a similar structure to assist in more quickly arriving at the elements that the planners and stakeholders select to include in their ideal vision.

An alternative to deriving a new ideal vision is to select a preliminary ideal vision from elsewhere and ask the planners to modify it as required and justified by hard data. Because all ideal visions, if prepared correctly, are almost identical, ownership of a system's ideal vision may be quickly obtained.

MISSION STATEMENT AND MISSION OBJECTIVES

As discussed in Chapter 4, objectives should never state *how* results will be achieved, only (1) what performance will be exhibited, (2) by whom or what will it be demonstrated, (3) where it will be demonstrated, and (4) what criteria will be used with which it will be measured.

The New Paradigm School District's Strategic Planning Committee developed a mission statement and then related mission objectives. A sample of their work is provided below. The mission statement and the mission objective must be derived from the elements included in the ideal vision that has been reached by consensus of the stakeholders.

Mission Statement: the New Paradigm School District's graduates and completers will be self-sufficient, self-reliant, productive citizens of society.

An Example Mission Objective: By January 1, 2010, all graduates of the New Paradigm School District since 2000 will have become self-sufficient and self-reliant, productive citizens of society as certified reliable and valid data are required, such as published reports of the government or credible experts and/or officials (such as coroners offices, secretary of state, etc.), by follow-up data such as job placement and job tenure at least at or above subsistence level verified by employing agencies, and/or graduation and job placement and keeping of jobs, and/or placement at graduation at advanced educational institutions that are verified by those institutions.

Once the end result(s) has (have) been identified — in this case the description of self-sufficient and self-reliant, productive citizens — it is important to list the role that various subsets of the school district have to play in the process that leads to the ultimate delivery of the desired result(s). That is, once the high school's tasks and responsibilities toward achieving the stated result(s) are determined, the middle school's or junior high school's tasks and responsibilities must be defined and its results must be measured. Next, the elementary schools' tasks and responsibilities must be defined and its results measured. Of course, if possible, the state of results achieved by parents or guardians prior to school entry should be assessed; and follow-up results data should be collected from post-high school educational institutions and employers to complete the *"results chain."* All segments of the results chain were included as assessment criterion measurements by the strategic planners and managers of the New Paradigm School District.

NEEDS ASSESSMENT

As illustrated in Chapter 5, Table 5.1 provides a format that can be utilized in conducting a *needs assessment audit.*

A vital task of the strategic planners is to identify the needs. Then, and only then, should the planners select the means, solutions, or processes that are designed to close the gap in the results.

To begin the process, the New Paradigm School District's Strategic Planning Committee conducted a comprehensive needs assessment by collecting two major types of data from a variety of sources, using the format found in Table 5.1. These data then formed the basis for the committee members to identify all existing needs, and for the members to reach consensus on the priorities established for each of the needs. The two sources of data consisted of:

- *Hard Data* includes student drop-out rates, post-high school employment and advanced education records, test score results, and other independently verifiable data. An example of the data collected indicated that the student body as a whole had a twenty percent drop-out rate. Later, the committee would have to determine if this was acceptable during our ever increasing technology and knowledge-based age; and they would have to determine the priority level given to this mission objective element to close the gap between what existed and what were desired results.
- *Soft Data* includes information collected by attitude surveys, questionnaires, and personal — not independently verifiable data. Soft data collected by the strategic planning committee consisted

of an assessment of the school climate, as determined by the results of a randomized and proportional attitudinal survey completed by students, parents, and employees. The results indicated that both the learners' families and the employees perceived the school climate to be grossly inadequate. Later, the strategic planning committee would have to determine specific objectives, the priority of each objective, the action plan to be put into place, and the resources to be allocated to the action plan designed to close the gap between what exists and the desired future school climate. In addition, the planners had to link, using the results chain, that this school climate improvement would also have a positive effect on decreasing the number of drop-outs and the societal contributions of this learner group. This should be confirmed later by collecting hard data.

To clarify, *needs assessments* are utilized by planners to identify and document gaps in results, to identify what should not be changed as well as recognizing what should be changed. Needs assessments will also uncover opportunities. The identification and prioritizing of needs provides the firm basis for later initiation of actions that will cause the desired changes to occur—that is, close the results gap between ''what is'' and ''what should be.''

Once these data were collected, the New Paradigm School District's Strategic Planning Committee members approached the task of conducting a *needs analysis.* The procedures used in conducting the needs analysis were designed to discover the causes and reasons behind the identified currently existing and prioritized needs previously identified. They clarified the types of results, the level of planning, and the needs assessment foci required.

An example of the process and some examples of the data sources utilized by the New Paradigm School District's Strategic Planning Committee are listed in Table A.4.

A useful way of thinking about the tie between the function analysis and the mission analysis is to visualize a matrix in which the *width* of the matrix is formed by the *mission analysis,* and the *depth* is provided by the *function analysis.* The function analysis takes its start from the mission analysis.

The New Paradigm School District's planners had to provide the human, temporal, and financial resources to initiate action plans

Table A.4. Examples of Data Sources.

1. Two examples of outcome results at the mega-level focus included the following:
   - Graduates who were self-sufficient, self-reliant, and productive members of society as indicated by such as continued employment, voter registration, earnings above subsistence, etc.
   - A school district and community environment that is crime free (e.g., 0 crime rate, decreased recidivism rate for incarcerated)
2. Two examples of outputs results at the macro-level focus included the following:
   - Graduated with a diploma
   - Successfully obtained acceptance to enter an accredited institution of higher education
3. Two examples of the products results at the micro-level focus included the following:
   - Courses successfully passed
   - Specific competencies attained

designed to complete each of the tasks listed in the function analysis. Without these required resources, the actions following the mission analysis and the function analysis would merely produce interesting busy work.

A TASK ANALYSIS

There were a series of steps that were followed by the New Paradigm School District's planners as they completed the processing of a task analysis. These steps are listed below:

- List *all* the detailed tasks necessary to complete the function being analyzed.
- Place the tasks in the sequential order in which they are to occur.
- List the input requirements—data that will be required by the person(s) responsible for completing the task(s).
- List the action requirements that spell out the number of times each task will occur and the time necessary to complete each task.
- List the support requirements—the material, equipment, and personnel required to complete the task.
- List the performance criteria—or required result upon task completion.
- Specify the prerequisite knowledge and/or skills the person(s) who is to perform the task must possess.

At this phase the focus becomes more detailed on the process of tactical planning.

A SCHOOL DISTRICT DEVELOPS TACTICAL AND OPERATIONAL PLANS

Now begins the important matter of locating and assessing the variables that may influence the level of success that the New Paradigm School district's planners and managers can achieve related to the ideal vision. The technique used for this purpose by the district's planners is called a SWOTs (Strengths, Weaknesses, Opportunities, and Threats) Analysis, and it is completed for both the external and the internal environments.

New Paradigm School District Completes a SWOTs Analysis

Once the New Paradigm School District's Strategic Planning Committee completed the scoping phase of strategic planning, the members decided that now was the time to lay the groundwork for action. The members decided to create two ten-member sub-committees to conduct the SWOTs Analyses; one charged with collecting the required data and trends for the *external* environment, and the other committee with collecting the required data and trendlines for the *internal* environment. These data will be shared with the full committee for action. Also, it was made clear to the committees that the SWOTs analysis begins not with the ideal vision but with the basic mission objective and the closer-in mission. (See Figure 4.4.)

As described in Chapter 6, the keys to successfully utilizing the results of the SWOTs Analyses lie in the following:

- *Strengths* are those identified variables that the school district should capitalize upon to help ensure the success of the district's plans. These strengths could be of both the external or internal variety. These identified supports (strengths) are available to assist in implementing strategies and possible future tactics which ultimately will achieve the ideal vision and mission of ''what should be'' for the New Paradigm School District.
- *Weaknesses* are those identified variables that action plans have

to overcome. If the weaknesses are not overcome, the probability of successfully achieving the district's plans are hampered. Again, the weaknesses may be of both the external or internal variety. The identified weaknesses should, as much as possible, be corrected in order to achieve the ideal vision.

- *Opportunities* are those identified variables that exist in the internal and external environments that have not yet been capitalized upon; but that would be very helpful, if properly utilized, in achieving the desired mission objectives and the ideal vision. If these opportunities have not been utilized in the past, they should immediately be used to moving continuously closer to meet the missions *and* assist in achieving the ideal vision.
- *Threats* are those identified variables that exist in the internal and external environments which must be eliminated or lessened. If they are not, there is not much probability of successfully achieving the mission objectives and the district's ideal vision. If possible threats should be completely eliminated; but, at the very least, tactics should be developed to diminish their negative impact.

We provide examples of the specific sources of external and internal sources of SWOTs data (Tables A.6 and A.7), and provide examples of the types of variable data collected. Now, let's summarize the cost items to be considered for doing the internal and external SWOTs Analyses (Table A.5). The cost items expended by the New Paradigm School District for these purposes are provided below; but no cost items related to the actions of the main New Paradigm School District's Strategic Planning Committee are included because they handled the work load related to the SWOTs as part of their normal meeting agenda.

MAKING OPERATIONAL DECISIONS WHICH WOULD BE COMPATIBLE TO THE STRATEGIC PLAN

Each school, program, activity, and operation was provided with the strategic plan. Each person and group decided how they would, by applying their unique expertise, knowledge, and experience, move increasingly closer to the mission objective and the ideal vision.

Each time a decision was to be made, they referenced the elements of the strategic plan to be achieved, and used the objectives for guidance.

Each individual and group used the following format (Table A.8) to

Table A.5. Summary of Expense Items Considered as Related to a SWOTs Analysis for the New Paradigm School District.

External SWOT Expense Items:	
Travel for data collection and discussion with external sources	$ ——
Sub-committee meetings	$ ——
Purchase of copies of data reports	$ ——
Administrative time	$ ——
Clerical time	$ ——
Materials and supplies	$ ——
Outside consultants' fees	$ ——
Internal SWOT Expense Items:	
Outside consultants' fees	$ ——
Sub-committee data gathering and transportation fees	$ ——
Sub-committee meetings	$ ——
Administrative time	$ ——
Clerical time	$ ——
Materials and supplies	$ ——

Table A.6. The External Environment's SWOT Analyses Subcommittee's Data Sources and Example Findings.

Many sources of information were contacted by the External SWOT Subcommittee. Some of the prime sources of information were:
- Chambers of Commerce
- State, city, and university libraries
- City, regional, state and federal agencies
- Financial institutions
- Major corporations
- Marketing and demography specialty firms
- United Way and other charitable groups
- Civic organizations
- Marketing and demographic specialty firms
- Political institutions
- State Department of Education
- U.S. Census Bureau
- Realty associations
- State Bar Association

The most important types of data collected and arrayed to indicated trends were of the following categories:
- Demographic trends
- Mental and physical health statistics
- Financial trends
- Volunteerism prevalence
- Business and housing trends
- Voting frequency
- In and out migration of people and business trends
- Crime statistics
- Attitudinal trends toward the school district and its expenditures, administration, teaching, products, outputs, and outcomes
- Strategic plans that have been developed by financial, realtor, business, civic, and governmental institutions

Table A.7. The Internal Environment's SWOT Analyses Subcommittee's
Data Sources and Example Findings.

The Internal SWOT Committee collected data from students, teachers, principals,
classified personnel, central administrators, and board of education members. The
types of data they collected and arrayed along historical trends included the
following:

- Student norm referenced and criterion referenced test scores that were item
  analyzed and disaggregated
- Student drop-out rates and absenteeism data
- School climate assessments
- Employee attitudinal surveys
- Percentage of students going on to higher education
- Percentage of students becoming gainfully employed at an adequate salary level
  upon completion of high school
- Turnover rates for all categories of personnel
- Percent of students engaging in co-curricular activities

Once the New Paradigm School District's Strategic Planning Committee has received
the reports of the two SWOT sub-committees, its members are ready to turn to the
development of a management plan or a mission profile.

Table A.8. Relating Mega-, Macro-, and Micro-Objectives to Learner Objectives and
Educational Activities.

Mega/Outcome Objectives (Societal and Community)

Macro/Output Objective (Organizational)

Micro/Product/School Objectives

Learner Objectives

Activities/Programs/Projects

Alternatives Considered

238

help assure that the sum total of educational activities, resources, and methods would contribute, synergistically, to the total effort and payoffs. In order to assure that everyone knew how to make the strategic plan translate into operational success, the Quality Management Plus (QM +) process was installed. Each person and group formally identified their progress toward the objectives and made revisions as required. Each time there was a breakdown—an objective not accomplished—they used that data for fixing and not for blaming. They made the fourteen points of TQM + a part of their organizational life in order to move ever closer to success.

TACTICAL PLANNING: DISCOVERING WHAT IS AVAILABLE TO GET FROM WHERE YOU ARE TO WHERE YOU WANT TO BE

A system analysis is a dynamic process. It allows planners to:

- determine if there are any ways and means to get the mission and functions accomplished
- conduct a feasibility study to determine whether or not there is any possible way of getting to the desired results
- identify the advantages and disadvantages of each alternative methods and means identified to get to the desired results

The planners should compile a list of possible solutions and identify the advantages and disadvantages of each, and to select from this list those solutions that are most feasible for allowing the desired results to be achieved. This tally of possible solutions, with the accompanying list of advantages and disadvantages, becomes the databank for further design and development. The process by which this databank is produced is called a methods-means analysis.

Methods-Means Analysis

Before we select how to meet our mission objective(s) and accomplish all related functions, the planning partners have to compile a databank listing the possible techniques and tools (methods and means) for achieving the mission objective(s). Methods-means analysis not only identifies the tools and techniques available; but it provides a feasibility study by

Table A.9. The School District Operates Its Own Child Care Program.

Advantages:
1. Quality assurance and control would be directly under the supervision of the school district.
2. Most parents would welcome the school district's entry into this program.
Disadvantages:
1. Some taxpayers would object to the district taking on more programs when they are not particularly pleased with current "mainline" program results.
2. Commercial child care agencies housed within the school district boundaries and the local Chamber of Commerce would object to the school district competing with commercial firms.

considering the advantages and disadvantages associated with each of the methods and means.

Table A.9 is an example of a possible methods-means the New Paradigm School District considered.

In summary, let's examine the prerequisites for conducting a methods-means analysis. The planners and managers should have available to them the following:

(*1*) Mission objective(s) and the related performance objectives, based upon the ideal vision

(*2*) Mission profile

(*3*) Mission analysis

(*4*) Functions and their performance requirements

(*5*) Tasks and their performance requirements

Once these items are on hand, the planners and managers can:

- identify ways and means of accomplishing each function and task
- identify the advantages and disadvantages for each possible methods and means suggested
- identify constraints—where no methods-means possibility exists—to performance and eliminate them when possible

Once the lowest level of function and/or task analyses have been completed and the final methods-means analysis has been carried out, two products result:

(*1*) A database of feasible *whats* for problem resolution exists.

(2) A database of possible *hows* and the advantages and disadvantages of each exists.

Putting the Strategic Plan to Work

Continuing our hypothetical and partial example, New Paradigm School District finished the plan and published it (using a format like the one suggested in Chapter 2). They later realized that when decisions were made, few people were using the plan to guide them. They had to find out what went wrong and how to fix it.

The district planners convened a small sub-group of the larger committee and became strategic themselves. They reviewed the six critical success factors (Table 1.1) that characterize what any useful plan has to look like and provide. They next reviewed the characteristics of a strategic plan and the basic questions any organization must ask and answer. Then they went to work in the "strategic plan—revise as required" process. First, they wanted to know what might have gone wrong. They sought to find out what worked (and was useful) and what didn't and should be revised, added, or eliminated.

What Might Be Wrong with the Plan

So many strategic plans sit on the shelf or languish on desks. A strategic plan is worthless if it is not used and does not result in continuous striving toward the ideal vision. If a strategic plan is not used, there might be a number of common flaws associated with it. The subcommittee noted the possible problems which could get in the way of the transition from strategic to tactical to operational planning and thus to implementation. It might be:

(*1*) Too long

(*2*) Too complex

(*3*) Not representative of the stakeholders

(*4*) Too concerned with means and resources without linkages

If the plan is not used, then learn from the weaknesses and improve on the plan and the planning process. The hallmark of a successful strategic plan is the extent to which, when decisions are to be made, the strategic plan is pulled out and used.

The "revision" sub-group found that their report had gotten to be over sixty pages and had included many means and resources and not enough linking to the mission objective and the ideal vision. They fixed the problems and submitted the revisions to the whole committee and then obtained approval from the Board.

Celebrating Success

Real celebration happens when the odds are overcome. It is not much of a happening when the usual occurs. When there is genuine continuous improvement toward the objectives, time should be taken to recognize the individual and collective contributions to learners, staff, parents, and community. Success is habit-forming.

Final Words

All educational partners—learners, parents, employers, citizens, board of education members, superintendent of schools, school district administrators—are often critical when a school district decides to become involved in strategic planning and continuous improvement. This is not a *quick fix* process; it will take time, human and financial resources, and commitment to do it in a quality manner.

These important members must become decision makers who:

- are strategic thinkers, facilitators, and leaders in the planning, implementing, monitoring, and continuous improvement phases of the strategic, tactical, and operational planning processes
- are strong believers in the requirement and payoffs from strategically planning the best way to achieve the ideal vision and the related mission objectives for the school or district
- develop and execute an effective and efficient MIS (Management Information System) that allows formative and summative data collection which, in turn, provides measures of the degree of successful or unsuccessful impact of each strategic, tactic, and action plan
- have control of the allocation of resources and provide those necessary to complete all tasks and functions related to the strategic, tactical, and operation plans. They must ensure that the proper types and amounts of temporal, human, financial, and

material resources are devoted to the various elements of the plans in a manner that optimizes the positive impacts that result from the plans
* serve as the communications conduits to the employees, stakeholders, and the community as a whole

SUMMARY

The New Paradigm School District was used to provide an example of how a stakeholders' committee was organized, how advanced training was provided to committee members, and how the projected costs were computed. Also, brief examples of the ideal vision and a mission objective were provided. It is important to remember that this is a continuous improvement process; and that items may have to be revised, as required, any place, any where, or any time.

Finally, a comprehensive needs assessment process was developed. A need is defined as a gap, or discrepancy, between what results currently exist and the desired results. Needs assessment is a process in which the strategic planners identify the array of existing needs, and prioritize them in a manner that will allow the school district to develop action programs and provide the required human, temporal, and financial resources to overcome the identified gaps and deficiencies that currently exist—attacking the highest priority needs initially, and then moving to those of lower priority.

Finally, as related to the school building levels, these members must also carry out certain responsibilities: assist the building-level functionaries (teachers, principals, and classified employees) in the development of the structures and processes that will ensure high quality successful results related to students' products, outputs, and outcomes; and ensure this appropriately takes place within the various organizational and community cultural environments.

* A SWOTs analysis is conducted to identify strengths, weaknesses, opportunities and threats for the school district's internal and external environments. The data from this analysis is used by the planners to determine future strategies and tactics.
* Once the SWOTs analysis is completed, en route strategic objectives can be identified or substantiated. They are the

stepping stones that the organization utilizes while moving toward the ideal vision.

- The tools strategic planners use for determining the requirements for getting from where the district is to where it should be in the future are termed *mission analysis* and *function analysis*. If likened to lenses on a microscope, the mission analysis provides a broader overview, whereas the function analysis magnifies a smaller piece of the overall problem.

- All of the above pieces are nested interrelated parts of what is called a *system analysis*. A system analysis depends upon priority *needs* (gaps in results between what is and what should be) having being identified, selected, and prioritized. It is results-oriented, identifying the functions necessary to meet the needs.

- Once the priority functions have been identified within the organizational mission and within the specific mission objectives, each function is logically sequenced and becomes a map or *management plan*. This management plan permits the coordinated activities to efficiently and effectively take place.

- Planning should permit you, or the group of planners to identify (1) where you want to arrive (result); (2) why you and your school district want to get to that result (an ideal vision); (3) the functions necessary to get from the present state to the desired future state (results); and (4) the best methods and means to get you where you want to go.

- Putting the strategic plan to work involves (1) developing structures within the school district that will achieve the strategies that have been decided, (2) monitoring the activities and evaluating both the activities that have been undertaken and the strategies that have been decided, (3) developing an integrated MIS (Management Information System) to assist those who are responsible for the management of the strategic plan, (4) making in-process adjustments—continuous improvement—in strategies, tactics, and activities when the monitored data indicate a requirement for change to take place, (5) ensuring the effectiveness and the efficiency of the activities, and (6) ensuring the success of the strategies employed.

Dealing with Beliefs and Values

MANY times people will include an exploration of the beliefs and values of their planning partners. We don't recommend a procedure that explores distinct beliefs and values within strategic planning, although the collection and inclusion of beliefs and values are almost *de rigeur* for many strategic planners. We recommend that it *not* be an initiating part of strategic planning nor do we recommend that it be a formal part of the strategic planning process. The reason we exclude it as a formal activity within the strategic planning process is that it is already a natural part of the development of an ideal vision. Bringing it up as a separate activity simply re-opens the agenda for slipping back into unexamined personal biases and predispositions about educational means and resources.

As the ideal vision is being developed, planning partners' beliefs and values come into play. Beliefs and values usually are imposed first by planning partners as methods, means, resources, and programs which partners want to be included in the ideal vision. As it is realized that beliefs and values usually relate to means and not ends, then they may be reserved—usually on a "place-holder list" for consideration when alternative methods-means are being considered.

For those planners who insist on the formal inclusion of the determination of beliefs and values, the following procedures are provided.

IDENTIFYING BELIEFS AND VALUES

Beliefs and values are usually unexamined and strongly held perceptions. They represent the planning partners' current realities, for people's perceptions are their realities. Beliefs and values usually focus on means, resources, and "how-to's." They often have such names as "my educational philosophy" or "my view of education."

Beliefs and values may not be supported by data and research, but they may be important to each educational partner. Dredging them up usually results in emotional responses. Keep away from your own value judgments and allow the responses to surface.

Ask the partners to use the ideal vision in deriving their beliefs and values. They should compare the expressed beliefs and values to the ideal vision to see if they are compatible. Often the beliefs and values are really biases and stereotypes and will be replaced after further reflection. By comparing beliefs and values to the ideal vision, self-examination and critical thinking should emerge. Allow for and encourage enlightened shifts, modifications, and growth. Paradigms *do* shift, frames of reference *do* modify.

An open and objective discussion concerning beliefs and values is useful. With each partner listening (not just waiting to talk) to the positions of the others, common understandings and directions may be formed. In guiding the mutual exploration of beliefs and values, an ends/means analysis will be helpful:

(*1*) Collect individual statements of beliefs and values.

(*2*) Sort common and unique beliefs and values.

(*3*) Present the common and unique beliefs and values to the group and ask them to sort each into ends and means.

(*4*) Ask the group to identify those that will contribute to the ideal vision and those that will not.

(*5*) Construct a list of agreed-upon beliefs and values.

USES OF BELIEF STATEMENTS WITHIN THE PROCESS OF STRATEGIC PLANNING (IF IT IS ARBITRARILY REQUIRED)

Beliefs and values, to be effective and contribute to strategic planning, require (a) a basis in the ideal vision and (b) a consensus among the stakeholders. How does one go about achieving consensus? There are a variety of consensus building techniques available to strategic planners; a few of these helpful tools follow. All work best when discussions relate only to ends and never to means or resources.

Comparing Beliefs and Values with an Ideal Vision

By first deriving our ideal vision, people with strongly held beliefs and values (old paradigms) have the opportunity to compare their values with the ideal, and change their beliefs and values appropriately and rationally. Table 3.1 provides a format for obtaining planning partner perceptions of an "ideal vision" or preferred future and the commitment to link organizational results and efforts to that ideal. Use that data to consider any emerging beliefs and values.

CONSENSUS-REACHING TECHNIQUES

Three helpful consensus-reaching techniques are (1) the Delphi Technique, (2) the Fishbowl Technique, and (3) the Telstar Technique. In each case, formats are devised to cause consensus among disparate viewpoints. In each case, the length of time it takes to attain consensus will vary from group to group. Consensus reaching is a process that cannot be rushed; whatever time is required to reach consensus, is time well spent. Unity of purpose and action is the result if the planners are patient.

The Delphi Technique

The Delphi Technique is used for reaching consensus without face-to-face meetings. Select participants that are truly representative of the greater population. This should include learners, parents, community members, teachers, administrators, businesses, civic groups, government agencies, and the like. Each participant is asked to write out a list of beliefs and values that should be included in a consensus listing to guide the school, school district, or university.

The participants should have a copy of the ideal vision as a guide. Have each participant identify the part of the ideal vision to which his or her beliefs or values relate. An individual is assigned by the planning team to collect and collate all the initial beliefs and values statements. These initial statements would then be forwarded to all participants with the request that they indicate (1) which beliefs and values statements are compatible with the ideal vision, (2) which ones they agree and disagree with, and (3) what changes could be made to those statements to encourage agreement.

This process continues as many times as is necessary to arrive at a consensus of beliefs and values. In other words, unanimous beliefs and values, or at the very least, those beliefs and values which they will allow, can be used to guide further planning steps. This process continues until agreement at some rational level (eighty to ninety percent) is reached.

The Fishbowl Technique

The Fishbowl Technique has the planners divide a large group of representative stakeholders into sub-groups of six to eight persons who meet to reach consensus on a statement of beliefs and values. They should each have a copy of the ideal vision to guide them. When each of the sub-groups have finished their statements, and related them to the ideal vision, each sub-group elects a representative to present their beliefs and values to the total membership of the large group. This is generally accomplished by having the representatives seated in a circle facing one another. All other members are seated outside the discussion circle.

However, to permit non-representatives to address any topic as the dialogue among the representatives proceeds, an empty chair is placed in the circle. If there were eight sub-groups involved in the process, a set of nine chairs would be placed in a circle. Eight of the chairs would be occupied by the representatives for each of the eight sub-groups; the ninth chair would be vacant so that a member of one of the sub-groups could enter the discussion circle, make his/her point, and leave.

Assuming that all sub-groups have presented their belief and values statements, this procedure then compares each statement to the ideal vision until consensus is achieved.

As the representatives negotiate beliefs and values with one another—based on the ideal vision—a member of the larger group may enter the circle and make any comment or statement he or she wishes to make. The comment may be a clarifying statement, a suggestion, or anything that they want to present. Immediately upon making the statement, however, the person occupying the previously empty chair must leave the discussion circle and cease to participate in the discussion.

This process, as was true with the Delphi Technique, has to be continued until final general consensus is achieved. Consensus can sometimes be quickly reached, while sometimes it takes longer.

The Telstar Technique

The Telstar Technique is similar to the Fishbowl Technique, but it differs significantly in the method of involving all participants and the degree of involvement that non-representative participants are afforded. The initial process is to divide the large group into sub-groups. If the process is designed for a school district, the planners may go through the process with each school. They have each school nominate two members to serve as their spokespersons to the district-wide group which has the ultimate responsibility of reaching a consensus on a list of beliefs and values, using the ideal vision to guide them. This list will guide the district stakeholders' planning group when they continue the work of strategic planning. In this case, let's assume that the number of persons involved at the school building levels varied from forty to six hundred persons, and there were eight school buildings in the district. The school levels represented included elementary, middle school, and senior high. The larger schools could be allocated a larger number of spokespersons.

Also, in this situation, we assume that all buildings have completed their listing of beliefs and values related to the ideal vision, and each building's group of participants has selected a spokesperson and an advisory committee of six persons. This configuration would provide a consensus-reaching discussion group of eight representatives, an advisory group to each spokesperson, and as many as wished to sit in the audience to view the consensus-reaching dialogue.

The eight spokespersons would negotiate with one another to achieve a final listing of guiding beliefs and values which are compatible with the ideal vision. During the process of negotiations, any member of any of the eight advisory committees could temporarily halt the discussion by calling "time out." This pronouncement would signal an opportunity for all spokespersons to have a caucus with their advisory persons. During the caucus the person calling the "time out," or any other members of the advisory group, could present a strategy, proposal, suggestion, or directive to the spokesperson. At the end of the time required for the caucus, as determined by the person calling the "time out," that same individual will call "time in." After "time in" is signaled all advisory groups cease discussion, and the negotiations within the spokespersons' group continues until final consensus is reached and beliefs and values have become compatible with the ideal vision. At times, the identification of beliefs and values may indicate missing elements of the vision which then require the vision to be modified.

GUIDELINES FOR STRATEGIC PLANNERS WHO ARE RESPONSIBLE FOR ARRIVING AT A STATEMENT OF BELIEFS AND VALUES

Here are guidelines that may be used for those persons responsible for the development of strategic plans for their university, school district, or school building:

- Strategic planning is a process that is worth doing correctly, with rigor and precision.
- Involve a truly representative stakeholders' group in the planning process.
- Planning may take place at the macro- and/or micro-level, but if it does, it must first demonstrate linkages and contributions to the mega-level and the ideal vision. It is very risky to start planning below the mega-level.
- Beliefs and values which focus on ends (rather than means) will be most useful in later planning steps.
- Techniques for consensus-reaching may be employed when dealing with large numbers of people.
- Require that all beliefs and values be compatible with and contribute to the ideal vision. Allow no exceptions.
- Existing beliefs and values should be examined for current fit with both the ideal vision and other stakeholder's perceptions. If they are not relevant, replace them with appropriate ones.
- Beliefs and values must be related to the ideal vision, needs, and the institutional mission. (Further discussion on missions is provided in the next chapter.) They should serve as guidelines when arriving at mission goals and objectives.

APPENDIX SUMMARY

Education occurs within an environment that is influenced by beliefs, values, and expectations. At the same time, education finds its expression through a series of interrelated results defined within the OEM to be products, outputs, and outcomes (micro, macro, and mega, respectively).

The relationship between beliefs and values to the ideal vision must not be ignored. One way to enlighten and inform the planning group is to identify, list, and discuss individual statements of beliefs and values as they relate to ends and means. As part of strategic planning, beliefs and values must contribute to the ideal vision. Therefore they best relate to ends. Beliefs and values that relate to means can be used as placeholders for later consideration when tactics become important.

Beliefs and values that are selected as relating to the ideal vision must be agreed upon by all planning participants. Such participants should be a truly representative sample of the population concerned with, of, and for educational results. Three techniques for facilitating consensus among participants are: The Delphi Technique, the Fishbowl Technique, and the Telstar Technique.

A Minimal Ideal Vision

EXAMPLES of ideal visions cited in the text, including performance indicators (or "standards") were developed on the basis of consensus. Worked out by planning partners, the ideal vision represents products that demonstrate how well people from very diverse backgrounds around the world agree on what kind of society they want for tomorrow's child.

What follows is another *minimal* ideal vision that reduces some of the "comfortable" methods and means and some of the enablers that consensus might derive. The following is a minimal ideal vision in that it refers to mega-level results only.

A GENERAL MINIMAL IDEAL VISION

There will be no losses of life nor elimination or reduction of levels of well-being, survival, self-sufficiency, quality of life, livelihood,[36] nor loss of property from any source including (but not limited to):

- war and/or riot
- unintended human-caused changes to the environment including permanent destruction of the environment and/or rendering it non-renewable
- murder, rape, or crimes of violence, robbery, or destruction to property
- substance abuse

[36]Livelihood is defined as the level that an individual's consumption is equal to or less than their production. Both consumptions and production are defined in terms of the expenditure or intake of units of monetary exchange.

252

- infectious disease
- pollution
- starvation and/or malnutrition
- child abuse
- partner/spouse abuse
- accidents, including transportation, home, and business/workplace
- discrimination based on irrelevant variables including color, race, creed, sex, religion, national origin, location

Poverty will not exist, and every woman and man will earn at least as much as it costs them to live unless they are progressing toward being self-sufficient and self-reliant. No adult will be under the care, custody or control of another person, agency, or substance: all adult citizens will be self-sufficient and self-reliant as minimally indicated by their consumption being equal to or less than their production.

Key Enablers[37]

Any and all organizations—governmental, private sector/for-profit, public service/not-for-profit, educational—will contribute to the achievement and maintenance of this minimal ideal vision and will be funded and continued to the extent to which it meets its objectives and the minimum ideal vision is accomplished and maintained.

People will be responsible for what they use, do, and contribute and thus will not contribute to the reduction of any of the results identified in this minimal ideal vision.

Minimal Ideal Vision Element	Possible Examples of Performance Indicators
There will be no losses of human life or elimination of survival of any species required for human survival, and there will be no reductions in levels of self-sufficiency, quality of life,	

[37]These will provide building-block results likely required to achieve the minimal ideal vision but are *not* mega-level results.

Minimal Ideal Vision Element	Possible Examples of Performance Indicators
livelihood, nor loss of property from any source including but not limited to:	
• war and/or riot	As certified by[38] the Secretary General of the United Nations and verified as correct by the national Secretary of State within the last calendar year.
• unintended human-created change to the environment including the permanent destruction of the environment and/or rendering it non-renewable	There will be no non-reversible human-created changes as certified by the United Nations Secretary for the environment, and no successful legal actions and findings as reported by the National Department of the Interior and/or documented and independently validated findings of irreversible environmental damage. No species will become extinct from unintended human action as certified by the National Department of Health and/or the United Nations Secretary for the environment.
• murder, rape, or crimes of violence, robbery, or destruction to person or property	There will be no murders, rapes, or crimes of violence, robberies, nor destruction to property as indicated by certified and audited reports of the chief law enforcement officer of the nation and/or those of each state and/or

[38] "As certified by" is to note that an official source is required to document and be accountable for the objectivity, and reliability results-referenced data. For example if an indicator is "as certified by the Secretary General of the United Nations" it could also be "or her or his official designees."

Minimal Ideal Vision Element	Possible Examples of Performance Indicators
	local region. These certified reports will be within the year.
• substance abuse	There will be no loss of life, reduction in livelihood, nor quality of life from abusive use of controlled and uncontrolled substances as indicated by certified and audited reports of the chief national health officer, and/or state and/or local health and human services officer(s).
• infectious disease	There will be no loss of life, reduction in livelihood, nor quality of life from infectious diseases and associated disorder as indicated by certified and audited reports of the chief national health officer, and/or state and/or local health and human services officer(s).
• pollution	There will be no loss of life, reduction in livelihood, nor quality of life from human produced pollutants and related toxic substances as indicated by certified and audited reports of the chief national health officer, and/or state and/or local health and human service(s) and/or the national chief health officer and/or the Secretary of the United Nations.
• starvation and/or malnutrition	There will be no loss of life, reduction in livelihood, nor quality of life from diagnosed starvation and/or malnutrition

Minimal Ideal Vision Element	Possible Examples of Performance Indicators
	as indicated by certified and audited reports of the national chief health officer, and/or state and/or local health and human services officer(s).
• child abuse	There will be no loss of life, reduction in physical and/or ability to function at or above the normative level for that individual, nor reduction of quality of life from documented child abuse by other children and/or adults as indicated by certified and audited reports of the chief national health officer, and/or state and/or local health and human services officer(s) and/or law enforcement officer(s).
• partner/spouse abuse	There will be no loss of life, reduction in physical and/or ability to function at or above the normative level for that individual, nor reduction of quality of life from documented partner/spouse abuse by other children and/or adults as indicated by certified and audited reports of the chief national health officer, and/or state and/or local health and human services officer(s) and/or law enforcement officer(s).
• accidents, including transportation, home, and business/workplace	There will be no accidents, including in the home/dwelling, public and private transportation, at and in the workplace that result in death, disability, loss or

Minimal Ideal Vision Element	Possible Examples of Performance Indicators
	reduction of livelihood, reduction of quality of life as indicated by certified and audited reports of the national and/or international chief officer(s) for transportation and/or health and human services and/or law enforcement.
• discrimination based on irrelevant variables including color, race, creed, sex, religion, national origin, location	There will be no significant statistical difference (.05 level of confidence or beyond) among people on the basis of these variables as certified by the chief health and economic officer of the appropriate state or nation.
Poverty will not exist, and every woman and man will earn at least as much as it costs them to live unless they are progressing toward being self-sufficient and self-reliant. No adult will be under the care, custody or control of another person, agency, or substance: all adult citizens will be self-sufficient and self-reliant.	As certified in independently audited reports of the Secretary General, and/or national and/or state/regional chief officer for labor and employment security.

Key Enablers

Any and all organizations — governmental, private sector/for-profit, public service/not-for-profit, educational — will contribute to the achievement and maintenance of this minimal ideal vision and will be	As indicated by certified and audited reports by the international and/or national and/or state/regional chief officer(s) • no successful lawsuits and/or damage recovery related to any public or private organization

Minimal Ideal Vision Element	Possible Examples of Performance Indicators
funded and continued to the extent to which it meets its objectives and the minimum ideal vision is accomplished and maintained.	• no public funding for any organization that does not document that they have contributed to no reduction or negative impact for any of the above elements in the ideal vision as certified by an independent TaxWatch organization and/or other independent agency or agent

Basic strategic planning questions Those questions that every organization faces. They include:

(*1*) Do you care* about the success of learners after they leave your educational system?

(*2*) Do you care* about the quality—competence—of the completers and leavers when they leave your educational system?

(*3*) Do you care* about the specific skills, knowledge, attitudes, and abilities of the learners as they move from course to course, and level to level?

(*4*) Do you care* about the efficiency of your educational programs, activities, and methods?

(*5*) Do you care* about the quality and availability of your educational resources, including human, capital, financial, and learning?

(*6*) Do you care* about the worth and value of your methods, means, and resources?

(*7*) Do you care* about the extent to which you have reached your educational objective?

*and commit to deliver

Beliefs and values The usually unexamined and strongly held perceptions about life and how it should be lived. They represent the planning partners' current perceived realities. Beliefs and values usually focus on means, resources, and "how-to's." They often have such names as "my educational philosophy" or "my view of education." It is urged that belief and values not be independently solicited but only come into play when the ideal vision is being derived. This "integrated" process will assure that beliefs and values are examined in the context of creating a better world rather than on allowing an emphasis on current ways and means.

Comfort zone The areas and situations where one feels unthreatened; the usual familiar territory where one's current paradigm works well, or appears to work well.

Constraint The situation when it seems that a mission objective, a performance requirement, or a set of performance requirements is not achievable. A constraint is a condition that makes it impossible to meet one or more performance requirements. Identifying a constraint requires planners to (1) change the mission objective and/or its performance requirements (and risk not meeting the needs); (2) be creative—develop a new methods-means or combine two or more methods-means that alone would not get the job done; or (3) stop, because it does not make sense to proceed with a problem if you now know that the effort will fail.

Continuous improvement The process of everyone in the organization constantly working individually and together to improve the quality and usefulness of what the organization does and delivers.

Cost/results analysis The process for comparing what it costs to deliver a result as compared with the consequences and payoffs of what is delivered. It will ask the two simultaneous questions of "What do you give?" and "What do you get?" for each possible how-to (or cluster of methods and means). Cost/results analysis may be made at each of the three levels of planning: mega/outputs, macro/outputs, and micro/products. This type of analysis is sometimes termed *costs/consequences analysis.* When there is a requirement that the output costs are covered by the savings or returns, there is said to be a *positive return on investment.*

Critical Success Factor(s) The vital ingredients required for any strategic planning process to deliver plans which will achieve required and useful results. There are six recommended critical success factors:

Critical Success Factor #1: Move out of today's comfort zones and use newer and wider paradigms for thinking, planning, doing, and evaluating/continuous improvement.
Critical Success Factor #2: Differentiate between ends and means (focus on what not how).

Critical Success Factor #3: Use and link all three levels of results (mega/outcomes, macro/outputs, and micro/products).

Critical Success Factor #4: Use an ideal vision as the underlying basis for planning (don't be limited by current restraints or only develop a vision for your organization)

Critical Success Factor #5: Prepare objectives – including mission objectives – that include indicators of how you will know when you have arrived (mission statement plus success criteria).

Critical Success Factor #6: Define "need" as a gap in results (not as insufficient levels of resources, means, or methods).

Distant and closer-in missions   The missions, derived from the ideal vision, that identify a temporal set of linked results the organization commits to achieve:

IDEAL VISION
↓
BASIC MISSION OBJECTIVE
↓
MISSION FOR THE YEAR 2010
↓
MISSION FOR THE YEAR 2000
↓
MISSION FOR NEXT YEAR
↓
MISSION FOR THIS YEAR

Ends   The results, consequences, accomplishments, and payoffs delivered. There are several different levels of ends that all deal with results. Ends include citizens who are self-sufficient and self-reliant, graduates, completers, people earning a license, and learners who acquired a specific skill, passed a test or course, or completed a recital.

Evaluation   The comparison of obtained results and payoffs with intended ones for determining what to keep, what to modify, and what to discontinue. Because of frequent use of evaluation data for blaming and not fixing, this book emphasizes the quality management process of *continuous improvement.*

Function analysis   The identification of the specific detailed aspects of each part of accomplishing a mission; what have to be the building-block results (again without selecting any how-to's) to get each function in the mission analysis accomplished. Function analysis defines the whats that must be completed in order to achieve the mission objective and satisfy its performance requirements. Function analysis, like mission analysis, identifies what has to be delivered as well as the order in which the products are to be completed.

Hard data   Data based on independently verifiable performances.

Ideal vision   The future, stated in measurable terms, we desire to attain. It is the ideal condition of the world in which we want tomorrow's children to live.

Inside-out planning   When one plans *for* the organization as the primary client it is as if one were looking from within the organization outside onto the operational world where learners complete, graduate, or get certified; and where citizens live, play, and work. This focus is on what is good for the organization and its continuation—a macro-level-limited perspective. Inside-out planning is reactive and usually projects the current educational mission(s), goals, purposes, and activities forward in time. This is also termed rolling-up planning.

Macro-level planning/thinking   A focus where the primary client and beneficiary of what gets planned and delivered is the school or educational system itself.

Means   The ways to deliver ends. For strategic thinking and planning, means include the resources (time, money, people, facilities) and methods (teaching, learning, supervising, planning, thinking, developing).

Mega-level planning/thinking   A focus where the primary client and beneficiary of what gets planned and delivered is the society and community.

Methods-means analysis   The determination of what ways and means exist, and the advantages and disadvantages of each, for the delivery of products. Methods-means analysis finds out whether there are one or more methods and means (solutions or processes) to achieve each product or group of products. If there are no possible methods-means, one has identified a *constraint* which must be overcome before proceeding. Thus, this analysis is a *feasibility study* in that it identifies feasible ways and means to get the necessary results. In order to make the best selection of ways and means (inputs and processes) for each function, the planning partners should compile a list of possible solutions and the advantages and disadvantages of each. This tally serves as a databank for selection and further design and development.

Micro-level planning/thinking   A focus where the primary client and beneficiary of what gets planned and delivered are the individuals and small groups within the school or system.

Mission analysis   The identification of the requirements for overall problem resolution to get to the ideal vision and getting our mission accomplished. Mission analysis reveals (1) what is to be achieved, (2) what criteria will be used to determine success, and (3) what are the building-block results and the order of their completion (functions) required to move from the current results to the desired state of affairs. Mission analysis is one of several tools in a cluster called *system analysis*. When the mission analysis incorporates the outcome level of concern, it is a process of mega-planning. When it deals only with the output level, it is a component of macro-planning. If it begins at the product level, it is a process of micro-planning.

Mission objective   A mission statement plus the criteria for measuring (on an interval or ratio scale of measurement) when one has or has not arrived.

Mission profile   The flow-charted graphic of the ''major'' milestones, or the central pathway, for the building-block results to be accomplished — moving from ''what is'' to ''what should be'' in solving a given problem such as accomplishing the mission. A mission profile identifies, in logical sequence, the major functions that must be performed while meeting the performance requirements. This is the major results pathway for meeting the mission objective.

Mission statement   Where one is headed — the destination — in general descriptive terms.

Need   The gap between current and desired/required results. It is not a gap in resources, processes, or how-to's.

Needs analysis   An analysis — which sensibly comes after a needs assessment — that finds the causes and reasons behind the existence of the needs — they examine the linkages between adjacent organizational elements.

Needs assessment   The process of identifying gaps in results (needs), placing them in priority order, and selecting the most important for reduction or elimination on the basis of what it costs to close versus what it will cost to ignore the need.

Needs assessment matrix A format that allows gaps in results (needs) to be recorded:

Type of Result	Current Results	Desired Results
Outcome (Mega)		
Output (Macro)		
Product (Micro)		

NOM assessment The identification of Needs, Opportunities, and Maintenance requirements. This is important so that (a) needs are identified, (b) opportunities are sought to remove oneself from a problem-solving mode and (c) you maintain that which is currently successful.

Objective A statement of intended results that includes (a) what results are to be obtained, (b) who or what will display the result, (c) under what conditions the result will be observed, and (d) what criteria (using interval or ratio scale measurement) will be used. An objective never includes how a result will be obtained.

Organizational Elements Model (OEM) The elements that make up that which every organization uses (inputs), does (processes), accomplishes (products), delivers (outputs) outside of itself, plus the external consequences of all of it (outcomes) in and for society; results at the micro-level are products; those at the macro-level are outputs; and those at the mega-level are outcomes.

The OEM may be placed in two levels: "what is" and "what should (or could) be." Use of the two-tiered OEM may help identify what exists and what is missing in any organization.

The organizational elements are:

- *inputs:* the ingredients, or starting conditions, used by the organization
- *processes:* the methods, means, activities, programs, and "how-to's" used to turn the inputs into accomplishments
- *products:* the building-block results accomplished by working with the inputs and using the processes (micro-level results)

- *outputs:* the results that are or could be delivered to society (macro-level results)
- *outcomes:* the external—outside the school or system—payoffs and consequences of the inputs, processes, products, and outputs in and for the society and community (mega-level results)

Outside-in planning   When one plans for society as the primary client and beneficiary. Planning in this way is as if one were looking into the organization from outside—from the vantage point of society—back into the organization. Social good, now and in the future, becomes paramount. The role of the educational organization as only one of many means-to-ends (providers) becomes obvious. In this type of planning, the client is all of society, as well as all of the educational partners. Outside-in planning is proactive. This is also termed rolling-down planning.

Paradigm   The boundaries and ground rules we use to filter and respond to our external world. Paradigms, or *frames of reference,* are with us for everything we experience and do in education, economics, society, and life.

Paradigm shift   The situation where old boundaries and associated ground rules don't square with reality; they have shifted to a new reality where revised boundaries and ground rules are appropriate.

Planning partners   The partners and clients for planning include learners, educators, and society/community members. By including vital stakeholders in the planning process, valid guidance is provided to the planning process, and ownership of the plan is transferred from the organization to all community members.

Practical dreaming   The process of identifying mega-level results and using them as the basis for all subsequent planning and doing.

Problem identification and resolution model (six steps)   A framework and steps for (1) identifying problems (based on needs); (2) determining detailed performance requirements and identifying possible methods and means for meeting the requirements; (3) selection of methods and means; (4) implementation; (5) determining effectiveness and efficiency of performance; and (6) constant revising as required. These six steps are often shown as a flow chart of five functions [items (1)−(6) above] with the sixth step showing a revision pathway between any or all of the steps.

Quasi-need/quasi-needs assessment   A gap in processes or resources (but not a gap in results); sometimes confused with needs assessment, which, when made, causes means, methods, and/or resources to be selected without linking them to gaps in performance.

Results chain   The linking of results at the mega-, macro-, and micro-levels with processes and inputs.

Soft data   Data based upon individual perceptions that are not independently verifiable.

Strategic planning   A systematic process for defining useful (and possible new) objectives and the linkages to effective and efficient tactics. The framework offered here has three phases: scoping, planning, and implementation and evaluation/continuous improvement. This differs from conventional planning approaches that assume current objectives as useful and valid and tend to react to existing problems.

Strategic Planning Agreement Table   A series of questions provided to internal and external partners to allow them to (a) understand the full array of questions and responsibilities an educational agency faces, and (b) buy-in or reject any or all. When an individual opts to not pursue any question then they have some responsibility for the consequences of not achieving those results. The suggested Strategic Planning Agreement Table is:

	Response			
	Stakeholders		Planners	
	Y	N	Y	N
1. Each school, as well as the total educational system, will contribute to the learner's, as well as society's, current and future success survival, health, and well-being.				
2. Each school, as well as the total educational system, will contribute to the learner's, as well as society's, current and future.				
3. Learners current and future survival, health, and well-being will be part of the system's and each of its school's mission objective.				

	Response		
	Stakeholders		Planners
	Y	N	Y	N

4. Each educational function will have objectives which contribute to #1, #2, and #3.
5. Each job/task/activity will have objectives which contribute to #1, #2, #3, and #4.
6. A needs assessment will identify and document any gaps in results at the operational levels of #1, #2, #3, #4, and #5.
7. Educational learning requirements will be generated from the needs identifed in #6.
8. The results of #6 may recommend non-educational intervention.
9. Evaluation will use data from comparing results with objectives for #1, #2, #3, #4, #5.
10. Data from evaluation will be used to continuously improve the contributions of #1, #2, #3, #4, and #5.

Strategic Planning Plus (SP+)   An approach that extends conventional strategic planning and tactical planning by also identifying the kind of future we want to create for tomorrow's children (mega-level results) while also taking care of today's housekeeping problems. The '' + '' is the addition of the mega-level to planning.

Strategic thinking   The way that an individual approaches her or his world: knowing what to achieve, being able to justify the direction, and then finding and implementing the best ways to get there. Being strategic is proactive and differs from being reactive to problems as they surface. Strategic thinking is the most important product of strategic planning.

SWOTs   Strengths, weaknesses, opportunities, and threats.

System   The sum total of individual parts, working alone and together, to achieve a common purpose.

System analysis   A rational and systematic process that identifies (1) what should be accomplished in terms of a measurable objective (which might be a mission objective) and is based upon selected needs; (2) the building-block "functions" (results or products) required to get from "what is" to "what should be" — each function, because it is results-based, has measurable performance requirements; and (3) the order and relationship among the functions in a flow chart format.

System approach to education   Treating the entire educational enterprise as a system where a change in one part causes changes in all other parts; creates a total school system, not a system of schools.

Systems analysis   The process for identifying possible ways and means to meet objectives; see cost/results analysis. Tools for systems analysis include (but are not limited to) operations research; simulating; planning, programming, budgeting system (PPBS); queuing; relevance trees; decision theory; strategic market planning; portfolio analysis; market attractiveness assessment; operational gaming; game theory; Delphi Technique; nominal group technique; pooling; and cross-impact analysis.

Tactical planning   The identification and selection of results to be obtained to meet previously specified (or assumed) objectives; tactical planning usually deals with micro-level results and concerns, such as a single course, activity, or group of students or teachers.

Task analysis   The optimal lowest level of a system analysis; it is derived from a mission analysis and the related function analysis. It yields the most discrete level of detail required to identify all the whats for problem resolution. Task analysis can consist of two parts, (1) the identification and ordering of the steps to be taken (task inventory), and (2) the description of the salient characteristics and requirements of successful job and/or task accomplishment (detailed task analysis, or task description).

Taxonomy of Educational Results   Everything is measurable when considering the four scales of measurement: nominal, ordinal, interval, and ratio. They form a taxonomy of results based on the reliability of each:

Type of Result	Description/Label	Scale of Measurement
Naming — no implied direction	Goal, Aim, Purpose	Nominal
Rank Order — relative position		Ordinal

Type of Result	Description/Label	Scale of Measurement
Equal Scale distances with arbitrary zero-point	Objective, performance Indicator, Performance Criteria	Interval
Equal Scale distances with known zero-point		Ratio

Total quality management (TQM) One of several labels given to Juran's and Deming's process for assuring client satisfaction. It is a process, built upon rational, data-based decision making, that enlists everyone in an organization in constantly improving the quality of what is delivered.

Total Quality Management Plus (TQM+) The extension of TQM to include a focus on the mega-level: current and future societal benefits, not just client satisfaction.

Value-added The extent to which we recover costs and deliver beyond the break-even point for a delivered output, or result.

References and Related Readings

Abell, F. F. and Hammond, J. S. (1979). *Strategic Market Planning: Problems and Analytic Approaches*. Englewood Cliffs: Prentice-Hall, Inc.

Ackoff, R. L. (1972: April 20). The Second Industrial Revolution. Philadelphia: Wharton School of Business, Fordyce House.

American Society for Quality Control. (1987: June 19). *American National Standard: Quality Systems — Model for Quality Assurance in Design/Development, Production, Installation, and Servicing* (ANSI/ASQC Q91 – 1987). Milwaukee, WI.

American National Standards Institute. (1992: Sept. 9). *American National Standard Draft Document: Quality Systems — Requirements for Using Quality Principles in Education and Training* (ANSCI/ASQC Z-1.11 1992.). Accredited Standards Committee Z-1 on Quality Assurance. Milwaukee, WI: ASQC.

Alkin, M. C. and Bruno, J. E. (1970). System approaches to educational planning. Part IV of *Social and Technological Change: Implications for Education*. Eugene, OR: ERIC/CEA.

Argyris, C. (1991: May-June). Teaching smart people to learn. *Harvard Business Review*.

Banathy, B. (1987). Instructional systems design. In R. M. Gagne (Ed.), *Instructional Technology: Foundations*. Hillsdale, NJ: Lawrence Erlbaum Associates, Publishers.

Banathy, B. H. (1991). *Systems Design of Education: A Journey to Create the Future*. Englewood Cliffs, NJ: Educational Technology Publishers.

Banathy, B. H. (1992). *A Systems View of Education: Concepts and Principles for Effective Practice*. Englewood Cliffs, NJ: Educational Technology Publications.

Banghart, F. W. (1969). *Educational Systems Analysis*. Toronto, Ontario: The Mac-Millan Co.

Barker, J. A. (1989). *The Business of Paradigms: Discovering the Future*. Videotape. Burnsville, MN: ChartHouse Learning Corp.

Barker, J. A. (1992). *Future Edge: Discovering the New Paradigms of Success*. New York: William Morrow & Co., Inc.

Barker, J. A. (1993). *Paradigm Pioneers. Discovering the Future Series*. Videotape. Burnsville, MN: ChartHouse Learning Corp.

Beals, R. L. (1968: Dec.). *Resistance and Adaptation to Technological Change: Some Anthropological Views. Human Factors*.

271

Bell, C. R. and Zemke, R. (1992). *Managing Knock Your Socks Off Service*. New York: American Management Association.

Bell, R. and Coplans, J. (1976). *Decisions, Decisions: Game Theory and You*. New York: W. W. Norton.

Bennis, W. and Nannus, B. (1985). *Leaders: The Strategies for Taking Charge*. New York: Harper and Row.

Bertalanffy, L. Von. (1968). *General Systems Theory*. New York: George Braziller.

Blanchard, K. and Peale, N. V. (1988). *The Power of Ethical Management*. New York: William Morrow & Co.

Block, P. (1993). *Stewardship*. San Francisco, CA: Berrett-Koehler Publishers.

Branson, R. K. (1988: 4). Why schools can't improve: The upper limit hypothesis. *Journal of Instructional Development*.

Branson, R. K. (1991: April). Restructuring public education: Imagining, visioning, or reforming? Paper presented at the *Annual Meeting of the American Educational Research Association*, Chicago.

Bryson, J. M. (1988). *Strategic Planning for Public and Nonprofit Organizations*. San Francisco: Jossey-Bass.

Buckley, W. (Ed.). (1968). *Modern Systems Research for the Behavioral Scientist*. Chicago, IL: Aldine Publishing Company.

Can corporate America cope? (1986: Nov. 17). *Newsweek*. Quotation of H. Ross Perot.

Caplan, F. (1990). *The Quality System: A Sourcebook for Managers and Engineers*. Radnor, PA: Chilton Book Co.

Carlson, R. V. and Awkerman, G. (Eds.) (1991). *Educational Planning: Concepts, Strategies, Practices*. New York: Longman.

Carnoy, W. and Levin, H. M. (1976). *The Limits of Educational Reform*. New York: David McKay.

Carter, L. F. (1969). *The Systems Approach to Education: The Mystique and the Reality*. System Development Corporation, Report SP-3921.

Carter, R. K. (1983). *The Accountable Agency* (Human Service Guide No. 34). Beverly Hills: Sage Publications.

Churchman, C. W. (1969, 1975). *The Systems Approach* (1st and 2nd eds.). New York: Dell Publishing Company.

Cleland, D. I. and King, W. R. (1968). *Systems Analysis and Project Management*. New York: McGraw-Hill Company.

Cleland, D. I. and King, W. R. (1968). *Systems, Organizations, Analysis, Management: A Book of Readings*. New York: McGraw-Hill Book Company.

Conner, D. R. (1992). *Managing at the Speed of Change*. New York: Villard Books, Division of Random House.

Cook, W. J., Jr. (1988). A series of four video tapes in association with *Strategic Planning for America's Schools*. Arlington, VA. National Academy of School Executives and the American Association of School Administrators.

Cook, W. J., Jr. (1990). *Bill Cook's Strategic Planning for America's Schools*. Revised edition. Birmingham, AL and Arlington, VA: Cambridge Management Group, Inc. and the American Association of School Administrators.

Corrigan, R. E. and Corrigan, Betty O. (1985). *SAFE: System Approach for Effectiveness*. New Orleans, LA: R. E. Corrigan Associates.

Corrigan, R. E. and Kaufman, R. (1966). *Why System Engineering?* Palo Alto, CA: Fearon Publishers.

Crosby, P. B. (1979). *Quality Is Free: The Art of Making Quality Certain.* NY: McGraw-Hill Book Co.

Cuban, L. (1994: June 15). The great school scam. *Education Week.*

Cuban, L. (1990: Jan.). Reforming again, again, and again. *Educational Researcher,* pp. 3–13.

Deal, T. and Kennedy, A. (1982). *Corporate Cultures: The Rites and Rituals of Corporate Life.* Reading, MA: Addison-Wesley Publishing Co., Inc.

Deming, W. E. (1982). *Quality, Productivity, and Competitive Position.* Center for Advanced Engineering Study, Massachusetts Institute of Technology, Cambridge, MA.

Deming, W. E. (1986). *Out of the Crisis.* Cambridge: MIT, Center for Advanced Engineering Technology.

Deming, W. E. (1990: May 10). A System of Profound Knowledge. Washington, DC, Personal memo.

Det norske Veritas Industry. (Undated). *9000 & 9: Most Often Asked Questions on ISO9000.* Houston, TX, DNV Industry, Inc.

Dick, W. and Johnson, F. C. (Eds.) (1993). Special issue on quality systems in performance improvement. *Performance Improvement Quarterly.* Vol. 6, No. 3.

Drucker, P. F. (1973). *Management: Tasks, Responsibilities, Practices.* New York: Harper & Row.

Drucker, P. F. (1985). *Innovation and Entrepreneurship.* London: William Heinemann, Ltd.

Drucker, P. F. (1988: Sept.-Oct.). Management and the world's work. *Harvard Business Review.*

Drucker, P. F. (1992: Sept.-Oct.). The new society of organizations. *Harvard Business Review,* pp. 95–104.

Drucker, P. F. (1993). *Post-Capitalist Society.* New York: HarperBusiness.

Drucker, P. F. (1994: Nov.). The age of social transformation. *The Atlantic Monthly,* pp. 53–80.

English, F. W. (1988). *Curriculum Auditing.* Lancaster, PA: Technomic Publishing Co.

Florida Department of Education. (1992). *Needs Assessment for Florida Schools: School Improvement Materials.* Tallahassee, FL, Office of Organizational Development and Educational Leadership.

Gagne, R. M. (1962). *Psychological Principles in Systems Development.* New York: Holt, Rinehart & Winston.

Galagan, P. A. (1991: June). How Wallace changed its mind. *Training & Development,* Vol. 45, No. 6.

Garratt, B. (1987, 1994). *The Learning Organization.* London: HarperCollins.

Garratt, B., (Ed.). (1995). *Developing Strategic Thought: Rediscovering the Art of Direction-Giving.* London: McGraw-Hill Book Company.

Gilbert, T. F. (1978). *Human Competence: Engineering Worthy Performance.* New York: McGraw-Hill.

Greenwald, H. (1973). *Decision Therapy.* NY: Peter Wyden, Inc.

Greenwald, H. and Rich, E. (1984). *The Happy Person: A Seven Step Plan.* New York: Avon Books.

Hammer, M. and Champy, J. (1993). *Reengineering the Corporation: A Manifesto for Business Revolution.* New York: HarperBusiness.

Harless, J. H. (1975). *An Ounce of Analysis is Worth a Pound of Cure.* Newman, GA: Harless Performance Guild.

Harless, J. H. (1986). Guiding performance with job aids. In M. Smith (Ed.), *Introduction to Performance Technology, Part 1.* Washington, DC: National Society for Performance and Instruction.

Hedges, L. V., Laine, R. D., and Greenwald, R. (1994: April). Does money matter? A meta-analysis of studies of the effects of differential school input on student outcomes. *Educational Researcher,* 23(8), pp. 5–14.

Hodgkinson, H. L. (1985). *All One System: Demographics of Education, Kindergarten through Graduate School.* Washington, DC: Institute for Educational Leadership, Inc.

Hodgkinson, H. L. (1986: Dec.). Reform? Higher education? Don't be absurd! *Phi Delta Kappan,* 68(4).

Hogan, R., Curphy, G. J., and Hogan, J. (1994: June). What we know about leadership: Effectiveness and personality. *American Psychologist,* 49(6).

Imai, M. (1956). *Kaizen: The Key to Japan's Competitive Success.* NY: McGraw-Hill Book Co.

Ishikawa, K. (1986). *Guide to Quality Control.* White Plains, NY: Quality Resources.

Joiner, B. L. (1985: Aug.). The key role of statisticians in the transformation of North American industry. *The American Statistician,* Vol. 39, No. 3.

Joiner, B. L. (1986: May). Using statisticians to help transform industry in America. *Quality Progress,* pp. 46–50.

Juran, J. M. (1988). *Juran on Planning for Quality.* New York: The Free Press.

Kanter, R. M. (1989). *When Giants Learn to Dance: Mastering the Challenges of Strategy, Management, and Careers in the 1990's.* New York: Simon & Schuster.

Kaufman, R. A. (1968). A system approach to education—derivation and definition. *AV Communication Review,* 16, pp. 415–425.

Kaufman, R. A. (1972). *Educational System Planning.* Englewood Cliffs, NJ: Prentice-Hall.

Kaufman, R. (1988). *Planning Educational Systems: A Results-Based Approach.* Lancaster, PA: Technomic Publishing Co., Inc.

Kaufman, R. (1988: Sept.). Preparing useful performance indicators. *Training & Development Journal.*

Kaufman, R. (1991). Asking the right questions: Types of strategic planning. In Carlson, R. V. and Awkerman, G. (Eds.), *Educational Planning: Concepts, Strategies, and Practices.* New York: Longman.

Kaufman, R. (1991b: Dec.). Toward total quality "plus." *Training.*

Kaufman, R. (1992a). *Strategic Planning Plus: An Organizational Guide.* Newbury Park, CA: Sage (Revised).

Kaufman, R. (1992b). *Mapping Educational Success.* Newbury Park, CA: Corwin Press.

Kaufman, R. (1992: April). The challenge of total quality management in education. *International Journal of Educational Reform.*

Kaufman, R. (1992: May). 6 steps to strategic success. *Training & Development.*

Kaufman, R. (1992: July). The magnifying glass mentality. *Performance & Instruction Journal.*

Kaufman, R. (1992: July). Comfort and change: Natural enemies. *Educational Technology.*

Kaufman, R. (1992: Oct.). A University for Florida's Future. *Ideas in Action.* Tallahassee, FL, Florida TaxWatch, Vol. I (7).

Kaufman, R. (1993: Mar.). Educational restructuring which will work: Beyond tinkering. *International Journal of Education Reform.*

Kaufman, R. (1993:Apr.). The vision thing: Florida's salvation. *Ideas in Action.* Tallahassee, FL, Florida TaxWatch, Vol. II (5).

Kaufman, R. (1993: Oct.). Mega planning: The argument is over. *Performance & Instruction.*

Kaufman, R. (1994: Feb.). A needs assessment audit. *Performance & Instruction.*

Kaufman, R. (1994). Needs assessment and analysis. Chapt. 87 in Tracey, W. R., *Human Resources Management & Development Handbook,* 2nd edition. New York: American Management Association.

Kaufman, R. (1994: April). A Synergistic Focus for Educational Quality Management, Needs Assessment, and Strategic Planning. *International Journal of Education Reform.* Vol. 3(2), pp. 174−180.

Kaufman, R. (1995). *Mapping Educational Success Revised.* Newbury Park, CA: Corwin Press.

Kaufman, R. (1995). Mega-planning: A framework for education. *International Journal of Education Reform.* Vol. 4(3), pp. 259−270.

Kaufman, R. and Carron, A. S. (1980). Utility and self-sufficiency in the selection of educational alternatives," *Journal of Instructional Development,* 4(1), 14−18, 23−26.

Kaufman, R. and Gavora, M. J. (1993). Needs assessment and problem solving: A critical appraisal of a critical reappraisal. *Performance Improvement Quarterly,* 6(2), pp. 87−98.

Kaufman, R. and Grise, P. (1995). *Auditing Your Educational Strategic Plan: Making a Good Thing Better.* Newbury Park, CA: Corwin Press.

Kaufman, R. and Herman, J. (1991). *Strategic Planning in Education: Rethinking, Restructuring, Revitalizing.* Lancaster, PA: Technomic Publishing Co., Inc.

Kaufman, R. and Hirumi, A. (1992:Nov.). Ten steps to "TQM plus." *Educational Leadership.*

Kaufman, R. and Stolovitch, H. (1991: Feb.). Planning, perspective, creativity, and control. *Educational Technology.*

Kaufman, R. and Thiagarajan, S. (1987). Identifying and specifying requirements for instruction. In Gagne, R. M. (Ed.) *Instructional Technology: Foundations.* Hillsdale, NJ: Lawrence Erlbaum Associates, Publishers.

Kaufman, R. and Valentine, G. (1989: Nov./Dec.). Relating needs assessment and needs analysis. *Performance & Instruction Journal.*

Kaufman, R. and Zahn, D. (1993). *Quality Management Plus: The Continuous Improvement of Education.* Newbury Park, CA: Corwin Press.

Kaufman, R., Rojas, A. M. and Mayer, H. (1993). *Needs Assessment: A User's Guide.* Englewood Cliffs, NJ: Educational Technology.

Kaufman, R., Stith, M., and Kaufman, J. D. (1992: Feb.). Extending performance technology to improve strategic market planning. *Performance & Instruction Journal.*

Kaufman, R. A. (1972). *Educational System Planning.* Englewood Cliffs, NJ: Prentice-Hall [Also *Planificacion de Systemas Educativos* (translation of *Educational System Planning*). Mexico City: Editorial Trillas, S.A., 1973].

Kirst, M. W. and Meister, G. R. (1985: Summer). Turbulence in American secondary schools: What reforms last? *Curriculum Inquiry*, 15, p. 2.

Kuhn, T. (1970). *The Structure of Scientific Revolutions.* Second Edition. Chicago: University of Chicago Press.

Lessinger, L. M. (1970). *Every Kid a Winner.* New York: Simon & Schuster.

Levin, H. M. (1983). *Cost Effectiveness: A Primer* (New perspectives in evaluation). Beverly Hills: Sage Publications.

Mager, R. F. (1975). *Preparing Instructional Objectives* (2nd ed.). Belmont, CA: Pitman Learning, Inc.

Mager, R. F. (1988). *Making Instruction Work: Or Skillbloomers.* Belmont, CA: David S. Lake Publishers.

Mager, R. F. and Beach, K.M., Jr. (1987). *Developing Vocational Instruction.* Palo Alto, CA., Fearon Publishers, Inc.

Marshall, R. and Tucker, M. (1992). *Thinking for a Living: Education & the Wealth of Nations.* New York: Basic Books.

Martin, R. (1993: Nov.-Dec.). Changing the mind of the organization. *Harvard Business Review.*

Martino, J. P. (1983). *Technological Forecasting for Decision-Making* (2nd ed.). New York: North-Holland.

Morgan, R. M. and Chadwick, C. B. (1971). *Systems Analysis for Educational Change: The Republic of Korea.* Tallahassee: Florida State University, Department of Educational Research.

Murrary, C. (1984). *Losing Ground: American Social Policy 1950−1980.* New York: Basic Books.

Naisbitt, J. (1982). *Megatrends: Ten New Directions Transforming Our Lives.* New York: Warner Books.

Naisbitt, J. and Aburdene, P. (1990). *Megatrends 2000: Ten New Directions for the 1990's.* New York: William Morrow & Co.

Nanus, B. (1992). *Visionary Leadership.* San Francisco: Jossey-Bass.

Nelson, F. H. (1992: July). The myth of high public spending on American education. *International Journal of Educational Reform.*

Newmann, F. M. (1991: Feb.). Linking restructuring to authentic student achievement. *Phi Delta Kappan*, Vol. 72 (6), pp. 458−463.

Nolan, T. M., Goodstein, L. D. and Pfeiffer, J. W. (1993). *Shaping Your Organization's Future; Frogs, Dragons, Bees, and Turkey Tails.* San Diego, CA: Pfeiffer and Co.

Ohmae, K. (1982). *The Mind of the Strategist: Business Planning for Competitive Advantage.* New York: Penguin Books.

Osborne, D. and Gaebler, T. (1992). *Reinventing Government: How the Entrepreneurial Spirit Is Transforming the Public Sector.* Reading, MA: Addison-Wesley Publishing Co.

Peddiwell, J. A. (H. Benjamin). (1939). *The Sabertooth Curriculum*. New York: McGraw-Hill.

Perelman, L. J. (1989: Nov. 28). Closing education's technology gap. *Hudson Institute Briefing Paper*. No. 111. Indianapolis, IN.

Perelman, L. J. (1990: May). The "acanemia" deception. *Hudson Institute Briefing Paper*, No. 120. Indianapolis, IN.

Peters, T. (1987). *Thriving on Chaos: Handbook for a Management Revolution*. New York: Alfred A. Knopf.

Peters, T. J. and N. Austin. (1985). *The Passion for Excellence: The Leadership Difference*. New York: Random House.

Peters, T. J. and R. H. Waterman, Jr. (1982). *In Search of Excellence: Lessons Learned from America's Best Run Companies*. New York: Harper & Row.

Pfeiffer, J. W., Goodstein, L. D., and Nolan, T. M. (1989). *Shaping Strategic Planning: Frogs, Bees, and Turkey Tails*. Glenview, IL: Scott, Foresman and Co.

Phi Delta Kappa. (1984). *Handbook for Conducting Future Studies in Education*. Bloomington, IN: Phi Delta Kappa.

Pipho, C. (1991: Feb.). Business leaders focus on reform. *Phi Delta Kappan*, pp. 422–423.

Popcorn, F. (1991). *The Popcorn Report*. New York: Doubleday.

Rappaport, A. (1986). *General System Theory*. Cambridge, MA: Abacus Press.

Rasell, E. and Mishel, L. (1990: Jan.). *Shortchanging Education*. Economic Policy Institute, Washington, DC.

Reigeluth, C. (Ed.) (1983). *Instructional Design Theories and Models. An Overview of Their Current Status*. Hillsdale, NJ: Lawrence Erlbaum Associates.

Ricoeur, P. (1986). *Lectures on Ideology and Utopia*. G. H. Taylor (Ed.). New York: Columbia University Press.

Roberts, W. (1987). *Leadership Secrets of Attila the Hun*. New York: Warner.

Roberts, W. (1991). *Straight A's Never Made Anybody Rich*. New York: Harper Collins.

Roberts, W. (1993). *Victory Secrets of Attila the Hun*. New York: Doubleday

Rodriguez, Stephen R. (1988). Needs assessment and analysis: Tools for change. *Journal of Instructional Development*. Vol. 11, No. 1, pp. 23–28.

Rojas, Alicia M. (1988). Evaluation of sales training impact: A case study using the organizational elements model. *Performance Improvement Quarterly*. Vol. 1, No. 2, pp. 71–84.

Rummler, G. A. and Brache, A. P. (1990). *Improving Performance: How to Manage the White Space on the Organization Chart*. San Francisco: Jossey-Bass Publishers.

Schaaf, M. (1986: Oct. 24). Wants: Whether we need them or not, *Los Angeles Times*, Part V, p. 3.

Scriven, M. (1973). Goal free evaluation, in *School Evaluation: The Politics and Process*. E. R. House, ed., Berkeley, CA: McCutchan.

Senge, P. M. (1990). *The Fifth Discipline: The Art & Practice of the Learning Organization*. New York: Doubleday-Currency.

Shanker, A. (1990: Jan.). The end of the traditional model of schooling – And a proposal for using incentives to restructure public schools. *Phi Delta Kappan*.

Shewhart, W. A. (1931). *Economic Control of Quality of Manufactured Product.* New York: D. Van Nostrand Co., Inc.

Sobel, I. and Kaufman, R. (1989). Toward a "hard" metric for educational utility. *Performance Improvement Quarterly,* Vol. 2 (1).

Stevens, S. S. (1951). Mathematics, measurement, and psychophysics. In S. S. Stevens, ed., *Handbook of Experimental Psychology.* New York: John Wiley & Sons.

Stolovitch, H. D. and Keeps, E. J. (1992). *Handbook of Human Performance Technology: A Comprehensive Guide for Analyzing and Solving Performance Problems in Organizations.* San Francisco, CA: Jossey-Bass Publishers (with the National Society for Performance & Instruction, Washington, DC).

Stufflebeam, D. L., W. J. Foley, W. R. Gephart, R. L. Hammon, H. O. Merriman and M. M. Provus. (1971). *Educational Evaluation and Decision Making.* Itasca, IL: Peacock.

Toffler, A. (1970). *Future Shock.* New York: Random House.

Toffler, A. (1980). *The Third Wave.* New York: Morrow.

Toffler, A. (1990). *Powershift: Knowledge, Wealth, and Violence at the Edge of the 21st Century.* New York: Bantam Books.

Tosti, D. T. (1986). Feedback systems. In M. Smith (Ed.) *Introduction to Performance Technology, Part 1.* Washington, DC: National Society for Performance and Instruction.

Towers, James M. (1994: April). The perils of outcome-based teacher education. *Phi Delta Kappan,* 75(8), pp. 624–627.

U.S. General Accounting Office. (1991: May). Management practices: U.S. companies improve performance through quality efforts. GAO/NSIAD-91-190. Washington, DC.

U.S. General Accounting Office. (1993: April). Systemwide education reform: Federal leadership could facilitate district-level efforts. GAO/HRD-93-97. Washington, DC.

Van de Ven, A. and Delbecq, A. L. (1971: June). Nominal versus interacting group process for committee decision-making effectiveness. *Journal of the Academy of Management.*

Walton, M. (1986). *The Deming Management Method.* New York: Dodd, Mead, and Co.

Wang, M. C., Haertel, G. D., and Walberg, H. J. (1993: Fall). Toward a knowledge base for school learning. *Review of Educational Research,* 63(3).

Wheatley, M. J. (1992). *Leadership and the New Science: Learning About Organization from an Orderly Universe.* San Francisco: Berrett-Koehler Publishers.

Wiesendanger, B. (Sept.-Oct. 1993). Deming's luster dims at Florida Power & Light: A case study. *Journal of Business Strategy,* Vol. 14(5), pp. 60–61.

Windham, D. M. (1988). *Indicators of Educational Effectiveness and Efficiency.* IEES Educational Efficiency Clearinghouse, Learning Systems Institute, Florida State University for the U.S. Agency for International Development, Bureau of Science and Technology, Office of Education.

Witkin, B. R. (1984). *Assessing Needs in Educational and Social Programs.* San Francisco: Jossey-Bass.

Witkin, B. R. (1991). Setting priorities: Needs assessment in time of change. In R. V.

Carlson and G. Awkerman (Eds.), *Educational Planning: Concepts, Strategies, and Practices.* New York: Longman.

Witkin, B. R. (1994). Needs assessment since 1981: The state of the practice. *Evaluation Practice,* Vol. 15 (1), pp. 17–27.

Zemke, R. and Bell, C. (1990; June). Service recovery. Doing it right the second time. *Training.*

Zemke, R. and Kramlinger, T. (1982). *Figuring Things Out: A Trainers Guide to Needs and Task Analysis.* Reading, MA: Addison-Wesley.

ROGER KAUFMAN is professor and director of the Center for Needs Assessment and Planning at Florida State University. He is also associated with the faculty of Industrial Engineering and Management Systems at the University of Central Florida. He has been a professor at both the United States International University and Chapman University, and taught at the University of Southern California and Pepperdine University. He was the 1983 Haydn Williams Fellow at The Curtin University of Technology in Perth, Australia. His Ph.D. in communications is from New York University, with graduate work in industrial engineering, psychology, and education completed at University of California at Berkeley and Johns Hopkins University (M.A.). His undergraduate studies consisted of psychology, statistics, sociology and industrial engineering at George Washington (B.A.) and Purdue Universities.

Before entering higher education, he was assistant to the vice president for research, as well as assistant to the vice president for engineering at Douglas Aircraft Company; director of training system analysis at US Industries; and head of human factors engineering at Martin Baltimore and earlier at Boeing. He has served two terms on the U.S. Secretary of the Navy's Advisory Board on Education and Training.

His clients—working in the areas of strategic planning, quality management, needs assessment, and organizational improvement—include or included: Andersen Consulting (world headquarters and Australia); Chase Manhattan Bank; the Los Alamos National Laboratories; AT&T, MIM Holdings, Ltd; the Public Service Commission of Australia; Florida Power & Light; the Australian Department of Defence; the Leon County (Florida) School Board; EastConn Regional Education Service Center; Florida Department of Education; Niagara

285

Wires Division of Niagara Lockport; IBM; U.S. Department of Veterans Affairs; American Society for Curriculum and Development (ASCD); Parke-Davis; Pioneer Cement; M&M Mars; Sydney Water Board; the U.S. Coast Guard, the Florida Department of Health and Rehabilitative Services; Texas Instruments; Florida Governor's Office of Planning and Budget; UNISYS of Australia; Fireman's Fund Insurance; Bankers' Institute of New Zealand; Boatmen's Bancshares; New Zealand Department of Health; McDonnell-Douglas; the U.S. Centers for Disease Control; and the Florida Department of Corrections, to name a few.

He is a Fellow of the American Psychological Association, and a Diplomate of the American Board of Professional Psychology. He has served as president for the National Society for Performance and Instruction and has been awarded their highest honor by being named "Member for Life." He has published twenty-seven books on strategic planning, quality management, continuous improvement, needs assessment, management, and evaluation, and is the author of over 155 articles on those topics.

JERRY HERMAN is a Professor of Administration and Planning at the University of Alabama-Tuscaloosa. He holds a Ph.D. in educational administration from the University of Michigan. He has taught in a variety of public school environments from elementary to high school. He has also been an instructor at junior college and university settings, working with both undergraduate and graduate students.

He is the recipient of many awards in the area of staff development and educational administration, including North America's 100 Top School Executives (Executive Editor), Boss of the Year (Agape Chapter of American Business Women's Association), and Distinguished Alumni Award (Northern Michigan University).

He has served as superintendent of schools in several states and has served on the editorial board of the *Clearinghouse Journal,* has been a consulting editor to the *National Staff Development Journal* and *School Business Affairs,* and is editor for several professional journals published by Corwin Press. He lectures nationally on the topics of strategic planning, leadership, and quality management. His vast consulting experiences have had him closely involved with school districts, universities, foundations, and various organizations within the business and industry sector.

He has authored 150 articles on management, evaluation, total quality management, and strategic and operational planning. He has also authored and co-authored eight books on educational administration, quality management, and planning.

KATHI WATTERS is an Associate in Research at the Center for Needs Assessment and Planning, Florida State University. She holds a bachelor's degree in communications and a master's degree in instructional systems, both from Florida State University. She is concerned with both communication and learning theories as they may apply to the strategic planning of public education and distance learning. She is actively engaged in research regarding education's impact on students and society.

Her research and development interests include alternative education, distance learning, needs assessment, and strategic planning. Her varied professional and volunteer experiences have included working with the mentally disabled, juvenile offenders, and at-risk youth. She is a member of the Phi Kappa Phi National Honor Society.